CARRYING THE FLAG

Also by Gordon C. Rhea

The Battle of the Wilderness: May 5–6, 1864

The Battles for Spotsylvania Court House and
the Road to Yellow Tavern: May 7–12, 1864

To the North Anna River:
Grant and Lee, May 13–25, 1864

Cold Harbor: Grant and Lee, May 26–June 3, 1864

CARRYING THE FLAG

★ ★ ★

The Story of
Private Charles Whilden,
the Confederacy's Most Unlikely Hero

GORDON C. RHEA

BASIC
BOOKS

A Member of the Perseus Books Group
New York

Published by Basic Books
A Member of the Perseus Books Group

Books published by Basic Books are available at special discounts for bulk purchases in the United States by corporations, institutions, and other organizations. For more information, please contact the Special Markets Department at the Perseus Books Group, 11 Cambridge Center, Cambridge MA 02142, or call (617) 252-5298, (800) 255-1514, or e-mail specialmarkets@perseusbooks.com.

Text design by Trish Wilkinson

Library of Congress Cataloging-in-Publication Data
Rhea, Gordon, C.
    Carrying the flag : the story of Private Charles Whilden, the Confederacy's most unlikely hero / Gordon C. Rhea.
        p.   cm.
    Includes bibliographical references and index.
    ISBN 0-465-06956-8 (alk. paper)
    1. Spotsylvania Court House, Battle of, Va., 1864. 2. Whilden, Charles Edmonston, 1824–1866. 3. Soldiers—South Carolina—Biography. 4. Confederate States of America. Army. South Carolina Infantry Regiment 1st. 5. Virginia—History—Civil War, 1861–1865—Campaigns. 6. United States—History—Civil War, 1861–1865—Campaigns. 7. South Carolina—History—Civil War, 1861–1865—Regimental histories. 8. United States—History—Civil War, 1861–1865—Regimental histories. 9. Charleston (S.C.)—Biography. I. Title.

E476.52.R4745 2003
973.7'36—dc21   2003011852

04 05 06 / 10 9 8 7 6 5 4 3 2 1

CONTENTS

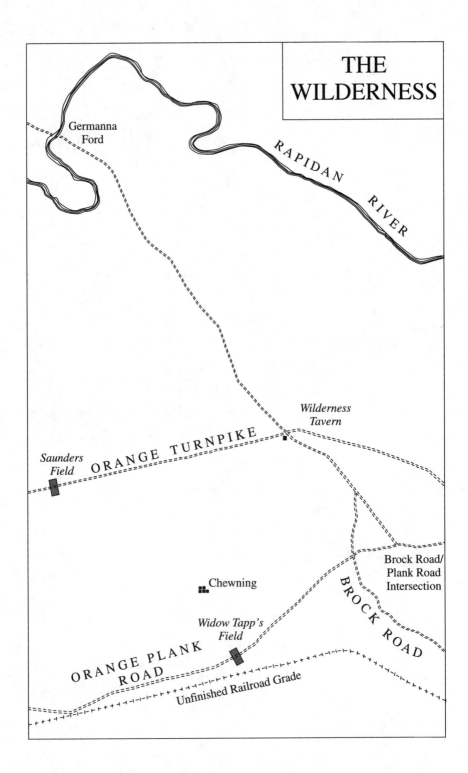

THE
WILDERNESS

Germanna
Ford

RAPIDAN

RIVER

Wilderness
Tavern

Saunders
Field

ORANGE TURNPIKE

Brock Road/
Plank Road
Intersection

Chewning

BROCK ROAD

Widow Tapp's
Field

ORANGE PLANK
ROAD

Unfinished Railroad Grade

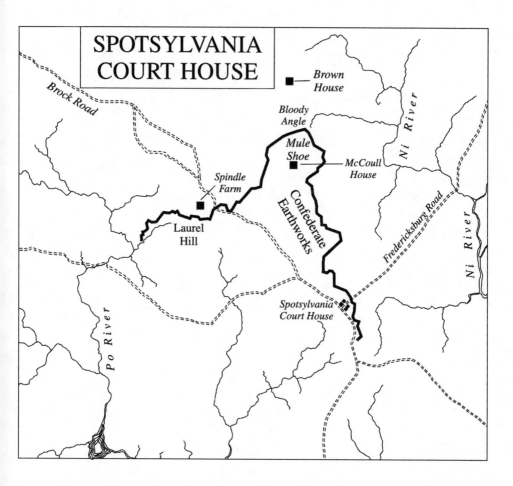

SPOTSYLVANIA
COURT HOUSE

Brown
House

Brock Road

Bloody
Angle

Mule
Shoe

McCoull
House

Ni River

Spindle
Farm

Confederate
Earthworks

Laurel
Hill

Fredericksburg Road

Ni River

Po River

Spotsylvania
Court House

INTRODUCTION

A few years ago, I moved with my family to Mt. Pleasant, South Carolina, a small town across the Cooper River from Charleston. The local historical society invited me to give a talk about the bloody fights between Grant and Lee in central Virginia, and after my presentation, a lady in the audience took me aside and handed me a sheaf of papers. Several young men from the surrounding area, she explained, had fought in General Lee's army, and she had collected materials about them and their experiences. I took the papers, thanked the owner, and promptly forgot about them, because people often give me copies of old diaries and letters when I speak at similar groups. A few days later, I came across the bundle of documents and began reading.

Buried in the packet were several letters from Charles E. Whilden of nearby Charleston and miscellaneous scraps of paper relating to his experiences. As I read the material, I realized that I had stumbled onto one of the American Civil War's most unlikely heroes.

For the first forty years of his life, Charles Whilden led an existence noteworthy for mediocrity and failure, be it in earning a living or finding a wife. Then, in a remarkable chain of events, the aging, epileptic desk clerk from Charleston found himself plunged into some of the war's most brutal killing fields at the Wilderness and

1

Spotsylvania Court House. Chance placed him near a bend in the Confederate line—dubbed the Bloody Angle—that became the focal point of Grant's massive spring offensive. There Charles performed an astounding feat of bravery foreign to anything he had accomplished in the past. The war would continue for another ten months, in part due to Charles's courage.

Charles's story fascinated me. What was his background, and what drove such an unlikely figure to risk his life in combat? Over the years I searched for materials about Charles, his family, and his compatriots in libraries and archives across the country. I did not expect to find much, because Civil War privates rarely left many letters behind. To my surprise, Charles was a well-educated and prolific writer. Nosing through dusty repositories, I assembled a treasure trove of letters that he sent to family members detailing his experiences both before and during the war. I expanded my search to encompass people who had known Charles or had served with him and found still more material, some of it corroborating Charles's heroic deed and adding important details. I also tracked down descendants of Charles's commanding officers and of his fellow privates. Many of them shared their ancestors' personal papers with me, filling in still more of the story. I visited Charles's childhood haunts and came to recognize the cultural and intellectual influences that drove him as an adult. I also contacted a genealogist and historian of the Whilden family who helped me flesh out more of Charles's background and understand his family's place in the community. Most interesting was a pamphlet published in the 1890s recounting the life and experiences of the Whilden family slave who helped raise Charles from birth. And I spent inordinate amounts of time visiting the battlefields where Charles fought, standing where he stood and trying to fathom what those places must have looked, sounded, smelled, and felt like to him.

The material collected here—much of it never before published—is surprisingly complete. Charles's letters, along with numerous first-hand accounts by his contemporaries, make it possible to recount the story of the man and his times. His remarkable tale underscores the capacity of insignificant players to alter the course of history. Generals set armies in motion; privates are cogs in the wheels of military machines. But what privates do can irretrievably affect the meshing of the martial gears and determine the outcome of battles and wars.

Heroes sometimes emerge from unlikely figures. Modern readers might find it hard to sympathize with a private who risked his life in a war to establish a slave-holding republic. We must remember, however, that inhabitants of Charles's world gauged things differently than we do, and that Charles was a creature of his time. But his story also embodies universal values that speak to the capacity of the human spirit to shine, according to its own lights, in times of stark adversity.

Battle studies, regimental histories, and biographies of generals and major actors in the American Civil War appear every year by the score. But books about privates are rare. The men who fought the war's battles remain obscure and are illuminated only fleetingly in those priceless diaries and letters that have managed to escape the ravages of time. None tell a story half as fascinating as that of Charles Whilden, the unsung hero of the Bloody Angle at Spotsylvania Court House. This book is an attempt to tell Charles's tale as it really happened, warts and all. The story is true—or at least as close to the truth as historians writing more than a century later can hope to get—and so its heroes have failings and its villains are never all bad. The people in this book were living, breathing beings that cause us to reflect on our humanity. And Charles's story inspires us to wonder whether we, too, might possess reserves that lie dormant within us, waiting for a special occurrence to bring them forth.

The Fate of
Two Nations

Spring came late to Virginia in 1864, and rain lashed the countryside, burying low-lying meadows under sheets of water and turning creeks into raging torrents. Roads dissolved into quagmires, ankle-deep in muck and treacherous for horsemen and wagons alike. Snow covered the Blue Ridge peaks well into April, and dense mist cloaked the valleys.

Swollen nearly to flood stage, the Rapidan River coursed eastward across the Old Dominion, joined the Rappahannock near Fredericksburg, and emptied its muddy flow into Chesapeake Bay. The river drew a physical and psychological divide between Virginia's northern region, occupied by Union forces, and the southern area, which was loyal to the Confederacy. Hostile armies faced each other from camps on opposite sides of the stream all winter, their pickets within shouting distance. North of the Rapidan, around the village of Culpeper Court House, the Union Army of the Potomac stirred restlessly in its log-and-earthen encampments, preparing to cross the river and advance on the Confederate capital of Richmond, sixty miles away. On the Rapidan's south bank, in camps around Orange Court House, the rebel Army of Northern Virginia girded to counter the Union offensive. Battle lines along opposite sides of the Rapidan ran not far from where they had lain when the war began three long years before. Soon the weather would clear, the roads would firm, and the tramp of armies would announce the start of another spring campaign.

War had transformed central Virginia into a wasteland. Armies had leveled the rich native forests to satisfy their voracious appetite for firewood. Farms stood untended, and the land seemed almost uninhabited, with neither the bark of a dog nor the song of a bird to break the silence. Hollow shells of mansions, abandoned by their owners and looted by troops, their doors gaping and their walls stripped of boards, presided over yards filled with weeds and debris. A mood as desolate as the surroundings had seized the white population of women, children, and old men. The region's able-bodied males of military age were with Robert E. Lee's army, dead, or disabled. A New Englander voiced a low opinion of the denizens of this storied land, formerly home to the likes of Jefferson, Madison, and Monroe. "Not a smile was on their faces but instead a scowl or frown," he remembered. "Even the little boys and girls looked the same and as for the men they were saucy and ugly."

Statesmen North and South had predicted a quick conclusion when hostilities opened in the spring of 1861. But victory had proved elusive. In the western theater—the broad swath of country encompassing everything from the Appalachian Mountains west to the Mississippi River, and from the Gulf Coast north to the Ohio River—Union armies had achieved resounding successes. The architect of those triumphs was an unlikely figure. An Ohioan by birth and upbringing, Ulysses S. Grant graduated from the Military Academy at West Point and went on to win laurels in the war against Mexico. In the decade before the Civil War, however, his fortunes spiraled downward. Assigned to remote outposts on the Pacific Coast, Grant succumbed to boredom, loneliness, and—according to rumors that hounded him all his life—drink. He resigned from the army, returned to his family, and tried farming, which proved unprofitable. The outbreak of war found him employed in his father's leather-goods store.

The story of Grant's metamorphosis from failure to chief of the United States armies would strain the credulity of Hollywood. Political connections landed Grant a colonelcy, followed by a brigadier generalship. In January 1862, he won the North's first major victory by taking Forts Henry and Donelson, driving the Confederates from Kentucky and much of Tennessee. He followed that success with another triumph at Shiloh and topped both those feats the next year by a brilliant campaign of maneuver and siege that captured the Mississippi River fortress of Vicksburg and ensured Union domination of the vital western waterways. After accepting the surrender of one rebel army at Vicksburg, Grant masterminded a bold attack that drove another rebel force from its mountain fastness above Chattanooga. By 1864, the Yankees were winning the war in the west, and Grant was the reason for their ascendancy.

The eastern theater—the relatively narrow band of land between the Appalachian Mountains and the Atlantic Ocean—presented a different picture. The flag of rebellion still waved proudly over the heartland of secession at Charleston, South Carolina, in open defiance of a Union blockade. But it was Virginia that riveted the attention of the political and military leaders on both sides. A little more than a hundred miles separated Washington, D.C., from Richmond, the Confederacy's capital, and the rolling hills, fields, and forests between the rival cities were the preserve of Robert E. Lee and his Army of Northern Virginia. Since assuming command of the rebel host in June 1862, Lee had administered humiliating defeats to a string of Northern generals. General George G. Meade, the federal army's most recent commander, had won his nation's applause by repelling Lee's foray into Northern territory with his victory at Gettysburg in July 1863. But summer, fall, and winter had come and gone, and Meade had accomplished nothing to reap the fruits of his Gettysburg victory. By the spring of 1864, Lee had brought his army back up to strength, and the defensive mind-set of the Union high command had dissipated whatever promise of success Gettysburg had offered the North. A frustrated President Abraham Lincoln could only wonder whether the years of bloodshed had been in vain.

By most estimations, 1864 loomed as the war's decisive year. President Lincoln was up for reelection, and his conduct of the war was at issue in the contest. Dissatisfaction was sweeping the North, and Lincoln needed military successes if his administration were to survive. In later years, historians would debate the relative importance of the eastern and western theaters. But in the spring of 1864, all eyes were on Virginia, the Confederacy's capital and the base of the rebellion's chief army.

Lincoln's political task was uncomplicated. A Union victory in Virginia would likely preserve his presidency. A Union defeat there would doom his administration and imperil his goal of preserving the United States.

Pondering his fledgling nation's precarious fortunes, the Confederacy's president, Jefferson Davis, reached much the same conclusion as had Lincoln. The North's overwhelming edge in manpower and industry, Davis reasoned, foreclosed the South's chance of winning independence by force of arms. The South's only hope lay in the political arena. If Confederate armies could stave off Union victories—or better yet, could score telling successes of their own— the burgeoning peace movement in the North would grow and

Lincoln would face defeat at the polls. Lincoln's successor, Southern politicians urged, would negotiate a settlement with the South to bring the bloodshed to an end. In short, a war-weary North would deliver to the South through political means the independence that it could not win militarily. "Every bullet we can send is the best ballot that can be deposited against [Lincoln's] election," a Georgia newspaper reminded its readers. "The battlefields of 1864 will hold the polls of this momentous decision."

To Lincoln, the prospects seemed alarming. The past two springs, Union armies had marched toward Richmond with high hopes, only to meet General Lee and his tatterdemalions and tumble back in defeat. This year had to be different; otherwise, the war, and with it his presidency, would be lost. Impressed with the gravity of the situation, Lincoln decided to bring his best general east. And so in March 1864, Grant came to Washington.

★ ★ ★

Grant reached the nation's capital on March 8 and checked into the Willard Hotel with his son Fred. The desk clerk did not recognize the demure general at first, but a glance at the signature on the registry revealed the distinguished guest's identity and prompted the clerk to offer him the best suite. Grant took Fred to the hotel dining room, expecting a quiet meal, only to find himself the object of everyone's attention. Whispers went around, heads turned, and an enthusiastic guest leaped onto a chair and proposed a toast to the hero of Chattanooga. Diners cheered and pounded their tables until Grant stood shyly and bowed. No sooner had he finished eating than a congressman began introducing him all around.

The general broke free of the throng at the Willard and strolled to the White House with Fred. Passing through a knot of gawking admirers, he walked into the East Room. He had never met the president but recognized the tall, gangly man on the chamber's far side from his pictures, and Lincoln recognized Grant as well. "This is General Grant, is it not?" he asked, extending his hand with a broad smile. "Yes," Grant answered, reaching out with a firm handshake.

The insistent crowd gave the president and his general no time to talk. Everyone wanted a glimpse of Grant, and the self-conscious man was coaxed into an uneasy perch atop a crimson couch so that everyone in the throng could see him. A newspaperman who witnessed the commotion reported that Grant blushed like a girl. But the tumultuous reception left no doubt about the importance of the uncomfortable-looking figure on Lincoln's couch. The fate of the Union depended on him.

Lincoln and his war secretary, Edwin Stanton, rescued Grant from the crush and ushered him into a private room, where the president informed the general that he was to receive his new commission the following day. He would become a lieutenant general, the first man to hold that rank since George Washington, and his assignment would be to coordinate the Union war effort and defeat Lee.

The president gave Grant a draft of the speech that he intended to make and suggested a response that he thought would be appropriate for his new commander in chief. "First say something which shall prevent or obviate any jealousy of you from any of the other generals in the service," Lincoln advised. "Second, [say] something which shall put you on as good terms as possible with the Army of the Potomac." The next day, Lincoln presented Grant his commission in front of the cabinet and delivered his prepared speech. Grant stood and haltingly made a few brief remarks that he had penciled on a scrap of paper. Nothing that he said resembled the president's suggestions, making it clear that he meant to do things his own way.

The two men, however, forged a working relationship that pleased them both. Lincoln, for his part, promised to give Grant a free hand running the war as well as all the troops and supplies he needed to win. It was best, the president jocularly suggested, that Grant keep details of military operations to himself, because Lincoln feared that he would leak information to the press. In return, Grant promised Lincoln victories, sealing perhaps the most compatible working relationship between president and commander in chief that the nation has seen. Lincoln's political fortunes, a New York newspaper noted, "not less than the great cause of the country, are in the hands of General Grant, and the failure of the General will be the overthrow of the President."

Grant set about changing the way the North was fighting the war. By his estimation, the North's prime advantage was its massive edge in men and material. Northern leaders, however, had squandered those advantages by permitting armies in the war's various theaters to function like independent fiefdoms. In Grant's homespun language, forces east and west had behaved like a team of balky mules, each pulling without regard to the other. The absence of coordination had undermined the Union's war effort by permitting the Confederates to shuttle troops from one theater to another, magnifying their numbers.

The unhurried pace of combat also made little sense to Grant. Lincoln's generals had conducted the war in a leisurely fashion, fighting the enemy in big battles that lasted two or three days and then withdrawing to rest. Sometimes the lull lasted for months and afforded the rebel armies time to repair their losses and return as strong as ever.

Finally, by Grant's assessment, Union commanders had paid too much attention to conquering Confederate territory. Captured ground quickly became a hindrance, because Union armies had to relinquish troops to man garrisons, and attenuated supply lines were vulnerable to rebel attacks.

Grant's vision for the spring campaign avoided these pitfalls. He foresaw a coordinated offensive in which armies east and west would move in tandem, bringing the Confederacy's main armies to battle at one fell swoop. The days of short encounters were also over. Henceforth, Union armies would engage rebel armies and hold on like bulldogs, fighting every step of the way. And no longer would the Union objective be to occupy territory. Some places, of course, remained important goals. Richmond had psychological value and worth as a rail and manufacturing center, as did Atlanta, Georgia. But Grant's chief aim was the destruction of the Confederate armies, and he determined to press them, as he put it, "until the military power of the rebellion was entirely broken." In short, Grant meant to "hammer continuously against the armed force of the enemy and his resources until by mere attrition, if in no other way, there should be nothing left to him but an equal submission with the loyal section of our common country to the constitution and laws of the land."

Lincoln had finally found his man. The logic underpinning Grant's remorseless style of warfare was compelling, and the outcome was predictable. Assuming Grant kept his resolve, the Union must surely win. "Grant is like a bulldog," the president was heard to remark with satisfaction. "Let him get his teeth in, and nothing can shake him loose."

Grant gave his friend and trusted subordinate William Sherman the assignment of coordinating Union forces in the west. Suspicious of political intrigues and hoping to avoid the corrupting influences of Washington, Grant elected to travel with the Army of the Potomac and personally supervise the campaign against Lee. He decided to leave gruff, hook-nosed Meade as the army's titular head, freeing him from the minutiae of army administration and enabling him to focus on broad objectives. He also resolved to keep a close eye on Meade and to infuse the eastern army with some of his western tenacity.

Throughout April and into the first days of May, Grant bent his energies to strengthening the Army of the Potomac in its campaign against Lee. He ordered officers and soldiers on furlough back to their commands, arranged for the recruitment of men, and ripped garrison troops from their comfortable quarters in the North's urban centers and sent them to the front. His quartermaster gathered vast stores of food and military accouterments in Alexandria, Virginia, and dispatched those stockpiles by train to depots near Culpeper Court House. Stevedores in Alexandria readied more supplies for transport by boat down the Potomac River, to be unloaded and brought cross-country by wagons keeping pace with the army as it marched south. The enterprise was phenomenal. Busy hands packed more than a million rations, a hundred rounds of ammunition for each of the army's 120,000 soldiers, and medical supplies for 12,000 wounded troops. Purveyors gathered fodder for the sixty thousand horses hauling the army's 4,300 wagons, 835 ambulances, and 275 field guns, along with their caissons, battery wagons, and forges—more than enough wagons, a reporter estimated, to form a train extending from the Rapidan River to below Richmond. Grant also arranged for a herd of cattle to accompany his vast force as a commissary on the hoof. "Probably no army on earth ever before was in better condition in every respect than was the Army of the Potomac," Grant's quartermaster general effused.

The commander in chief's resolve and industry impressed even his critics. Meade, who was inclined to be wary of his new boss, wrote home that Grant's "great characteristic is indomitable energy and great tenacity of purpose." Meade's staffer Theodore Lyman agreed, adding that Grant "habitually wears an expression as if he had determined to drive his head through a brick wall, and was about to do it." Even Grant's opponents across the Rapidan expressed grudging admiration. Although Southern wags suggested that U. S. Grant stood for "Up the Spout Grant," those who knew the man counseled caution. Lee's vaunted lieutenant James Longstreet had been a close friend of Grant before the war and best man at his wedding. "That man," Longstreet predicted, "will fight us every day and every hour until the end of the war."

★ ★ ★

The mood in Richmond matched the dreary Virginia spring. For three years, war had scoured the state, and even homes that had escaped the tread of troops felt the conflict's heavy hand: Inflation reached into everyone's pocket, goods were scarce, and widows kept lonely vigils, striving to preserve what remained of their families and property. News from the front grew bleaker by the day. After Vicksburg and Gettysburg, the Confederacy's hopes for foreign intervention had become half-forgotten dreams. Now Grant was assembling a juggernaut on the Rapidan River, sixty miles north of the Southern capital. Reports suggested a second Union army gathering at Fort Monroe, southeast of Richmond on the James River, and a third enemy force menacingly congregating in the Shenandoah Valley, poised to attack from the west. Grant held Richmond and its defenders in a three-jawed vise, and his intentions were apparent. When the skies cleared, he would close the vise's jaws, crushing the rebellion's capital and the Confederacy's premier army.

Richmond's fate and the fortunes of the Confederacy were in the able hands of General Lee, whose victories during the past two years had made him a symbol of the rebellion's determined spirit. The Virginia aristocrat was the Army of Northern Virginia's prime asset, and his threadbare veterans trusted him implicitly. "General Robert E. Lee is regarded by his army as nearest approaching the character of the great and good [George] Washington than any man living," a Confederate wrote home. "He is the only man living in whom they would unreservedly trust all power for the preservation of their independence."

The general was fifty-seven years old—fifteen years Grant's senior—and his cropped beard had gone almost entirely gray. At first glance, the proud Virginian seemed strikingly unlike the plebian Grant. The two men, however, shared remarkably similar military temperaments. Both possessed well-honed aggressive instincts, and both reveled in surprising their foes with innovative and unexpected maneuvers. Lee's most brilliant successes were against armies that outnumbered him better than two-to-one, coincidentally the same numerical advantage that Grant held over him this spring.

The Army of Northern Virginia had suffered through the hard winter of 1863–1864 in camps south of the Rapidan River. Food was scarce, and desertions ran high. But wayward soldiers began returning by the score as spring advanced, and new recruits poured in from the Deep South. Food, however, remained a problem. "Short rations are having a bad effect upon the men, both morally and physically," Lee cautioned the authorities in Richmond.

By the end of April, Lee commanded a force of nearly sixty-four thousand soldiers. Facing an enemy more numerous and better supplied, Lee's troops nonetheless held important advantages. Most were veterans, and new recruits were generally assigned to veteran outfits, where they could fight alongside experienced troops. Lee's men were also fighting on home ground: They knew every road and path, every farmer was an ally and potential spy, and they had the élan of men defending their native soil. Most importantly, they had General Lee. Years later, a Virginian reminisced, "The thought of being whipped never crossed my mind."

But several concerns troubled Lee. One was his health. Assisted by only a small staff, the rebel army commander habitually immersed himself in the minutiae of command, often retiring late and rising by three in the morning. Heavy responsibilities and countless nights on hard cots had exacted a toll. "I am becoming more and more incapable of exertion, and am thus prevented from making the personal examinations and giving the personal supervision to the operations in the field which I feel to be necessary," the general admitted after Gettysburg. Writing one of his sons during the spring of 1864, Lee confessed a marked change in his strength that he feared rendered him "less competent for duty than ever."

Lee's chief worry centered on the Union force growing larger by the day north of the Rapidan. It was clear by mid-April that Grant meant to launch his major effort in the Old Dominion. "Every preparation must be made to meet the approaching storm which will burst in Virginia," Lee warned the Confederacy's war secretary. Ever aggressive, he preferred to seize the initiative and attack. A Confederate victory in Virginia, Lee urged, would disarrange Grant's plans and compel Lincoln to recall his forces in defense of Washington. But deficiencies in supplies required Lee to curb his belligerent instincts. "To make this move I must have provisions and forage," he reminded Richmond, and he expressed concern over the proximity of the contending armies to the Confederacy's capital. "If I am obliged to retire from this line," Lee predicted, referring to his hold on the country below the Rapidan, "either by flank movement of the enemy or want of supplies, great injury will befall us." Lee seldom used such dire language, and his resort to it here commanded President Davis's attention.

The heavy spring rains worked to Lee's advantage. Mud held the Union army fast while Virginia's pastures erupted in brilliant green, providing ample forage for the rebel army's horses. But the down-pours that shackled the Union army also immobilized the Confederates. Lee was troubled besides by the auxiliary federal army on the James River, southeast of Richmond, which was growing larger by the day. Concerned that he might have to detach part of his army to help defend Richmond, Lee decided to await Grant's move before committing his forces.

The curtain of gray clouds lifted during the last week of April, and Lee prepared for the inevitable onslaught. High ridges along the Rapidan's south bank bristled with artillery, ready to repel the blue-clad army on the far shore. Near the center of the rebel defenses, the ridges rose several hundred feet to form a commanding eminence named Clark's Mountain. A signal station on top gave a bird's-eye view across the river to Culpeper Court House and the plains beyond. Smoke from cooking fires curled from the Army of the Potomac's tents and winter quarters. Daily the fires multiplied, heralding the arrival of Grant's reinforcements. Lee frequently rode his horse Traveller onto Clark's Mountain to contemplate the enemy's encampment, searching for clues to Grant's possible movement. The massive concentration of troops, wagons, and cannon confirmed Lee in his impression that Grant meant to attack. It was not apparent, however, whether Grant intended to launch his offensive head-on or avoid the rebel fortifications by slipping around Lee's defensive line. About one matter Lee was confident. "Everything indicates a concerted attack on this front," he warned Richmond.

Hindered by circumstances from going on the offensive, Lee settled on a defensive strategy. The greater part of his army occupied twenty-five miles of fortified entrenchments south of the Rapidan, and rebel horsemen patrolled the country past each end of the rebel position, prepared to sound the alarm if enemy troops tried to slip around Lee's flanks. The Confederate commander resolved to hold the line of the Rapidan and attack the federal army as soon as it ventured across. At all costs, he would resist falling back to Richmond. Retreating, he insisted, would curtail his ability to maneuver, costing him the trump card in his deck of military tricks. Pinned against Richmond, his army would be immobilized, and the war would settle into a siege, which the North would win.

Thus was the stage set for the Civil War's decisive campaign. In later years, popular historians would tout Gettysburg as the turning point of the war. Gettysburg was a bloody fight, but its importance in deciding the conflict's result has been vastly overblown. By the spring of 1864, Lee had largely repaired his Gettysburg losses of ten months before. Ensconced in his Rapidan fastness, he faced Grant with only slightly fewer men than he had taken into Pennsylvania. This was several thousand more troops than he had wielded to deadly effect at Antietam and in his signal victory at Chancellorsville. Contrary to popular lore, the Army of Northern Virginia was in fighting trim. Supplies were short, but Lee's lean veterans would lose no battles because of hunger, nor would they run short of ammunition. They were firm in their determination to beat Grant and to send him packing, as they had his predecessors. "I don't have any fears but what we will give the Yanks the worst whipping they have got if they do attempt to take Richmond," a Southerner penned to his family.

The campaign would be a duel to the death between Grant and Lee, the best generals either side could field. The prize was the fate of two nations.

★ ★ ★

On April 27, with the campaign imminent, Lee reviewed several thousand soldiers recently returned from Georgia and Tennessee. The troops stood in double columns across a broad field, artillery posted on each end of the line. Lee rode between gateposts and into the clearing. This was the first time these men had seen their revered commander for several months, and they could not restrain their enthusiasm. A bugle sounded, artillery fired, and drums and fifes struck up "Hail to the Chief." Hats flew high as soldiers cheered at the top of their lungs. The sound, an onlooker recalled, was a "wild and prolonged cheer, fraught with a feeling that thrilled all hearts, [and that] ran along the lines and rose to the heavens." Lee trotted to the center of the clearing and watched the troops parade past. When the review ended, Lee and his staff rode up and down, inspecting the threadbare soldiers. Hands reached out to touch the general and his horse. "There was no speaking, but the effect was of a military sacrament," a participant remembered. Lee, too, was overcome with emotion. A chaplain riding with the staff saw tears tracing down his face. "Does it not make the general proud to see how these men love him?" the chaplain asked an aide. "Not proud," the staffer responded. "It awes him."

Sprinkled among the Army of Northern Virginia's veterans was a liberal allotment of new recruits. Early in 1864, faced with the prospect that constant campaigning was bleeding its armies dry, the Confederate government had broadened compulsory military service to include all white males from seventeen to fifty, extended terms of enlistment for the war's duration, abolished the hiring of substitutes, and tightened exemptions from military service. The dragnet pulled men into the army who were formerly ineligible, and Lee's veterans greeted the newcomers with derision, as worthwhile only for cannon fodder.

On a raw, wintry day, a train chugged into Lee's camps with a collection of greenhorns from South Carolina, some volunteers and some swept up in the new conscription law. Alighting from boxcars, they shuffled to the camps of General Samuel McGowan's

South Carolina brigade, in the shadow of Clark's Mountain. One volunteer from the Carolina Low Country seemed especially out of place in these martial surroundings. Five feet, seven inches tall and almost forty years old, he looked every bit his age. His beard and thinning hair, red in youth, were now mostly gray, and his stooped shoulders and ample belly suggested a lifetime of inaction. The man's medical record, had it been available, would have revealed that he suffered from epileptic seizures. A confirmed bachelor, the recruit—Charles Whilden was his name—had an abiding fondness for meerschaum pipes and good books. A dispassionate observer would have gauged him more at home in a clerk's office than on a battlefield.

War was a young man's game. The place for an unfit, aging epileptic was not at all apparent, except as a target to draw fire while veterans did their work. No one could have imagined on that cold Virginia day that the incongruous hunched figure would soon emerge as the unsung hero of the campaign's bloodiest battle.

This book is Charles Whilden's story.

2

A City by a Harbor

A visitor to Charleston in 1824 would likely have missed Magazine Street. It was only three blocks long, unlike Charleston's grander thoroughfares, and it boasted none of the imposing mansions that graced the broad avenues along the harbor. This was a working-class neighborhood, home to clerks, tradesmen, and occasional free blacks. The dwellings were mostly wooden and of the unique Charleston single-house style, built perpendicularly to the street with rows of front doors opening onto the ends of covered porches called piazzas. The piazzas of Magazine Street overlooked small yards and offered inviting places where families could congregate on summer nights to escape the stifling heat inside. This was a comfortable neighborhood, scented by mingled odors of cooking fires and jasmine and ringing with the chatter of children.

Magazine Street was part of a subdivision developed in the mid-1700s from land owned by Isaac Mazyck, a Huguenot immigrant to Charleston. Local lore held that it was named after powder magazines formerly located in the area. The steeple of St. John's Lutheran Church, its bell tolling out the quarter hours, towered over the northern end of Magazine Street, and a sixteen-foot-high concrete wall bounding the city jail looked back from the street's southern end. In former times, the jail quartered notables such as William Moultrie, imprisoned for debts after his term as South Carolina's governor. More recently, following the construction of a new jail in 1802, the building served as home to the city's incorrigibles, including brigands such as John and Lavania Fisher, hanged in 1820 for a string of brutal highway robberies and murders. The cells, six feet by eight feet, were crammed with as many as twenty inmates. Sanitation was primitive and disease commonplace. On still nights, screams rent the air from prisoners stretched on a pulley-and-rope device called the crane, which held them in place while jailors whipped them.

On the west side of Magazine Street, next to the jail, loomed the workhouse. Originally intended as a place to confine runaway slaves, vagrants, and disorderly seamen, the workhouse had been established on the site of a former sugar refinery or sugar warehouse. White prisoners had been removed from the workhouse when the new jail was constructed next door at the turn of the century, and the structure now served as a place for punishing slaves. Some of the unfortunates were under sentences for crimes, most commonly for running away, and many had been brought there by their masters. For a small fee, slave owners could pay to have their human chattels incarcerated, whipped, or subjected to a diabolical torture known as the treadmill. Chained to a rotating drum, slaves were forced to walk for hours at a rapid pace on the treadmill; anyone who fell or fainted would be flayed by the revolving drum. Charlestonians called the workhouse the Sugar House, after its original use, and slaves well understood what their owners meant when they threatened to give them a "little sugar" unless they shaped up.

★ ★ ★

Charles Edmondston Whilden was born on April 3, 1824, into a modest household in the shadow of the workhouse. His father, Joseph Whilden, struggled to make ends meet as an obscure newspaper editor. His mother, Elizabeth, already had her hands full with two girls and two boys—seven-year-old Charlotte, four-year-old Bayfield, little Joseph, who was three, and Ellen Ann, who was not yet two. Sharing the home with them was Joseph's twice-widowed mother, who lived there since acquiring the property in the late 1790s.

The elder Joseph made a precarious living. In 1816, he and a gentleman named Samuel Skinner founded the Charleston *City Gazette and Advertiser,* but Skinner drowned on a trip home to New England and left Joseph the newspaper's sole proprietor. By 1820, he had established the *Carolina Gazette,* a weekly newspaper that appeared every Saturday. The publication, Joseph declared in its maiden issue, was dedicated to "advocate and support the great cause of Republicanism, as being best calculated to secure the rights of the individual, and to advance the great interests of the country." Only a few pages long, the *Carolina Gazette* reported congressional proceedings, shipping news, obituaries, and items of local interest, as well as foreign news, especially from England and South America. A section chronicled the arrivals and departures of ships, and advertisements for sales and notices for the return of runaway slaves were popular items.

The newspaper never did well, but Joseph's enthusiasm remained undampened, and he weighed in on the major controversies of his time. His outspoken editorials defending dueling marked him as a staunch champion of the manly arts, a trait he passed on to his children. "Be it barbarous or polite: of Teutonic or Saracenic origin, [dueling] is considered the *ultra ratio* of gentlemen," Joseph lectured his readers. "While we may deplore its effects, it must be confessed that in many instances, the anticipation of a duel preserves those courtesies of life which otherwise would be frequently violated."

Economic hardship did nothing to lessen Joseph's procreativity. Two years after the birth of Charles, Richard Furman—named after the Baptist preacher who baptized Elizabeth and later performed her marriage to Joseph—was born. By 1828, with the addition of another boy named William, the rambunctious Whilden brood consisted of seven children in all, five of them boys. With a growing family and dwindling financial means, Joseph never seemed able to make ends meet.

Although the Whildens were far from wealthy, they still considered themselves among the city's elite, at least by blood, a distinction that counted a great deal in Charleston. Ancestors on both sides of the family settled the area in the late 1600s. Elizabeth's forebear Reverend William Screven founded the First Baptist Church of Charleston in the 1680s, and Joseph's father ran away from home as a teenager during the Revolutionary War to fight with the "Swamp Fox," Francis Marion, a daring guerilla renowned for his Robin-Hood-like attacks against the British. Other members of the Whilden family—most notably Joseph's cousin Elias, whose family owned a plantation and a fine home in Mount Pleasant, across the Cooper River from Charleston—played prominent roles in local society.

In the early 1830s, when Charles was six or seven, a stroke left Joseph partially paralyzed, sapping even further his ability to provide for his family. Economic salvation came from an unlikely source. Years before, Joseph's stepfather, Bayfield Waller, a Charleston merchant, purchased a young slave girl as a servant for his wife Charlotte. Named Juno by her new owners—after the fashion of naming slaves after mythological figures—she became an integral part of the Whilden household, and the children fondly called her Maumer or Maum, common appellations for slave women. "From our earliest recollection, we picture her in a blue plaid homespun dress reaching to her ankles," one of Charles's sisters-in-law later reminisced, "a large apron either of checked homespun or gingham; a delicately colored, or white, cambric neckerchief, and a similar style for her head."

Maumer Juno never tired of telling her story. She claimed to be of the Fulah tribe of West Africa. Her real name, she said, was Cumbe, and she was the daughter of a king. She contracted small-pox as a child, and her mother, believing that bathing in the sea would help cure her daughter's affliction, had taken her to the coast. One day, when she was with her mother in the early morning, worshiping the sun, a rustle in the bushes interrupted her praying, and she turned to find the cause of the disturbance. Sensing that her daughter was distracted, her mother swatted her. Slavers suddenly jumped from the bushes and seized both of them. Her mother escaped, but the slavers carried Cumbe to a slave ship. It was the last she would see of her homeland.

The slavers took Cumbe to the French colony of St. Domingue—now Haiti—in the Caribbean and sold her. She had been there for only a short time when slave revolts rocked the island, and the ten-year-old slave girl was sold again and sent to Charleston, where Waller bought her. About the same age as Joseph, Juno would serve first Joseph's mother and later Joseph.

Maumer Juno was illiterate but fluent in English, French, and her native African tongue. She was also a spellbinding storyteller and delighted in enthralling the family and visitors with tales of her African upbringing and her travails in St. Domingue. She practically raised Charles and his siblings—a family member remembered her striding about the house with a baby tucked under each arm—and Charles became deeply attached to her. She had special names for the children, calling them B, Capin, Mass Boss, Doctor, Donkey, Miss Mog, and Todie. Which of these appellations she applied to Charles we do not know, although the nickname reportedly stuck with him for life.

After Joseph fell ill, Maumer Juno redoubled her labors. When the destitute family had to hire out its cook to bring in extra income, Maumer Juno took over management of the kitchen. All day she also minded the children, and after the young ones had gone to bed, she toiled into the night, taking in washing and ironing and remitting the pay that she received to the family. After Joseph's death in 1838—Charles was fourteen—she added a day job, hawking wares for a local merchant and turning her earnings over to Elizabeth. Joseph's death also caused a change in Maumer Juno's legal status; ownership of her passed to Joseph's children in undivided portions. At some point she married, but she never had children of her own. She and her husband most likely lived in a small shack in the Whilden yard, as was the custom in those times.

★ ★ ★

Unlike most ventures by Europeans in the New World, Charleston began as an economic proposition, not as a religious experiment. In 1670, settlers from England and the Caribbean island of Barbados sailed into the wide protected harbor formed by the confluence of two rivers, later named the Ashley and the Cooper after Lord Ashley Cooper, a lord proprietor of the new colony. They staked out a fortified village a few miles upstream, then a few years later moved to the narrow peninsula where the two rivers emptied into an expansive bay. Planners surveyed an orderly grid of streets, and the city of Charleston began taking shape.

Fortunes were made first in commerce. Situated athwart major shipping routes from Europe, Charleston became a bustling port. Sailing ships rode the trade winds from the Azores to the West Indies, hitched a ride on the Gulf Stream, and swept north to the Carolinas. Stevedores at Charleston's docks off-loaded finished goods, rum, and sugar from Europe and the Caribbean and refilled the empty hulls with skins, lumber, and pitch brought by wagons from the Carolina interior. Groaning with bounty from the New World, the ships departed for other American ports or returned directly to Europe, completing the triangular trade route.

The real source of Charleston's wealth, however, was rice, not trade. The Carolina Low Country's tidal estuaries afforded ideal environments for raising the grain, and plantations fanned out around the city. Rice cultivation was labor-intensive, and the fetid marshes were unhealthy places, particularly in the summer, when heat and malaria made the Low Country virtually uninhabitable. African slaves provided the answer. Accustomed to the unrelenting heat of the torpid summer and more resistant to tropical diseases than the whites, Negroes were bought in from Africa and the Caribbean in large numbers. Black slaves and rice seemed a natural fit. Charleston's Barbadian settlers were familiar with the slave economy from sugar plantations on their home island, and adapting the Barbadian system to rice plantations in the Carolinas proved a relatively simple matter. Rice was also a staple along much of the western coast of Africa, and the inhabitants were intimately familiar with the arts of cultivating, cleaning, and husking the grain. That expertise was invaluable to Charleston's burgeoning planter class, which avidly sought slaves from the rice-growing regions of the windward African coast. Indigo, another labor-intensive crop, also flourished in the Low Country marshes, further fueling the region's appetite for slave labor.

By the end of the colonial period, Charleston was the largest city south of Philadelphia and perhaps the wealthiest urban center in all of North America. It was also the most beautiful. To escape the oppressive heat and disease of summer on their plantations, planters built grand town houses and filled them with ornate furniture and artwork. Theaters and places of entertainment catered to the moneyed elite, and the city gained a reputation for extravagance. Horse racing, cock fighting, and rounds of balls and parties enlivened the existence of the aristocracy. "The inhabitants are the gayest in America," a European visitor effused, proclaiming Charleston "the centre of our beau monde." Some critics scoffed at the Charleston elite's decadence. "The men are of idle disposition, fond of pleasures that lead them into a system of dissipation to which they are in a manner wedded," a disapproving visitor remarked. Another wag reported that daylight often surprised the city's young males "at the gambling table exhausted with fatigue and tortured with unsuccess."

Charleston's affluence rested on the backs of slaves. As plantations multiplied along the coastal marshes and tidal rivers, so multiplied the commerce in human flesh. A quarter or more of all Africans brought into the colonies passed through Charleston's slave markets, and black faces populated the city. "Carolina looks more like a Negro country than like a country settled by white people," a foreign visitor observed. In addition to working the rice and indigo plantations, slaves cleaned the streets and toiled as bricklayers, carpenters, blacksmiths, bakers, and laborers. They swarmed over the bustling wharves, serving as dockhands and stevedores, and they grew the city's produce and brought it to market, where other slaves purchased the goods and carted them back to their masters' homes.

Slavery touched every aspect of Charleston's social, political, and economic life. By one estimate, three-quarters of the town's white families—the Whildens among them—owned slaves. So accustomed was the white populace to slaves performing household chores that cooking, cleaning, and other everyday duties were considered too menial for proper folks. "No white woman, however humble in the scale of society, would touch this domestic work if she could avoid it," opined one observer. Life in Charleston without slavery was unthinkable, and the Negro's position in society was fixed, often with unsettling consequences to masters as well as to servants. "I wonder if it be a sin to think slavery a curse to any land," reflected the diarist Mary Boykin Chestnut, wife of a South Carolina senator and daughter-in-law of one of the state's largest slaveholders. "The mulattoes one sees in every family partly resemble the white children. Any lady is ready to tell you who the father is of all the mulatto children in everybody's household but her own." Inquired another of Charleston's ladies to her pastor: "Is it possible that any of my slaves could go to Heaven, and must I see them there?"

The demographics of the Carolina Low Country became a matter of growing concern to the white population. Charleston's 1820 census showed 24,780 inhabitants; 12,652 were slaves, 1,475 were free blacks, and 10,653 were whites, giving the city an emphatic black majority. The surrounding country boasted an even heavier concentration of blacks, with slaves in some rural areas composing 90 percent of the population. Slaves, a visitor noted, did all the labor and hard work. "They are in this climate necessary but very dangerous domestics," he wrote, "their number so much exceeding the whites."

As the Carolina Low Country's slave population grew, so grew the white minority's unease about servile insurrection. Authorities made organized efforts to guard against that eventuality almost from the start. In 1696, the fledgling colony adopted a slave code modeled after that in Barbados. Masters were free to punish slaves as they saw fit, and slaves traveling from plantations required passes. Blacks who attempted violence against their masters faced whipping, branding, or having their noses split, and attempted insurrection was punishable by death. Charleston, at the heart of the Carolina Low Country's slave empire, retained its surface calm, but the currents of dread ran deep.

White Charleston saw a preview of its worst nightmare in 1739, when some twenty slaves met west of town, decapitated a white store owner and a clerk, stole firearms, and roamed south, burning houses and killing white inhabitants at will. Their objective was to reach the settlement at St. Augustine, where they expected the Spanish authorities to grant them freedom. Recruits poured in from nearby plantations, swelling the mob's numbers to more than a hundred. In a chance encounter, the colony's lieutenant governor came upon the fugitives, spurred away to safety, and rallied the white population. Bands of white militia brutally squelched the rebellion and skewered the heads of captured blacks on mileposts along the road to Charleston as a deterrent to anyone considering following their example.

The rebellion sent a disturbing message to white Carolinians, and the government responded with a flurry of repressive measures regulating relations between whites and slaves. Teaching slaves to read and write was strictly forbidden, and Charleston's police were authorized to forcibly enter places engaging in "mental instruction" of Negroes. The city fathers also imposed a curfew. At the sound of a drum at nine o'clock, all blacks were to disappear from the streets until sunrise.

Charleston's whites liked to affect an unhurried, cultured air, but fear of a slave revolt was palpable, and public criticism of human bondage was taboo. Charleston's delegates to the Continental Congress vigorously objected to Thomas Jefferson's first draft of the Declaration of Independence, which denounced King George for waging "cruel war against human nature itself, violating its most sacred rights of life and liberty in the persons of a distant people who never offended him . . . carrying them into slavery." The offending provision was omitted. Later, white Charleston's eyes turned nervously to St. Domingue, where African slaves threw off the yoke of French servitude through violent revolution. White refugees from the island poured into Charleston with lurid tales of atrocities at the hands of the blacks. More terrifying was the ascendancy of Toussaint L'Ouverture, the black Napoleon, and the establishment of the black republic of Haiti. White Charlestonians began to imagine the hands of black revolutionaries in every mischief in their city. "The Negroes have become very insolent," a newspaper reported, "in so much that the citizens are alarmed, and the militia keep a constant guard."

The year 1800 brought more shocking news from even closer to home. In Virginia, a slave named Gabriel Prosser masterminded a revolt—"the most serious and formidable conspiracy we have ever known of the kind," according to the state's governor—that provoked South Carolina into passing strict measures to stem the flow of dangerous ideas into the state. Free Negroes, numerous in Charleston and suspect because of their semiautonomous status, were subject to enslavement if they left the state and tried to return. New laws prohibited blacks from holding religious meetings after dark, curtailed emancipation, and tightened the rules governing oversight of slaves on plantations. In 1804, authorities in Charleston jailed a local printer for distributing pamphlets about the black revolution in Haiti, charging him with fomenting domestic insurrection and disturbing the peace of the community.

The national Constitution, ratified by South Carolina in 1788, permitted the importation of slaves until 1808, after which the trade was to cease. South Carolina briefly suspended its participation in the international slave trade to help domestic creditors and to prevent slaves infected with the rebellious Haitian spirit from entering the state and spreading their revolutionary doctrines. But greed finally trumped fear; other states had also outlawed the slave trade, and South Carolina jumped into the void with a vengeance. South Carolina reopened the slave trade in 1803, and from 1804 through 1808, nearly forty thousand slaves passed through Charleston. Most came directly from Africa, giving the city an even more exotic caste. But the law authorizing importation contained an important caveat. No slaves who had set foot in the French West Indies or had participated in an insurrection could enter the state, and all had to have good character. The influx of Africans spurred the city fathers to further restrict the conduct of blacks, be they free or slave. Assemblages in numbers greater than seven were forbidden, as was dancing for merriment, smoking pipes and cigars, walking with a cane, or whooping or hollering in the streets.

The slavery debate assumed national proportions with Missouri's petition for statehood in 1820. Slave and free states were equally balanced, and the admission of Missouri threatened to upset that delicate equilibrium. Bitter debates in the Senate underscored sectional differences over the "peculiar institution." A compromise was finally struck by admitting Missouri as a slave state and Maine as free, and by drawing a line of demarcation through the territories at thirty-six degrees, thirty minutes, to govern the status of future admissions. New states south of the line would permit slavery; those north of the line would be free. The Missouri Compromise was a temporary solution, and the message understood by white Charleston was clear: Northern abolitionists would go to any lengths to further their cause, placing slavery's very future at risk.

★ ★ ★

Two years before Charles was born, white Charleston's fear of a slave rebellion had assumed dramatic immediacy. At the center of the story was a sixty-year-old free black, whose single-story frame house stood but a few blocks from Magazine Street and who spent his final days imprisoned in the workhouse, a stone's throw from the Whilden residence.

Telemaque was born in West Africa or the Danish West Indies. At the age of fourteen, he was purchased on the island of St. Thomas by Captain Joseph Vesey, who captained a ship loaded with slaves bound for St. Domingue. Sold into bondage to work on the island's plantations, Telemaque proved unfit for hard work—he was diagnosed with epileptic seizures—and his new owner returned him to Captain Vesey. Impressed by the boy's intelligence and bearing, the captain made him his assistant and re-named him Denmark Vesey. For the next two years, the young slave traveled the Atlantic basin, becoming conversant in Danish, English, French, and the dialects current among the captain's recent acquisitions from West Africa.

Captain Vesey settled in Charleston in 1783 and kept Denmark with him. The black man became a carpenter and, in spite of strict laws forbidding literacy among slaves, learned to read and write. He also earned money hiring out his labor—with the captain's permission—and he prospered. In December 1799, he purchased a lottery ticket, and early the next year, he won the handsome sum of fifteen hundred dollars. With his winnings, he bought his freedom and set himself up at 16 Bull Street, where he continued his trade as a carpenter.

Over the next twenty years, Denmark Vesey transformed himself into a revolutionary. He had experienced slavery firsthand, from the horrors of the Atlantic crossing to the plantations of St. Domingue to the slave markets of Charleston. His travels and readings had acquainted him with growing abolitionist sentiments in Europe and in the Northern states of his adopted country. Did not the Declaration of Independence's ringing pronouncements embodying modern notions of equality and the rights of man apply to himself and his kinsmen as surely as to their white brethren? How could one square Negro slavery with the heady doctrines of the American and French Revolutions? Had not the slaves of St. Domingue risen successfully against their masters and established a black republic? Why could the slaves of Charleston not do the same? Was it not their right to do so?

Vesey also drew inspiration from religious texts. In 1815, a free black established an African Methodist Episcopal Church in Charleston, and the congregation had quickly grew to more than four thousand members, including free blacks as well as slaves. Vesey became active in the church, where he taught and recruited followers. "He studied the Bible a great deal," a slave who knew him later testified, "and tried to prove from it that slavery and bondage is against the Bible." According to a confidant, Vesey emphasized the Old Testament's more apocryphal passages. His favorites were reputedly Joshua 6:21—"And they utterly destroyed all that were in the city, both man and woman, both young and old"—and Zechariah 14:2—"For I shall gather all nations against Jerusalem to battle; and the city taken, and the houses rifled, and the women ravished . . ."

After years of groundwork, Vesey claimed the ears of thousands of slaves and free blacks in Charleston and on neighboring plantations. Jack Pritchard, originally from Angola, became one of Vesey's fervent supporters. Revered as a shaman by slaves who retained their African beliefs, the bewhiskered figure called Gullah Jack exercised strong influence among the African residents of Carolina's coastal islands. Vesey also developed contacts in the plantation country north of Charleston, where refugees from the rebellion in St. Domingue had settled. Their slaves, called French Negroes, were attracted by Vesey's revolutionary dogma, having seen a version of it work on their native island, and Vesey could speak to them in their own tongue. Many of

Vesey's followers also came from the households of South Carolina's elite white families. Two of his closest lieutenants—Ned and Rolla Bennett—were slaves in the home of Thomas Bennett, the state's governor. Another supporter, John Horry, worked for Elias Horry, a prominent Charlestonian.

By spring of 1822, Vesey had matured his plan. What he envisioned—at least according to accounts later published by the city government—was the burning of Charleston and the slaughter of its white inhabitants. At the appointed hour, a lieutenant named Peter Poyas was to march into town, leading a mob of coastal slaves, and seize the government arsenal; Rolla Bennett was to lead a force and take the United States arsenal; and Gullah Jack was to bring slaves from north of town to join Bennett and parade through central Charleston, killing white people. More slaves directed by another of Vesey's adherents, Monday Gell, were to swarm through the docks and converge in the city's center. Ned Bennett was responsible for seeing that Governor Bennett and Charleston's mayor, James Hamilton, Jr., were murdered; then he was to join a contingent under Vesey at Bull Street. Meanwhile smaller bands were to steal horses and ride through town, killing any white people they met to prevent them from assembling or spreading the alarm. According to some accounts, once the city was in flames, Vesey intended for the insurrectionists to commandeer ships in Charleston harbor and sail to Haiti.

Vesey and his confederates made their preparations in secrecy. Slaves hid knives, clubs, and guns stolen from their masters, and French Negroes in the Santee region promised to make swords and spears after the African fashion. A blacksmith committed to preparing a hundred pikes, capped with sharp tips of iron. Monday Gell concealed a gunpowder keg, stolen by another slave, in his harness shop.

Vesey settled on Sunday, July 14, as the day of the uprising. The time was well chosen. It would be in the heat of summer, when

Charleston's white inhabitants traditionally left for cooler climates. And Sunday was the day when blacks were permitted to move about the city with relative freedom, congregating in large numbers around the market in the heart of town. The insurgents could assemble under the very noses of the unsuspecting white folks, whiling away the day in apparent idleness.

But too many people knew about the plan for it to remain secret. On May 26—a Saturday—a slave named Peter Prioleau made purchases for his mistress at the market and afterward went for a stroll along Charleston's wharfs, where he struck up a conversation with another slave, William Paul by name. "Do you know something serious is about to take place?" Paul asked. Taken aback, Prioleau averred that he had no idea what his new acquaintance meant. "We are determined," Paul explained, "to shake off our bondage, and for that purpose we stand on a good foundation; many have joined, and if you will go with me, I will show you the man who has the lists of names, and he will take yours down."

Disturbed by Paul's talk of revolution, Prioleau excused himself and sought advice from a free black named William Penceel. Penceel recommended that Prioleau tell his master what he had heard, and he did just that, first to his mistress and then to his master, when he returned from a trip five days later. Mayor Hamilton was alerted and had Prioleau and Paul brought to the workhouse for interrogation. Doubtlessly tortured, Paul named several conspirators, Peter Poyas and Ned Bennett among them. He also mentioned a sorcerer, most likely Gullah Jack, who carried a charm that made him invulnerable.

As the investigation widened and various conspirators were summoned for questioning, Vesey decided to advance the date for the uprising to June 16, also a Sunday. Another slave, however, passed word of the imminent revolt to the authorities, and this time they acted with resolve. Militia concentrated in the city, and the white inhabitants went on the alert. "I shall never forget the feeling of alarm and anxiety that pervaded the whole community from the time the danger became known, until all risk appeared to be over," a young boy later wrote. Charleston's white citizens spent a tense Sunday night, curtains drawn and weapons near at hand. "The passing of the patrols on the streets, and every slight noise, excited alarm," the boy remembered.

But the uprising did not come. Unable to reorganize his scattered followers and cognizant that the whites were now on to his game, Vesey called off the revolt.

Over the ensuing weeks, authorities rounded up Vesey and his accomplices. Acting according to the old Barbadian slave code, Mayor Hamilton convened a special court of seven prominent Charlestonians who were to serve as judge, prosecutor, and jury, and to conduct their proceedings in secret. Their verdicts, rendered at the end of June, surprised no one. Vesey was convicted and sentenced to death, and on July 2, he and five companions were escorted from the workhouse to the outskirts of Charleston and hung. The authorities deposited Vesey's body in an undisclosed grave.

An orgy of arrests followed. In all, 131 blacks were imprisoned, and 35 were executed. Authorities singled out the African Methodist Episcopal Church as a hotbed of revolutionary activity and had the building burned. The final executions took place near the end of July, when 22 conspirators were hung in a public display. The ceremony went awry when the fall from the scaffold failed to break the necks of several slaves. "Owing to some bad arrangement in preparing the ropes, they, in their agony of strangulation, begged earnestly to be dispatched," an onlooker reported, "which was done by pistol shot by the Captain of the City Guard, who was already prepared for such an emergency, i.e., shooting slaves."

Denmark Vesey's revolt was over, but the debate over the consequences of his intended insurrection had only just begun. To the horror of Charleston's whites, Northern newspapers expressed sympathy for the rebellion. "White men, too, would engender plots and escape from their imprisonment were they situated as are these miserable children of Africa," the New York *Daily Advertiser* predicted. Noted the Boston *Evening Gazette:* "Strictly speaking, nobody can blame the servile part of the population (the blacks) for attempting to escape from bondage, however their delusions may be regretted."

South Carolina's governor Bennett condemned the secret court proceedings as a travesty, suggesting that testimony coerced from slaves was less than trustworthy. But Bennett's views were in the minority, and with few exceptions, white Charlestonians closed ranks. As they saw it, they had barely averted being murdered in their beds. Joseph Whilden's editorials mirrored the popular suspicion that Northern abolitionists were somehow behind the plot. "When we think of the murder and violence and destruction of property which those deluded wretches might have committed, we cannot but be grateful to the Negro who gave the information," Joseph wrote. "While we shudder at the scenes which might have been acted, and contemplate its origin and progress in a society, we cannot but hope that our southern fellow citizens will hereafter be permitted to manage their own concerns in their own way. They have as much humanity and intellect, and more experience on this subject, than the people of the non-slave holding states can be supposed to have." The editor applauded the hanging of the conspirators. "In all cases involving such ingratitude to humane owners, such indiscriminate mischief to the unsuspecting, such demonical passion for blood and plunder and conflagration—we confess ourselves to be among the number of those, who deem the punishment cannot be too sudden, sure and final."

Denmark Vesey's slave revolt stirs controversy to this day. A recent review of the written trial record raises the intriguing prospect that the nation's largest planned slave rebellion might have been nothing more than a concoction by Mayor Hamilton to advance his own political fortunes. The mayor, the argument goes, used the secret kangaroo court, replete with coerced testimony from slaves, to create the illusion that Charleston was in danger and that he had saved the city. Exploiting the political capital that he gained as savior of white Charleston, Hamilton was subsequently elected to Congress, followed by a term as South Carolina's governor. Turning conventional interpretations on their heads, this view sees the Vesey episode, according to a proponent of the theory, not as "a plan by blacks to kill whites but rather a conspiracy by whites to kill blacks, which resulted in the largest number of executions ever carried out by a civilian court in the United States."

For purposes of our story, it matters not whether Vesey's rebellion was a real event or the figment of a conniving mayor's imagination. What matters is that Charleston's white community believed that the threat of rebellion was real. That perception lay at the root of emotions that would ultimately bring the country to war. And it also shaped the unique mix of attitudes that formed the world into which Charles Whilden was born.

★ ★ ★

The Vesey trial ended once and for all white Charleston's illusions that its slaves were complacent, and the truth hit men such as Elias Horry hard. When constables came to lead away his trusted servant John, Horry protested that John must be innocent. He would just as soon suspect himself, he insisted. Later, he confronted John in captivity. "Tell me, are you guilty?" he asked. "What were your intentions?" John minced no words. "To kill you," he told his former master, "rip open your belly, and throw your guts in your face."

The Vesey affair made controlling the slave population a prime matter of interest for all whites, whether or not they owned slaves. Some South Carolinians cautioned against the dangers spawned by the hysteria, but their call for restraint was drowned out by the clamor for action. "I fear nothing as much as the effects of the persecuting spirit that is abroad in this place," Governor Bennett wrote his friend Thomas Jefferson. "Should it spread through the state and produce a systematic policy founded on the ridiculous but prevalent notion—that it is a struggle for life or death, [then] there are no excesses that we may not look for—whatever be their effect upon the Union."

Excesses were indeed quick to come. New curfews governed the movements of blacks at night, and vigilante committees patrolled the roads, dispensing summary justice to wayward slaves and to white strangers suspected of harboring abolitionist views. To further stem the introduction of abolitionist ideas, a law required the incarceration of all black sailors on ships entering Charleston harbor and demanded that the captains pay the price of their men's imprisonment until their ships departed. A military presence was secured with the establishment of a guardhouse that evolved into the South Carolina Military Academy, now called the Citadel.

Charles's formative years—the 1830s and 1840s—saw white Charleston come increasingly under sharp criticism. In 1831, William Lloyd Garrison of Boston published the *Liberator,* urging the immediate abolition of slavery. That year also witnessed Nat Turner's bloody slave revolt in Virginia, a rebellion that Charlestonians and like-minded Southerners reflexively attributed to Garrison's agitation. Two years later, the American Anti-Slave Society emerged in Philadelphia, and the British Parliament ended slavery in the British West Indies. As Northern states abolished slavery within their borders, Northern politicians waxed shrill in their denunciation of human bondage.

South Carolina's response was to go on the offensive, arguing to the outside world that slavery was a practical and moral necessity. Alexis de Tocqueville, visiting from France, was struck by the vehemence of white Southerners, who insisted that relaxing control over slaves would incite a racial conflagration. The outcome, Tocqueville predicted, might well be "the extirpation of one or the other of the two races." Noted he: "Such is the view that the Americans of the south take of the question, and they act consistently with it. As they are determined not to mingle with the Negroes, they refuse to emancipate them." Benjamin Yancey of Alabama echoed a similar sentiment. "It is not with us merely a question of principle," he urged, "but of our very existence."

White Charleston's message was uniform: African bondage must be preserved at all costs. The city's economic, religious, and political leaders repeated the consistent theme that emancipation would sound the death knell of Southern civilization. Shortly after the Denmark Vesey conspiracy, Richard Furman, pastor of Charleston's First Baptist Church, where the Whildens worshipped, publicly addressed the governor of the state on behalf of South Carolina's Baptists, expounding a Biblical defense of slavery as a positive social good. Following Dr. Furman's lead, editors of denominational periodicals in the South filled the columns of their papers with scriptural justifications of slavery. "Slavery is a necessary element towards the composition of a high and stable civilization," insisted the *Charleston Southern Episcopalian.* Southern politicians such as South Carolina Senator John C. Calhoun also picked up and advanced the argument for slavery as a "positive good." In 1844, the Methodist

Church split into Northern and Southern factions over whether bishops might own slaves, and the next year the Baptist Church also divided along sectional lines over slavery.

Charleston's constant patrols and conspicuous show of armed might reminded one Northern visitor of the old fortified frontier towns of Europe. The difference, he observed, was that white Charleston did not fear an outside invasion; it directed its concern toward the internal threat of a slave rebellion within the city. The renowned architect Frederick Law Olmstead also passed through Charleston and noted that the cannon on the parade ground, the militia parades, and the armed police "might lead one to imagine that the town was in a state of siege or revolution." A prominent South Carolina lawyer described Charleston as living under a "reign of terror."

Charles came of age during this chaotic time. His views on slavery matched those of his parents, his peers, and his Southern contemporaries; it is difficult to imagine how they could have been otherwise. Throughout his life, Charles voiced deep distrust for abolitionists, and he gladly risked his life to fight for a breakaway republic dedicated to preserving slavery. Yet his family owed its very economic survival to a slave, the same slave who had raised him and for whom he expressed heartfelt love and respect. Charles was to travel widely and experience a varied range of people and cultures, but he never relaxed his emotional and intellectual attachment to Charleston and its institutions. He was a Southern patriot to the core, and that loyalty would become a defining precept of his life.

3

LIFE AMONG SCOUNDRELS AND GRASSHOPPERS

W e know little of Charles's early years. Illness ended Joseph Whilden's life in 1838 and doomed the family to genteel poverty. Charles and his brothers doubtless whiled away their childhood much like Charleston's other young boys, exploring the city's byways, playing along the waterfront, fishing, and casting for shrimp in the tidal creeks that wound through the marshes around the city.

At least two of Charles's brothers attended the College of Charleston, but existing records are silent about Charles's education. Letters that he wrote later in life reveal a well-schooled man conversant in history and politics, observant, and possessed of a quick and agile mind. His grammar was nearly faultless, his handwriting impeccable, and he exhibited a gift for expression that he likely acquired from his father. The doubt is not whether he received a formal education but where. The choices were limited. If the family had sufficient funds, he would have attended an all-male school run by a one-eyed Englishman named Christopher Cotes. Tuition was one hundred dollars a year, and the curriculum emphasized mathematics and the classics. In 1839—Charles would have been fourteen —the city council established the High School of Charleston, a public institution for boys that charged a more modest ten dollars a quarter. Reading, writing, and arithmetic were stressed, along with Greek, Latin, geography, history, and readings from Cicero, Homer, Caesar, and Virgil. Located on Society Street, the school was an easy walk from the Whilden home.

As the Whilden boys grew to manhood, they took different paths. Bayfield, Charles's oldest brother, turned to the Baptist ministry. In 1849—the same year that their mother Elizabeth died—Bayfield sailed to China with his wife, Eliza Jane. Not long after her death in Canton in 1850, Bayfield returned to South Carolina and continued with his ministry in the interior part of the state, called the Upstate, and in Georgia. Furman, two years younger than Charles, worked for several years as a schoolteacher and then followed in Bayfield's footsteps and became a Baptist minister. Joseph, nearly four years older than Charles, tried his hand at bookkeeping and later at selling insurance but had little success with either. For much of the 1850s, he lived with his brother William and depended on family members for support.

It was William, the youngest of the brothers, who had the head for business. Married on Christmas Day 1850 to a minister's daughter named Ellen Taylor, William secured promising employment as a clerk in the prestigious retail firm of Hayden and Gregg. The firm's founders, Nathaniel and Sidney Hayden, were Connecticut natives who had moved to Charleston in the 1820s and had formed a partnership with a silversmith from Columbia,

South Carolina, named William Gregg. Specializing in silver goods imported from New York and England, Hayden and Gregg sold wares that graced Charleston's prominent households. Customers drew on an inventory that included watches, jewelry, silver dinnerware, teakettles, pocket knives, scissors, and all manner of accessories. The store also featured weapons and martial accouterments such as swords, dirks, sashes, and guns. Always alert to business opportunities, the Hayden brothers advertised their shopping trips abroad in advance and offered to procure items on request. They also broadened their lines to offer life and casualty insurance. "Risks on the lives of slaves taken on reasonable terms," one of their notices promised.

The store occupied a three-story building at the corner of King and Hassell Streets, in the heart of Charleston's business district. It was a grand brick structure, rebuilt after the great fire of 1838 in the Greek Revival style. Masons had scored the exterior stucco to resemble stone blocks, and a row of bay windows displayed the firm's wares. The store was crowned by a parapet roofline and sported false-eyebrow windows lined with cast-iron grilles in a lotus-and-palmetto design, and cast-iron lion's heads that peered down at pedestrians ambling past. In 1852, William's employers made him a partner. Three years later, when Nathaniel Hayden moved to New York to become president of the Chatham Bank, his younger brother Augustus went into business with William, renaming the firm Hayden and Whilden. The *Charleston City Directory and Stranger's Guide* for 1856 listed Hayden and Whilden as "importers and dealers in watches, clocks, jewelry, etc."

As William's prosperity increased, so did the size of his family, which soon included three daughters. Also living with William were Ellen Ann—Charles's unmarried sister—a nephew, and several servants. Befitting a person of his status, William purchased property at the corner of Wentworth and Rutledge, a decidedly more upscale neighborhood than the Whilden brood's former Magazine Street digs. And as consummate proof that he had arrived socially, he bought a billiard table. "It is one of the best games for exercise, and I think the best thing for ladies," Charles wrote William when he learned of his sibling's acquisition. "If everyone who could afford it had such things in his house, he would find enough happiness at home without seeking it elsewhere."

★ ★ ★

William was always Charles's favorite brother, and the two remained close throughout their lives. But while William established himself at a young age as a pillar of Charleston's retail community, Charles embarked on a whirlwind of ventures that all ended miserably. His attempts to find a wife and a suitable career failed with a regularity that was almost comical.

Charles first pursued a career in law; the bustling seaport town offered opportunities for enterprising attorneys, and the profession carried an enviable degree of respectability. He probably hired on with a local attorney as an apprentice, reading law and learning the trade well enough to sit for the state bar examination. Although details of Charles's apprenticeship have been lost to history, we do know that in 1845, at the age of twenty-one, he was admitted to the South Carolina bar in a ceremony in Columbia, the state capital.

But Charles's legal career quickly soured. As fortune would have it, his admission to the bar corresponded with a period of steep economic decline in South Carolina's Low Country, due to falling rice prices. Unable to make a living in Charleston, Charles moved to Pendleton, in the interior of the state, but he had no more success there than in his hometown. Like many other young South

Carolinians of his generation, he decided to leave the state and seek his fortune elsewhere.

For reasons that remain obscure, Charles moved to Detroit. Vast iron deposits had been discovered on the Upper Peninsula of Michigan in the mid-1840s, and speculators were flocking to the state. Several of Charles's acquaintances from Charleston had settled in the region, and they no doubt urged him to come. Charles's fling at speculating, however, was no more productive than his attempt at lawyering. He bought several hundred dollars worth of copper stocks, but the shares stubbornly refused to rise in value. He also purchased property on Lake Superior on the off chance that the land might contain minerals, but that speculation proved as unfruitful as the stock venture. The plot of land, Charles reluctantly concluded, was good only for raising potatoes.

Unable to make money the easy way, Charles settled for employment as a clerk at the United States Commissary Office in Detroit, boarding at the National Hotel downtown. The *Detroit Directory* for 1854 listed him as a clerk, this time at the Quartermaster's Office, and noted that his residence had changed to the Michigan Exchange hotel. He found it impossible to make ends meet and fell into debt, borrowing several hundred dollars from his brother William. His brother Joseph was also having financial problems and asked Charles for money, but Charles could do nothing to help. "I am very sorry to hear of brother Joseph's embarrassments and wish I was rich enough to advance him favors," Charles wrote William in frustration, "but as I cannot, we must console ourselves with the thought that not one business man in ten is uniformly successful and that most of them at some time or other experience a reverse of fortune."

Charles's social life, unlike his economic endeavors, prospered, and he hobnobbed with some of Detroit's leading figures. He became especially close with the family of Eber Brock Ward, one of

Detroit's most successful entrepreneurs. Ward was a self-made man, having started as a lowly deckhand at the age of twelve on his uncle Sam Ward's trading schooner. In 1853, when Charles got to know him, Ward was assembling a group of financiers to develop the Eureka Iron and Steel Works. The Ward family's widespread business interests included newspapers, railroads, shipping lines, insurance companies, and banks, as well as investments in timber and ore. "Their name was almost synonymous with success," Charles wrote home. He also used the Wards' experiences as an example to encourage Joseph. The Wards, he explained to his struggling brother, once owned a fleet of steamboats on the Great Lakes, but a series of accidents had chipped away at their fortune. Charles considered them possessed of such "unconquerable energy," however, that he was certain they would "come out richer than ever." Joseph, he predicted, had the perseverance of the Wards and was just as likely to succeed.

Some of the Wards' luck did indeed rub off on Joseph, if not on Charles. The year 1854 found Joseph running a stationery shop in Charleston, and the venture prospered. He did well enough to purchase a home near William, where he lived with his wife, his own burgeoning family, and Maumer Juno. The entire Whilden clan—Charles excepted—were settled into comfortable, middle-class lives.

★ ★ ★

As Christmas of 1854 approached, thirty-year-old Charles wrote William from Detroit. Money remained a problem, and cognizant of his advancing years, Charles regretted his failure to find a spouse. His friends the Wards tried to help by suggesting that Charles marry one of their relatives, but the romance never took root. "You may remember that I told you that one of them liked me so much, that he wished me to marry his Aunt who was not much over fifty and has red hair," Charles reminded William in December of that year. "I do not know whether I will accept the invitation, but as you have so kindly invited me when married to come with my lady to your house and spend the Honeymoon, do not be astonished if you see me one of these days enter your mansion corner of Wentworth and Rutledge with my venerable bride." The prospective liaison came to naught.

One Detroit contact, however, did pan out. John Breckinridge Grayson, a Kentuckian and military man of repute, befriended Charles. A graduate of West Point, Grayson served as General Winfield Scott's commissary officer during the Mexican War and had recently become chief of the Commissary Department of New Mexico. He invited Charles to come along as his personal secretary, and Whilden jumped at the chance to draw a steady salary and repay his debts.

Grayson's invitation also offered Charles a chance for adventure. The United States acquired New Mexico in 1848 as spoils from its recent war with Mexico, and its population was overwhelmingly Hispanic. Some prominent Southerners looked askance at the darker hue of the inhabitants and their reputedly loose morals. South Carolina's outspoken Senator Calhoun, for example, fulminated against granting a political voice to the new territory's "colored" inhabitants, somberly reminding his colleagues, "Ours, sir, is the Government of the white race." But for many men like Charles, New Mexico seemed an intriguing land of mystery.

Santa Fe, New Mexico's largest town, was the territory's political and commercial center, and getting there was no easy undertaking. Most visitors came by way of the Santa Fe Trail, an eight-hundred-mile path from Independence, Missouri, through the heart of Comanche country. The prize at the end of the trail was a drab sprawl of brown adobe buildings clustered around a dusty central plaza. The town numbered no more than five thousand permanent inhabitants, but a regular influx of traders, adventurers, and fortune-seekers kept it buzzing. Soldiers garrisoning nearby Fort Marcy protected the bustling trade center from marauding Indians and provided a visible Anglo presence.

Charles left Detroit in May 1855 and journeyed to St. Louis, where he was to join Colonel Grayson. The colonel was busy assembling an impressive wagon train at Fort Leavenworth made up of some five hundred soldiers, seven hundred mules and horses, and more than a hundred wagons. He had hoped to start right away, but the Missouri River was unseasonably low, making it difficult to bring in supplies by boat. But by June 30, the procession was finally off.

It took Grayson and his entourage two months to reach Santa Fe, and the trail more than satisfied Charles's yen for adventure. A few weeks into the trip, a servant dropped red-hot coals on the prairie grass, igniting an uncontrollable blaze that consumed a large portion of the expedition's tents and muskets. Stray bullets set off by the fire wounded four or five men, and countless others were left without shelter. "You have seen the Books at School pictures of the prairies on fire," Charles wrote his brother William in the first of several letters detailing his experiences, "and you can imagine how like the old Harry the fire goes when it has once started." Charles also witnessed a stampede—"imagine some seven hundred animals getting frightened and rushing through your camp at twenty miles an hour, overturning and trampling down everything in their way, and rushing over the plains like a whirlwind," he explained to William. Twice the expedition swam its horses and wagons across rivers swollen by rain, drowning two soldiers. "Suffered from pestilence and thirst," Charles informed William, "but I enjoyed it on the whole."

Western wildlife fascinated Charles, who marveled at the buffalo herds moving across the plains. "We also saw deer, antelope, and rabbits they call 'Jackass Rabbits,' from their resemblance to that animal being almost as large—with just as long ears; prairie dogs, a very harmless animal living in villages under ground, and looking more like large squirrels than dogs, having their own constitution and laws, and living as they say with perfect happiness in company with rattle snakes and owls," Charles wrote. "As for the rattle snakes, hundreds were killed every day—this is the country for them—big ants, hopper grapes with stomachs like aldermen, and every kind of insect and vermin—spotted lizards would crawl under our beds, but we had to get use to them—the wolves howled about our encampment every night, and would look us in the face in broad daylight."

But the highlight of the trip was the Comanches. "You should have seen these wild Indians," Charles effused, "all painted and decked off with feathers and their splendid horses which they rode as if they [had] been born in the saddle—the squaws dressed the same as the men, and armed with their bows and arrows tipped with steel or iron." The young boys he described as "hard cases" and marveled at their ability to kill an antelope with an arrow "as easily as one of our marksmen with a rifle."

One day, a force of Indians that Charles estimated at four thousand warriors swept across the plains. They were Comanches and Kiowas under Shaved Head, the preeminent Comanche chief who had recently negotiated a treaty with the Americans. Charles feared for his safety because most of the troops with the expedition were rank novices, and the earlier fire had destroyed most of their weapons. "They could have wiped out the whole command,"

Charles wrote, "but they did not know what we did, and professed peace." Shaved Head took a liking to Charles. "I rode along side of him and White Eagle, Buffalo Hump and other of their big chiefs for a dozen miles," Charles boasted. "Shaved Head seemed pleased with my red beard. He pointed to it, and then to the sun."

When the expedition reached within a hundred miles of Santa Fe, the town's commandant, General John Garland, rode out to greet the newcomers. Charles accompanied Grayson and Garland back into town, ahead of the wagons, and he was disappointed by what he saw. "Santa Fe is nothing but a collection of mud houses one story high," he concluded after looking around. Rain had washed away several buildings, including one intended for Charles, but he found temporary accommodations in a "splendid mud hotel." His overall impression was scathing. "It ain't worth keeping," he informed William. "Magnificent scenery and all that, but very little good land," he added, populated by "the most worthless set of scoundrels I have ever seen and the most ignorant." It would be best, he advised, to transport the inhabitants elsewhere, fence the territory, and then "give it up to the Indians and let them fight it out in their own fashion."

★ ★ ★

A good night's rest persuaded Charles to reserve judgment. "Perhaps I am wrong in giving such a hard character to the New Mexicans," he penned in his neat hand to William. "When I become more acquainted with them, I will no doubt find that they are better than they look at first sight, and I have not seen any of the better class—of which I hear there are very few." He was also heartened to learn that a house damaged in the recent rains was being repaired for Colonel Grayson and himself. "When I can have my own room and smoke my pipe, having on my morning gown and slippers, I will be happy," he predicted.

Within weeks, Charles and the colonel were ensconced in a single-story home with an office, a sitting room, two bedrooms, and a kitchen—and three servants, including an Italian cook. "I live very much as I did in Detroit," Charles informed his sister-in-law Ellen, "taking the world easy, and not bothering myself about what I cannot help." To William, he confided that he was "living as pleasantly as a man can do in New Mexico, and have got back into my regular, quiet habits. I get up, put on my dressing gown and slippers, and frequently forget to put on a coat all day, having nothing to call me outside the house." He wore old clothes, and his moustache had grown so long "that I can't eat soft boiled eggs comfortably," he admitted.

For companionship he befriended Dr. David Camden DeLeon, a fellow South Carolinian, and dined occasionally with him at the officers' quarters. He also looked forward to receiving the Charleston newspapers, which he had arranged to have sent to Santa Fe. The most exciting event in his otherwise humdrum existence was an introduction to Christopher "Kit" Carson, who invited Charles to visit him at his ranch in Taos. "He is an unpretending modest man, about my size only thicker," he wrote, "and has the reputation of being as noble hearted as he is fearless."

A few rides in the country set Charles crowing about the scenery—"the sunsets here are grand beyond description," he assured Ellen. Nothing, however, changed his opinion about the populace. The women, he professed, were "good looking enough with jet black eyes, but they are ignorant." As for the men, "they are for the most part the worst specimens of humanity I have ever seen, and I really don't know what they were made for." He felt nothing but disdain for the Catholics. "The priests have the reputation of being great rascals," he reported, "and yet if a Mexican girl meets one in the street, she drops on her knees to receive his blessing and remains on her knees in the dirt until he has passed."

Finding little to like in his new surroundings except the scenery, Charles grew nostalgic for Charleston and his family. "I should like it is true to have you setting alongside of me trying to smoke through politeness," he wrote William, "and to hear your wife upbraiding me for wishing to ruin her husband, but I hope one of these days to have that pleasure." Tongue in cheek, he insisted that Ellen come for a visit. "I think you would be delighted with the trip—everything would look so different from what it does in the States," he assured her. "It would be so romantic, too, to see you mounted on top of a mule, holding onto [your daughter] Julia and the mule's long ears to prevent being tumbled off." Several officers had brought their wives out, and they appeared to have withstood the rigors of the journey. "One thing I have noticed however," he admitted, "is that they no sooner get here, than they want to be at home again." His letters invariably closed with the salutation, "Please give my love to all the folks including Maum Juno."

Charles's first Christmas in Santa Fe triggered an intense spell of homesickness. "I recollect well how we used to look for this season when boys, and I would like to be with you now to fire off a few packs of firecrackers," he wrote William in late December, and then he proceeded to get in a dig against his new neighbors. "Here we have a celebration every now and then. There are so many saint days among these Hottentots that it is hard to recollect them. The men and boys build large bonfires on the plaza, and the priests on the top of the churches, so that occasionally Santa Fe looks like a city in a state of conflagration. This is the season too when the masked balls are the fashion, and fun generally prevails. Among other usages the girls have any quantity of colored eggs filled with cologne or some other sweet substances, and crack them over the heads of everyone they can. One poor bald headed gentleman of my acquaintance had to take more than his share, and was compelled to leave the ball and go home for protection."

* * *

The long winter's tedium, coupled with a dearth of mail occasioned by harsh weather, solidified Charles's disgust with his new home. "There being no theatres, libraries, lectures or concerts, with which you people in the States help to pass the time, makes it worse than one of the smallest towns in Carolina," he complained to William. "Occasionally we have an Indian foot race or something of the kind to stir us up a little," he added, "or an Express rides suddenly into town with the news that the Indians have run off the cattle of some neighboring ranch—and sometimes a fight or two on the plaza, or a court martial, but nothing like you have in a large city." Charles jumped into a whirlwind of civic activities to relieve the boredom and in due course became the warden of a Masonic Lodge, the president of a Literary Society, and an active member of a Territorial Democratic Central Committee.

With time on his hands, Charles had ample opportunity to pursue his interest in genealogy. He was hardly unique in his fascination with his family tree, as pride of ancestry ran strong among Low Country Carolinians. Aware that his grandfather had grown up on a plantation a short distance north of Charleston, he opened a correspondence with Elias Whilden, his father's second cousin and a rice planter in his late fifties. Elias once owned more than 250 slaves and was easily the most prominent Whilden in the state. Now semiretired, Elias graciously declined Charles's invitation to visit him in New Mexico.

A visit to the neighboring town of San Miguel only served to further harden Charles's jaundiced view of Mexican culture. "You could hardly see a vacant space on the halls of the inside of some of their houses," he informed William following his trip. "They are all covered with looking glasses and pictures of the saints, most of them ugly beyond description. The bedding is arranged around the room in the day time in the form of lounges, and spread out at night. Whenever you go into a Mexican house, the first thing the old lady does is to give you a terrible hug which is not as pleasant as they eat so much sheep. They have a strong flavor of mutton, and the young ladies make you a cigarette and also take a smoke with you. I regret that I have so little to do with them that I stand a poor chance of learning Spanish, but it is not the pure Spanish— it is corrupted very much from the language of Cervantes." The New Mexicans, it seemed, could do nothing right, including speaking their own language properly.

Charles tried to keep up his Detroit acquaintances, but sharpening sectional differences over slavery strained those contacts. "One of the Detroit editors sent me his paper with a request that I would drop him some news," he informed William. "I wrote a hurried account of our trip very similar to the one I wrote to you, to one of my friends, permitting him to publish it, if he thought proper—but I am almost sorry that I did so, as the paper since has turned a little abolition, and as my letter was not, presume it will not appear."

He still searched in vain for female companionship, counting only seven unmarried young ladies in the territory. In the dead of winter, he undertook a hundred-mile journey to Fort Union to bring two women back to Santa Fe, where they could socialize with the married ladies. Presumably he also wanted to have a look at them. The journey was bitterly cold, but the ladies, Charles reported, were "trumps" who feared neither the cold nor the Indians. "The only objection I have to them," he informed William, "is that they are so homely." In March, Charles learned that the daughter of Colonel Dixon S. Miles at Fort Stanton, three hundred miles from Santa Fe, was soon to be married. "This will leave six unmarried American ladies in New Mexico," he lamented, adding that he would "very much like to see an American young lady as there are none in Santa Fe, and I have not seen one for some time." After another year in Santa Fe, he began to sound desperate. "If there are any of my sweethearts in Carolina who want to come out, send them on," he urged William. "I will meet them halfway, viz., at the crossings of the Arkansas."

Finances also remained a problem. Charles left his copper stocks with a friend in Detroit named Palmer, and they continued to decline. Palmer had to sell some shares to cover assessments, and he finally recommended that Charles dispose of the remaining shares to minimize his losses. Before Charles could act, however, the stock market took a precipitous dive, and Charles in desperation authorized Palmer to forfeit his holdings. "As there was no certainty these stocks would be ever worth anything," he explained to William, "the best way was to cut them off." Charles's expectation that minerals would be found on his Lake Superior holdings also failed to pan out, but he decided to hold on to the land. Unlike his stocks, the property was at least not losing value, and he could use it to secure his debts.

Charles still had his government salary to fall back on, but even that was not what he had expected. Although Grayson promised him fifteen hundred dollars a year, Congress authorized only nine hundred dollars per annum, leaving him no course but to tighten his belt and save part of his meager salary to pay off his debts. "I can do it better out here than in the States," he assured William, "as there are no concerts, theaters, white kid gloves, subscriptions to charities or churches, or gallanting the ladies on sleigh rides, etc., to make a man's money fly." On the other hand, "everything costs twice as much as it does in the States," he admitted, and he "always found that it is these little daily expenses which amount to more at the end of the month, than board or clothing, how dear they may be."

The belt tightening paid off, and in mid-1856 Charles proudly wrote William that he had retired all his obligations, save what he owed William and the *Charleston Mercury* for his newspaper subscription. He had also brought current the taxes on his Lake Superior property, which he pledged to William in case anything happened to him.

The next spring, with his financial situation seemingly under control, Charles decided to try his hand once again at a commercial venture. This time he chose farming. "The other day I hired a ranch of 16 acres having on it a house with 17 rooms, about 28 miles from Santa Fe, bought provisions, etc., and started a man to superintend it in the planting thereof," he wrote William in April 1857. "I will take a ride out there every week or two and stay a few days for recreation," he went on, adding that he expected to grow cabbages, potatoes, beans, corn, and sugarcane. He was getting "tired (thoroughly so) of attending to Uncle Sam's affairs in this territory, and if the signs are encouraging may go live on my farm in a month or two, and let the government slide," he wrote. "If I can make a few hundred dollars, my deliberate object is to go to some part of Texas or other new country and commence the practice of law. All I want is a little money to support me for a time at the outset. If I fail in my plantation scheme, I will have to defer this intended sticking up of my shingle, until I pay up the debts which I have already contracted and will be obliged hereafter to contract for the farm."

But this venture too was doomed. "I have had to send 70 miles for potatoes to plant and if I do not succeed in getting them, I will not probably do so well, as potatoes are the most lucrative crop of the territory," he wrote William shortly after he acquired his plantation. "The grasshoppers are also a great scourge to the country and may eat up my crops. If so, well and good, I must grin and bear it. If I should not make anything I will have the satisfaction of trying to do something for myself, and shooting ducks, of which there are a great many, my ranch being right on the Rio Grande."

A chain of misfortunes undermined Charles's agricultural foray. Colonel Grayson became seriously ill with pneumonia, preventing Charles from leaving town. In Charles's absence, the overseer proved less than competent, and then the weather turned fickle. "I could have been entirely out of debt if I had not gone into the farm speculation," Charles sadly informed William. "All I have heard from the farm, after spending all my cash on it, was that a few cabbages and watermelons had made their appearance." Miserable as it seemed, Charles saw no course but to continue in his clerk's position until he paid off the new debts from his "plantation speculation."

Just when it appeared that things could not get worse, a swarm of grasshoppers descended on his crops. Charles, as usual, did his best to remain hopeful. "I have been out to my little farm at Pino Blanco, and if the grasshoppers do not eat up my cabbages, corn and beans may at least clear expenses," he wrote William. "If they do, I will be flat broke again, and somewhat in debt."

Through it all, Charles kept his sense of humor. "You tell me that last year was your 32nd birthday," he wrote William. "I think it was my 33rd, as I was born in 1824. If your whiskers are getting gray, mine are as red as ever. I regret to say, however, that my hair is extremely gray, and notwithstanding Maum Juno used to tell me that each one of them would be worth $1,000, I have never been worth $1,000 yet. I could sell out my head of hair at Maum Juno's calculation for about $100,000."

★ ★ ★

The 1850s—Charles's years in Detroit and Santa Fe—saw the national rift over slavery widen past repair. The war with Mexico and the annexation of the new territories raised vexing questions: Should new states be carved from the conquered lands, and if so, should they be slave or free? A compromise permitted California to enter the Union as a free state, deferred the status of further admissions, and enacted a stronger fugitive slave law requiring Northern citizens to return escaped slaves to their owners. Outspoken politicians in South Carolina considered the Compromise of 1850 a setback because California's admission skewed the balance in Congress in favor of the free states. It would only be a matter of time, Southerners warned, until the free states tried to abolish the South's peculiar institution. The choice, a South Carolina newspaper warned, was clear: "We must give up the Union or give up slavery."

Debates over the status of the Kansas and Nebraska territories in 1854 reopened sectional wounds. Both territories lay north of the line demarcated in the Missouri Compromise of 1820 and hence were eligible for admission only as free states. But the prospect of more free states was antithetical to Southerners, and bitter wrangling tied Congress in knots. A new negotiation, embodied in the Kansas-Nebraska Act, abrogated the Missouri Compromise and provided that persons living in the Kansas and Nebraska territories would decide by vote the status of slavery in their respective jurisdictions. Southerners felt mollified because the measure opened the possibility of slave states carved from Northern territory, and

President Franklin Pierce, a New Englander, backed the compromise because it cooled sectional tempers. But the consequences were dramatic as abolitionist and pro-slavery partisans poured into Kansas, precipitating a bloodbath that made any hope of reconciliation impossible. Impressive numbers of South Carolinians hurried west and actively participated in the tragedy known as Bleeding Kansas.

From the remoteness of Santa Fe, Charles closely followed the national debate over slavery from newspapers, particularly the outspokenly pro-slavery *Charleston Mercury*. His letters expressed strong pro-slavery views. "The country is getting into a pretty fix," he wrote William early in 1856, "when a set of abolition rascals can impede the whole business of a nation, and stop the wheels of government." Later that year he complained that "the Government is becoming more abolition every day, and did we not have Pierce and a few honest men at the helm of state, we would be shipwrecked." Like many of his contemporaries, he feared that the slavery issue would split the country. And like most of his fellow Charlestonians, he believed that the North should back down. "The Union may last a few years longer," he predicted, "but unless a decided change takes place in Northern politics, it must at last go under."

South Carolina remained in the forefront of the slavery controversy. In May 1856, Massachusetts Senator Charles Sumner derided a South Carolina senator for choosing "the harlot slavery" as his mistress. Congressman Preston Brooks of South Carolina avenged the slight by savaging Sumner with a cane in the Senate chamber. Brooks was lauded throughout the South, where pieces of the cane were distributed as souvenirs, but Northerners were appalled and denounced the vicious attack on an unsuspecting man as an act of barbarism. Brooks resigned his seat and was overwhelmingly reelected.

Charles followed the political machinations leading up to the 1856 presidential election with interest. "The last mail brought us the announcement of the nomination of [James] Buchanan and [John C.] Breckinridge, and all the Democrats here are highly delighted, and we think that we shall surely whip the Black Republicans and Know Nothings in the coming election," he wrote William. Charles was especially excited about Breckinridge, who was related to Colonel Grayson, and he hoped to get a lucrative appointment if Breckinridge was elected vice president. The Democrats won, but nothing in the way of a new job materialized for Charles.

While Southerners took heart from Buchanan's victory, the new Republican Party, which was fervently opposed to the expansion of slavery in the territories, did unexpectedly well, and sectional mistrust ratcheted higher still. In 1858, Senator William H. Seward, the leading Republican contender for president, warned of an "irrepressible conflict" in which the United States "must and will, sooner or later, become entirely a slaveholding nation, or entirely a free-labor nation." Congressman W. W. Boyce of South Carolina delivered an emotional rejoinder. "Mr. Seward's proclamation of his purposes is the logical result of the dogma of the Republican Party, that slavery is a crime," he asserted. "The principle of the equality of the races that underlies the philosophy of your movement would drive you on in vain wars against the higher laws of God to demand that the enfranchised blacks should be put on a social and political equality with the whites; this, and this alone, would be the finale of your irrepressible conflict." And such a finale, of course, was unacceptable to Southerners.

When the abolitionist John Brown launched an armed raid against the government arsenal at Harper's Ferry in October 1859, Southerners recoiled in terror. Here, they declared, was proof that white abolitionists were bent on inciting a race war on Southern soil. A map found in Brown's possession with X's marking dense black populations was read as targeting areas for rebellion, and South Carolina reacted much as it had after the Denmark Vesey affair: with a wave of repressive legislation. New laws restricted travel in the state by outsiders, banned writings or drawings intended to "disaffect" slaves, and directed postmasters to seize abolitionist mailings and turn them over to magistrates to be burned.

In April 1860, the Democratic convention opened in Charleston. The leading Democratic candidate, Stephen A. Douglas, was already a pariah in the South for advocating a stance on slavery in the territories similar to that of the black Republicans. The territories, argued Douglas, must have the right to determine whether or not to permit slavery within their borders. The slave states insisted on a plank confirming that neither Congress nor the territorial legislatures possessed "power to abolish slavery in any territory, nor to prohibit the introduction of slaves therein, nor any power to exclude slavery therefrom, nor any right to destroy or impair the right of property in slaves by any legislation whatever." The lines were drawn, and when the convention rejected the Southern proposal, delegates from the eight lower Southern states walked out amidst raucous celebration. "There was a fourth of July feeling in Charleston last night—a jubilee," an observer wrote the next morning. Northern Democrats met the next month in Baltimore and nominated Douglas; Southerners held their convention in Richmond and selected Breckinridge.

Bypassing Seward, the Republicans nominated Abraham Lincoln as their presidential candidate. Lincoln's anti-slavery views were well known, and many Southerners considered him even more objectionable than Seward. He professed, it was true, to lack constitutional authority to emancipate slaves in existing states, but few Southerners doubted his commitment to freeing their black bondsmen, and few questioned that he would persist until he found a way to succeed. With the Democrats divided, Lincoln's election was inevitable, and so was the slave-holding South's response. "Every negro in South Carolina and every other southern state will be his own master; nay, more than that, will be the equal of every one of you," the Reverend Richard Furman warned his white congregation. "If you are tame enough to submit, abolition preachers will be at hand to consummate the marriage of your daughters to black husbands." All Carolinians, whether they owned slaves or not, felt threatened by the specter of emancipation that they believed Lincoln's election presaged.

Following news of Lincoln's electoral victory, a Secession Convention met in Charleston, and South Carolina voted to leave the Union on December 20, 1860. The city went wild with celebration, although a few dissenters could be found. "South Carolina is too small to be a Republic, and too large to be an insane asylum," fumed James L. Petigru, a Charleston lawyer who argued long and hard against secession. Not wishing to go alone, South Carolina invited its neighbors to join in a "Confederacy of Slaveholding States." Six more states seceded by early March 1861 and sent representatives to Montgomery to form a provisional government. The convention adopted a constitution modeled after the United States constitution in most respects, save one. The new Confederate document forbade the passage of laws denying or impairing the right of property in Negro slaves.

War came soon afterward. Fittingly, the spark that ignited the conflagration flashed in Charleston. In late December 1860, Major Robert Anderson, commanding federal troops in the vicinity of the city, moved under cover of darkness to Fort Sumter in Charleston Harbor and stubbornly refused to relinquish his tiny outpost. Following Lincoln's inauguration, Fort Sumter became a highly visible pawn in the larger game of whether the federal government would recognize the secessionist authorities. Lincoln viewed abandoning Fort Sumter as tantamount to conceding the legitimacy of the breakaway republic; the Confederate government considered Anderson's occupation of the fort an affront to its sovereignty. The crisis came to a head when Lincoln sent a naval expedition to provision the fort. For the rebels to let the ships deliver their supplies would be a concession to federal authority; if they shot at the fleet, they would be blamed for precipitating a war. Confederate officials called upon Anderson to surrender, but he refused, and their response was an artillery bombardment of a day and a half that reduced the fort to rubble. Anderson surrendered, at noon on April 14, but Lincoln was the real winner in the fracas; he could point to the Southerners as the aggressors, and the North stood solidly behind him. When the new president called for seventy-five thousand volunteers to quell the insurrection, his demand provoked several border states, including Virginia, to join the secessionists. The lines were drawn for a bitter and protracted civil war.

4

A DESERT
BLASTED BY FIRE

Southerners in the national army faced an agonizing decision. With war inevitable, were they honor-bound to remain with the United States, or should they return home and join the forces their states and the new Confederate government were raising?

Men saw their duties differently. Some remained loyal to their home states while others honored the broader concept of nation. "If the Union is dissolved, I shall return to Virginia and share the fortune of my people," Colonel Robert E. Lee wrote from a remote outpost in Texas after a bout of reflection. Returning home, Lee was offered command of a Union army, but he declined the appointment, electing to cast his lot with his native state. "With all my devotion to the Union, and the feeling of loyalty and duty of an American citizen," Lee explained in a letter to his sister, "I have not been able to make up my mind to raise my hand against my relatives, my family, my home." Lee tendered his resignation to General Winfield Scott, another Virginian and commander of the Union armies who unlike Lee had chosen to stay with the Union and oversee the war against secessionists, be they Virginians or anyone else. And one of Lee's fellow officers, George Thomas, also a Virginian, likewise cast his lot with the Union. "Turn it every way he would," Thomas's wife later wrote of her husband's decision, "the one thing was uppermost, his duty to the government of the United States."

The Santa Fe contingent embarked on similar soul-searching. Colonel Grayson, a Southerner through and through, resigned his commission and accepted an appointment as brigadier general in the provisional Confederate army. For Grayson's personal secretary Charles Whilden, the choice was never in doubt. His loyalty and sympathy lay with Charleston and the Southern cause.

Grayson returned east during the summer and was assigned to duty in Florida, where he died soon afterward from disease. Charles, bent on enlisting in Confederate service, took his leave from the Masonic Lodge in Sante Fe in mid-September 1861 and started on his way toward Charleston. The return trip proved as tortuous as most of his other undertakings. He made his way to the seacoast of Texas or Louisiana, determined to secure passage to Charleston by ship, and surfaced next in the Bahamas, still trying to reach Charleston. According to family lore related twenty years later by one of William's daughters, Charles finally managed to engage a ship heading to the Carolina coast, but the craft was badly damaged in a storm, and Charles drifted for days in an open boat, exposed to the elements and broiling under an unforgiving tropical sun. He reached Charleston in late 1861 or early 1862 with his health seriously compromised. For the rest of his life, he suffered from severe epileptic seizures that he attributed to exposure during that arduous voyage.

★ ★ ★

During the war's early months, the firm of Hayden and Whilden enjoyed a boom. Federal ships had blockaded Charleston's harbor, but rebel blockade-runners at first had little difficulty making nighttime runs to the city's wharves, keeping the store's shelves crammed with goods. The market for swords, weapons, and uniforms remained strong, and the firm also branched into the flag business, a line that proved especially popular. Hayden and Whilden provided the cloth and prepared the flag, turning the needlework over to one of several local ladies proficient in the craft. One of its more spectacular banners was a silk flag for the newly formed 1st South Carolina regiment. Featured against a blue background was the state seal—a palmetto tree surrounded by a wreath, the left arm depicting magnolia leaves and berries, the right oak leaves and acorns, with a half-moon in the left corner—embroidered in white by a local merchant's wife.

Charleston's status as a major Confederate port and the seat of the rebellion made it an important objective for the Union war effort. The place was a "viper's nest and breeding place of rebellion," a New York newspaper insisted. "Should its inhabitants choose to make its site a desert, blasted by fire," the writer predicted, "we do not think many tears would be shed."

War edged closer in the fall of 1861 when Union forces captured Port Royal, fifty miles to the south, and the townspeople nervously monitored their newspapers as Yankee troops began advancing methodically toward the city. December saw another disaster—this one not attributable to Yankees—when a slave's cooking fire got out of control and reduced much of Charleston's downtown to ashes. William's and Joseph's residences were spared, although flames consumed several homes on neighboring streets.

As the Union chokehold on Charleston tightened, Hayden and Whilden's initial burst of prosperity dwindled. And then William was called away. Before the outbreak of hostilities, he had joined a military company named the Washington Artillery of Charleston. Made up of prominent young citizens, the outfit had the trappings of a snazzy social club. The state's war footing, however, inspired a frenzy of drilling, and after the firing on Fort Sumter, a portion of the unit left South Carolina for service with the Confederate army in Virginia. The part that remained was called Walter's Light Battery, and Lieutenant William Whilden was fourth in command.

Toward the end of 1861, state authorities assigned William and his companions to Adams Run, a railroad town twenty-five miles south of Charleston, where they were to keep watch on the federal force moving up from Port Royal. William remained in rural isolation for a year and a half, seeing his family only occasionally on furlough. Charlestonians breathed collective sighs of relief in mid-1862 when Confederate troops stopped the Union advance at the tiny settlement of Secessionville, a few miles from the city.

War had transformed the city of Charles's youth. Charleston sent its sons to the battlefronts in Virginia and to the west, where Union and Confederate armies were grappling in Tennessee. "The following two years were a succession of victories and defeats, alternate hopes and fears; battles fought and won," one of the Whilden girls later recorded. "Widowed women and mothers whose sons had fallen on many hard fought battle fields were weeping and working, caring for the sick, and doing all they could to make comfortable the suffering, praying all the while that the God of battles would bless the cause so sacred to our hearts, and crown our efforts with success. The cause was dear alike to all, everything was staked, and upon the result depended our destiny."

★ ★ ★

Arriving home to Charleston penniless and wracked by seizures, Charles likely moved in with William's family at their home on Wentworth Street. William was away, as was Joseph, who had enlisted as a private in the state militia, and Charles found himself in the unlikely position of senior male head of William's and Joseph's households.

William and Joseph, Charles soon learned, were not the only Whildens swept up in the war. The five sons of Elias Whilden, his cousin in Mount Pleasant, had gone off to war, and all of them would win distinction. One son, John Marshall Whilden, was with the Citadel cadet battery that claimed the honor of firing the first shots of the rebellion. Wounded at the First Battle of Manassas in Virginia, he returned to Charleston to convalesce. There he raised a company that he commanded and in which his brother Septimus held the rank of lieutenant. Promoted to major at the age of twenty-two, John met a hero's death in August 1862, riddled by five bullets while carrying his regiment's battle flag at the head of a charge at the Second Battle of Manassas. Septimus remained on active duty for another year, finally contracting a disabling disease in Mississippi in 1863 during the Vicksburg campaign. Another of Elias's sons—George—joined the famed Hampton Legion. He was severely wounded in the initial battles around Richmond in May 1862 and was shot in the arm the next year at Knoxville, but fought on to the end of the war. Elias's remaining sons, Augustus and Washington, joined a cavalry regiment that was ultimately assigned to Virginia in 1864. Augustus was mortally wounded in May of that year, in the battles around Richmond; Washington fought in all of those engagements and more but managed to survive the war unscathed.

Charles wanted nothing more than to join the Confederate military. His family, after all, boasted a proud martial tradition from

Revolutionary War times, William and Joseph were bearing arms at personal cost to their families, and Elias's branch of the Whilden clan was conspicuously advancing the family's honor. Charles's brothers Bayfield and Furman never enlisted, but both were ordained ministers. Bayfield frequently preached to troops in South Carolina during the war, and it is possible that Furman did likewise. In a world where most men his age were wearing uniforms, Charles must have felt very out of place.

Charles went to great lengths to volunteer for military service, but the stars, as usual, seemed aligned against him. The sticking point was his frail health. "He enlisted a number of times," one of William's granddaughters later wrote, "but when he had an [epileptic] attack he would be discharged. Then he would go somewhere else and enlist again."

★ ★ ★

War came closer to Charleston as the Union generals stepped up their efforts to capture the city with a combined land and sea attack. Determined to take Charleston's strategic port, Lincoln's naval secretary, Gideon Welles, arranged for a large expeditionary force to gather at Port Royal. The naval arm contained several of the Union navy's formidable ironclads and the armored warship *New Ironsides,* bristling with eleven-inch guns.

General Pierre G. T. Beauregard, charged with defending the city, laid careful plans to repel the onslaught. Rebel forts near the mouth of Charleston Harbor—Fort Moultrie on Sullivan's Island to the north; Fort Sumter in the center of the harbor; and Battery Wagner on Morris Island to the south—were armed with the best cannon available. Confederate engineers dotted the harbor with buoys to afford gunners precise ranges and strung booms laced with mines across the harbor mouth. Confederates also mounted guns on small islands nearer the city, in case enemy ships broke through the first string of forts, and they placed still more guns along the city's waterfront. And if the Yankees managed to overrun his gauntlet and gain a foothold in the town, Beauregard expected his scratch collection of regular troops and local militia to resist the invaders "street by street and house by house."

Sensitive to Charleston's political and strategic importance, the Confederacy's President Davis insisted that all citizens of Charleston able to bear arms and not subject to enrollment for military service organize to defend the city. Charles, of course, was eligible under the president's emergency plan, and he fervently desired to serve his hometown. Prevented by infirmities from serving in the regular forces, he likely volunteered for the local militia cobbled together in desperation to wage Charleston's last-ditch defense. Charles, at last, was a soldier of sorts.

The vast Union armada appeared outside the harbor in early April 1863, commanded by none other than Rear Admiral Samuel F. Du Pont, head of the Union navy. Beauregard directed the city's women and children to leave, and the remaining townspeople prepared for battle. "Ambulances were standing by on East Bay to carry the wounded to the hospitals," recorded one of the city's historians; "people were collected in groups, talking in low voices; women were preparing lint for bandages; the impoverished shops were still open."

The attack came on April 7, led by the ironclad *Weehawken*. Cannon from the outer line of Confederate forts opened, and the roar of artillery and the ringing sound made by shells ricocheting off steel hulls vibrated across the water. Citizens lined the battery to watch as a gusher spit into the air from a mine exploding near the *Weehawken*. More ironclads steamed up, only to be disabled by fire from the forts. Shells from Union boats pummeled Fort Sumter, blasting huge holes in the walls, but were ineffective at silencing the rebel artillery. Watching the action from aboard the *New Ironsides*—the massive warship sat too low in the water to enter the harbor—Du Pont deemed the attack a failure and ordered his ironclads to retire. The action lasted only a few hours. A Union general conceded that Beauregard had repulsed "the most powerful and gallant fleet the world ever saw." Charleston had much to celebrate that evening.

Du Pont's failure to take Charleston did not deter the Federal commanders, who decided next to focus their attention on Battery Wagner, the rebel fort on Morris Island guarding the southern approaches to Charleston Harbor. Their plan was to storm Battery Wagner from the south with infantry and use the captured fort to batter Sumter into submission, opening the way for the Union armada to safely enter the harbor.

As spring turned to summer, eleven thousand Federal infantrymen under Brigadier General Quincy Gillmore fought their way to within striking distance of Battery Wagner. Early on the morning of July 11, as the Northerners charged across an open stretch of sand, volleys from the fort slammed into them. Some of the attackers managed to scale the ramparts, but reinforcements failed to arrive, and supporting troops broke under withering Confederate fire. The rest of the assaulting force retired, coming again under heavy musketry and artillery fire as they ran across the open sand. Almost 350 Union soldiers fell in the brief but bloody fiasco. "The troops all fell back to their former positions of the day before," a New Englander who lived through the ordeal wrote, "with the same accompaniment of hot sun, hot sand, hot shot, and hot shell."

All the next week, artillery projectiles rained into Battery Wagner from Union warships off the coast and from batteries that Gillmore brought onto the southern end of Morris Island. On July 18, in preparation for another infantry assault, Union artillerists redoubled their rate of fire. Beauregard estimated that shells hit the fort at the rate of fourteen a minute; the chief of Confederate artillery put the number of enemy shells that day in the range of nine thousand. "No one would believe for a minute that a human being, or a bird even, could live on that fort," a Northerner observed.

The cannonade stopped at dusk, and six thousand of Gillmore's infantrymen started across the open expanse of sand toward the fort. Leading was the 54th Massachusetts, a regiment of black troops commanded by Colonel Robert Gould Shaw, a white Bostonian and war hero. Raised in the early months of 1863, soon after President Lincoln's Emancipation Proclamation, these black soldiers had never seen combat. As they moved forward, the rebel fort seemed to come alive in flame and smoke, and musketry and artillery fire cut deep swaths in Shaw's ranks. But the novices kept on, and in a burst of energy, the colonel led the survivors across a moat and onto the fort's parapet, where he and most of his followers were killed. White troops in blue also charged across the open stretch of sand and met the same fate as the black troops. "Men fell by scores on the parapet and rolled back into the ditch," a New Yorker who witnessed the scene recalled; "many were drowned in the water, and others smothered by their own dead and wounded companions falling upon them." Realizing that this attack was as hopeless as the previous week's foray, Gillmore ordered his troops to retreat, abandoning large numbers of Yankees in the rebel battlements to be killed or captured. Union losses totaled about fifteen hundred men.

The approaches to Battery Wagner presented a grisly scene. Bodies ground to mush by sheets of lead from close-in fighting floated in muddy craters left from the Union artillery bombardment. The victorious rebels pitched Colonel Shaw's body into an open ditch, along with the corpses of his black troops. The attack had failed, but the bravery of the 54th Massachusetts went far to change opinions about the fighting qualities of black soldiers. The performance of Shaw and his troops, a Northern newspaper observed, "made Fort Wagner such a name for the colored race as Bunker Hill has been for ninety years for the White Yankees."

Having twice failed to take Battery Wagner by storm, Gillmore decided to try a siege. Federal guns resumed their ruthless shelling while Union infantrymen slowly advanced, digging trenches and throwing up mounds of sand for protection. Conditions were miserable for men on both sides, as the treeless expanse offered no shelter from the baking sun, and the stench from bloated, decomposing bodies was overpowering. Water was scarce, and attempts to dig wells produced only foul pools polluted by the effluence of corpses. Swarms of biting insects feasted on Yankees and rebels alike.

As the summer ground on, Beauregard realized that Battery Wagner must soon fall to the enemy, and the Confederates evacuated the fort under cover of darkness, spiking their artillery pieces so that the Yankees could not use the guns. Suspecting that the rebels had abandoned the crumbling edifice, Gillmore sent a contingent of troops inside. "Dead bodies long unburied, heads, arms, feet (with the shoes still upon them) lay strewn all around," a member of the scouting party remembered, adding that the stench "was almost unbearable." A Southerner who had just left the fort informed anyone who would listen that he was "afeared of hell no more, it can't touch Wagner."

The blockade and the proximity of Gillmore's army spelled disaster for the Whilden family. Like many Charlestonians, William and his business partner watched their livelihood collapse, and William's obligations to the Washington Artillery kept him away from home. In William's absence, Augustus Hayden labored to hold the firm together, but it was an impossible task. By mid-summer, the firm of Hayden and Whilden had no choice but to auction off its inventory and close its doors.

★ ★ ★

While his infantrymen were digging their way toward Battery Wagner, Gilmore stationed artillery within firing range of Charleston. One gun—an eight-inch Parrott gun nicknamed the Swamp Angel—was destined to achieve special notoriety.

On August 21, 1863, Gillmore demanded that the Confederates agree within four hours to vacate Morris Island and Fort Sumter, in effect paving the way for a Union occupation of the harbor. The general threatened that if he did not receive an affirmative response within the prescribed time, he would "open fire on the city of Charleston from batteries already established within easy and effective range of the heart of the city." Not receiving a timely reply—Beauregard, it seems, was absent from his headquarters when the message arrived—Gillmore ordered his guns to bombard the city.

Beauregard was furious. "Among nations not barbarous the usage of war prescribes that when a city is about to be attacked, timely notice shall be given by the attacking commander, in order that noncombatants may have an opportunity for withdrawing beyond its limits," he lectured the Yankee general in his reply. "It would appear, sir, that despairing of reducing [the Confederate forts]," the irate general went on, "you now resort to the novel measure of turning your guns against the old men, the women and children, and the hospitals of a sleeping city, an act of inexcusable barbarity."

Chastened by Beauregard, Gillmore quieted his guns for a day; then he began directing them against Charleston in earnest. Early on the morning of August 22, the Swamp Angel lobbed a shell into the city. The projectile exploded in a house on Pinckney Street, in the heart of town, setting it ablaze. Shortly another shell screamed into the stricken neighborhood and exploded near the first. Panicked citizens poured from their homes and hurried inland where the guns could not reach. Families were seen carrying invalids to safety on mattresses. A war correspondent reported that the sound of descending artillery shells "resembled the whirr of a phantom brigade of cavalry galloping in mid-air."

The Swamp Angel burst while firing its thirty-sixth round, but other guns took its place, and the methodical bombardment continued. Union artillerists favored using the prominent steeples of Charleston's churches to sight their guns. The graceful steeple of St. Michael's Church served as their initial target, being located in the heart of town. When Gillmore felt satisfied that he had leveled that neighborhood, he shifted his sights to St. Philip's Church, farther inland. Then the Second Presbyterian Church, more inland still, became a preferred target. "Block by block of [Charleston] is being reduced to ashes," a Northern newspaper accurately reported. Fires invariably followed the shellings, and the city's list of refugees grew by the day. On Christmas, Gillmore's present was to pound Charleston without letup, igniting more of the central city.

January 1864 brought still more misery. By one count, Union guns fired more than fifteen hundred shells into the city. Mrs. St. Julien Ravenel, who experienced those terrible days, recorded that the portion of Charleston below Calhoun Street—the sector nearest the Union guns—resembled a ghost town. The area north of Calhoun Street and less vulnerable to the federal ordnance was crammed with refugees and hospitals for wounded soldiers. "To pass from this bustling crowded scene to the lower part of the town," she wrote, "was like going from life to death."

The Whilden residences—those of William and Joseph, as well as the Magazine Street house—stood within the exposed part of town, well south of Calhoun Street, and the family quickly realized that they had to abandon their homes. "We were startled from our sleep on a summer's morn, just at dawn," one of the Whilden girls later recorded, "by the explosion of a shell, and we awoke to the reality that the powerful mortars which had been placed on Morris Island had the city within the range of their shell, and there was safety no longer." Her fright remained vivid years later. "The panic produced by the knowledge that our heads might be blown off at any moment, each imagining they were to be the certain victim, brought about the wildest scenes of confusion," she remembered.

Some of the Whildens decided to flee to Columbia right away and hurried to the railway station, Maumer Juno in tow. Refugees packed the tracks, pushing and shoving to board the limited number of cars. "The writer," one of the evacuating Whildens later wrote, "with children and nurses, baggage, etc., was of course anxious to get to a place of safety, and after hours of waiting finally secured for a party of seven persons, two seats, and the only way we could gain admittance for our nurses was through the window by means of a ladder. One of the servants being very stout, it was with great difficulty she could be squeezed through, much to the amusement of lookers-on and the dismay and discomfort of Mauma." Reaching Columbia the next morning—after a dismal journey that "seemed as though it was to be a night without dawning"—the Whildens and their entourage went in search of lodging. They finally settled into the third story of a boardinghouse that they all agreed was gloomy.

William was away when the bombardment began—his battery was assigned to nearby John's Island—and it fell to Ellen to make arrangements for safeguarding the family's possessions. She scooped out a trench behind the house in Charleston and filled it with her valuables, including her daughter Julia's miniature china set. After covering the items with dirt, she concealed her excavation under a pile of kindling. The family's silver she sent on to Columbia. William remained with his battery, wheedling a brief leave to help his family resettle in Columbia, where he hoped they would at least be safe.

★ ★ ★

Toward the end of January 1864, Charles—now thirty-nine—tried once again to enlist in a formal Confederate unit, and this time he was accepted. His apparent change in fortune resulted from the Confederate armies' critical need for troops. The South's manpower well was running dry, and recruiters were willing to take anyone capable of locomotion to fill the dwindling ranks. Even sickly, over-aged men such as Charles looked attractive. The Confederate government's decision to conscript young boys and old men provoked criticism—President Davis expressed concern about grinding the seed corn of the nation—but harsh realities afforded no other solution. Charles, of course, viewed the army's new attitude as a windfall. At last he could fight for the Confederacy.

Soldiers enlisted in Confederate service for a variety of reasons. Some were motivated by patriotism, others by politics, and probably most by a sense of duty to family and friends. At least during the early stages of the war, men served with other men whom they had known since childhood, and social pressures made it impossible for eligible men to avoid service. This arrangement gave fighting units a sense of cohesion that explains their tenacity on the battlefield. No one wanted to let his friends down, and word about how each soldier acquitted himself in combat was certain to reach home. Few things were worse than being branded a coward by your hometown.

Charles never wrote about why he enlisted, but his reasons are readily apparent. Patriotism was undoubtedly a strong motivation. He had lived for almost a decade in Detroit and in the wilds of Santa Fe, but Charleston remained the standard against which he judged everything. Other visitors might have been fascinated by the western frontier with its exotic Spanish ways, but Charles reflexively measured the place against Charleston and found it sorely lacking, save perhaps for its mountain scenery and clear air. The men were useless, the women ignorant, and their Catholic religion a font of superstition. Although well read, Charles was unabashedly provincial.

The vicious Union bombardment of Charleston only strengthened Charles's loyalty to his hometown and his determination to go to war. Charleston was the center of his universe, and he was ready to risk his life to save it. He had seen Yankee shells explode in neighborhoods familiar to him since childhood, had watched fires rage, and had looked on as grief-stricken families hauled dead and wounded loved ones from the smoldering debris. The blockade and bombardment had wrecked his brother William's business, undermined his family's prosperity, and driven his siblings and close relatives from their homes. Yankees were not distant people whom Charles had read about in newspapers. They were here on his doorstep, bent on doing him harm, and it is no wonder that he rejoiced when he finally received the opportunity to strike back.

Charles also agreed absolutely with the Confederate war goal of seceding from the Union and establishing a slave-owning republic.

He, along with most Charlestonians of his generation, never tried to sugarcoat their pro-slavery opinions. They were secure in their belief that God had ordained the black race to serve white masters, and they advocated those views with conviction. Charles's racial views are repugnant to modern ears, but they mirrored the sympathies of virtually everyone around him. He had been raised in a world dedicated to the supremacy of the white race, and he felt strongly about fighting to preserve the social order built on that premise.

Desire to fight alongside friends from Charleston may also have played some small part in Charles's motivation. At this stage of the war, new recruits could be certain of being placed in units drawn from their state but not necessarily from their community. A major reason behind this change in philosophy was the need to prepare novices for the realities of combat. Rather than banding new men together, Confederate authorities now assigned greenhorns to veteran outfits. The plan made sense because the accelerated pace of combat left little time for drilling, and new recruits could best learn their trade by fighting alongside experienced men.

Charles was directed to report to Virginia for induction into the 1st South Carolina Infantry, a part of Robert E. Lee's army. Climbing into a railroad car packed with new recruits and conscripts, he headed off to war.

5

GENERAL LEE'S
SHOCK TROOPS

Charles and his new companions reached central Virginia on a bitterly cold day in early February. The sight that greeted the fresh recruits from the Carolina Low Country seemed a far cry from Charleston. Orange Court House, on the rail line three miles south of the Rapidan, served as the nerve center for General Lee's army. A wooden train station surrounded by a huge platform stood at one end of Main Street, and a block away an Italianate courthouse rose, an angular stone building strangely out of place in the rural setting. Snow, blackened by soot and churned under wagon wheels, covered the ground, and church spires could be seen in the distance, piercing the frozen, misty air. Warehouses, lodgings for teamsters, and buildings housing the army's quartermaster and postal officials spilled across the surrounding countryside.

All was bustle as engines puffed up, disgorged troops and supplies from Richmond, and disappeared south to pick up more men and provisions. Wagons jostled into town on farm roads, adding to the mountains of crates and sacks already heaped around the station. Teamsters sorted through the piles, extracted what they needed, loaded their wagons, and set off for the army's camps. Clusters of tents and makeshift huts fashioned from logs, tarps, dirt, and fence rails crammed the fields and woods around the town.

Charles enlisted with the rank of private on February 6, 1864, at Orange Court House, and Captain Edward D. Brailsford of Company I, 1st South Carolina, handled the paperwork. His period of service was for the duration of the war. Signing the document inducting him into the army, Charles must have felt that his run of misfortune had finally ended. He was now a soldier in an army whose reputation had already become legend.

If Charles wanted to see combat in something more than the militia, he was about to experience far more than he expected. Grant had chosen to focus his might against the very army to which Charles was assigned. Lee's veterans were accustomed to hard marching and fighting, but 1864 would exceed anything they had faced. And it would be Charles's lot to find himself in the very outfit destined to see the worst of the campaign's carnage.

As he settled into army life, Charles learned about the generals and officers whose decisions would control his future. Veterans explained that Stonewall Jackson's death the previous year had led General Lee to organize his army into three infantry corps, each containing between fifteen and twenty thousand men. James Longstreet, a burly Georgian affectionately dubbed the War Horse, now headed the army's First Corps. The Second Corps—comprised largely of Jackson's former command—was in the hands of Richard Stoddard Ewell, an eccentric, one-legged former subordinate of Jackson recently returned from sick leave. And the head of Lee's Third Corps, reputedly the most aggressive of the Confederate infantry commands, was a sallow-faced, hot-tempered Virginian named Ambrose Powell Hill.

Charles's orders directed him to report to Hill. Known by his men as Little Powell because of his slight frame, Hill hailed from nearby Culpeper Court House, now occupied by the federal army. He made his reputation early in the war at the head of his famed Light Division, a hard-hitting outfit accustomed to serving as the rebel army's shock troops. Lee would never forget the auburn-haired Virginian's timely appearance at Sharpsburg, urging his soldiers to the battlefield's critical sector in time to save the day for the Confederates.

But the thirty-eight-year-old general was not well. Rumor had it that his poor health was due to malaria, to a liver ailment, or perhaps to an elusive psychological malady aggravated by the weight of his heady responsibilities. It is also possible that Hill suffered from chronic prostate problems triggered by a venereal disease that he contracted while a student at West Point. The general certainly had an eye for ladies, and his prewar dalliances were the talk of the army. Most intriguing was his knack for courting women who ultimately married Union generals. He once dated Nellie Marcy, who later wed George McClellan, an early commander of the Army of the Potomac. He also wooed Emily Chase, a Baltimore beauty and future wife of Gouverneur Warren, who headed a corps under Grant. Hill was now married to Kitty Morgan McClung—sister of John Hunt Morgan, the famous Confederate cavalryman, and his sunken eyes and hollow cheeks served as visible reminders of his sickness.

Little Powell had organized his corps into three divisions. One division, commanded by Cadmus Marcellus Wilcox, contained most of the troops from Hill's former Light Division. A year older than Hill and a confirmed bachelor, Wilcox attended West Point with Little Powell and served with him in the Mexican War. He cut a colorful figure wearing a broad-brimmed straw hat and riding a white pony, and his wry humor and engaging personality made him popular with his men, who affectionately nicknamed him Old Billy Fixin. For his most difficult and bloody work, Little Powell liked to call on Wilcox's veterans. This, of course, was the division to which Charles was assigned.

Four brigades drawn from Georgia, North Carolina, and South Carolina made up Wilcox's division. Led by experienced commanders, the brigades numbered among Lee's elite combat outfits. By near-universal consensus, the best of Wilcox's brigades—and the best in Lee's army—was the South Carolina brigade of Samuel McGowan, an Up Country lawyer and politician. Brought up to strength with the infusion of new troops, the brigade numbered about 2,230 men. His luck running true to form, Charles drew an appointment to McGowan's famous outfit.

★ ★ ★

Charles likely saw little more of Hill and Wilcox than fleeting glimpses at reviews. But Sam McGowan's corpulent form, shuffling painfully about with the aid of a cane, was a common sight at the brigade's camp. The strong-willed general would play an important role in Charles's brief but eventful career as a soldier.

Born in the Laurens District of South Carolina to Scots-Irish immigrants of limited means, McGowan labored as a field hand in his youth. Impressed with the value of education, his father scrimped to send the boy to James L. Lessly's Classical School and then on to South Carolina College, where he graduated third in his class. He read law in the Abbeville office of Thomas Chiles Perrin, was admitted to the South Carolina bar in 1842, and embarked on a successful career as one of the Up Country's foremost attorneys. "He had a wonderful voice," a fellow barrister recalled of McGowan's oratorical prowess. "It could be heard in a whisper. Its middle tones were charming and beautiful. Its higher tones resembled the storm and the thunder. I have seen him so worked up in arguments before juries that his eyes beamed like the eagle's, his hair waved like the lion's mane. It was then that he took the ear prisoner and swept everything before him."

Young McGowan had been practicing law scarcely a year when he found himself embroiled in a scandal that became the talk of Abbeville. Miss Elizabeth Harrison, of Charleston, was serving as governess to Thomas Perrin's children, teaching them and other offspring of the town's elite families, when she caught the eye of John Cunningham, a promising lawyer and scion of nearby Rosemont Plantation. Taking a fancy to Miss Harrison, Cunningham sent her a note expressing his sentiments. She took offense at his advances and showed her employer the young lawyer's jottings. Perrin had come to regard Miss Harrison as a family member and rushed to defend her honor by confronting Cunningham at a Fourth of July picnic. The two men quarreled, and matters came to a head with Cunningham challenging Perrin to a duel. The older man refused Cunningham's invitation, explaining that he did not believe in dueling and that, in any event, he would not fight a man so many years his junior. To everyone's surprise, McGowan, who had no personal interest in Miss Harrison, took up the cudgel on Perrin's behalf. His zeal to uphold the honor of his friend and their law firm doubtless played a part in his decision, although town gossips suggested another motive. McGowan, it seems, had fallen in love with Susan Caroline Wardlaw, eldest daughter of Judge David Louis Wardlaw, one of Abbeville's distinguished jurists. By dueling Cunningham, the speculation went, young McGowan hoped to prove his worth to the judge and win Susan's hand.

On July 15, 1843, shortly before noon, Cunningham's cousin Benjamin Yancey handed a note to McGowan. The message, signed by Cunningham, expressed dissatisfaction with McGowan's refusal to apologize for Perrin's remarks. "I therefore demand of you that satisfaction which is due to a gentleman," the note concluded in words that unequivocally demanded a duel. "My friend, Mr. Yancey, who will hand you this note is authorized to make the necessary arrangements."

The two hotheaded lawyers decided to conduct their duel at Sand Bar Ferry, a small island in the Savannah River near Augusta, Georgia. The line between South Carolina and Georgia ran through the center of Sand Bar Ferry and afforded the protagonists easy escape if authorities from either state attempted to interfere. A reporter from the Abbeville newspaper described the island as "a sequestered place, a lovely white strand on each side, ideal for such high toned killings."

The tall, stalwart son of Scots-Irish immigrants and the noticeably smaller, cultured son of plantation owners met a few days later at Sand Bar Ferry. Their friends got wind of the impending tragedy and hurried to the island in a two-horse wagon, hoping to stop the fight, but they arrived too late. Armed with rifles, the attorneys were already facing off, twenty paces apart. Cunningham was draped in a broad cape, and when the referee gave the command to fire, he tossed his cape aside and squeezed the trigger. His bullet, according to later reports, "passed in at the orifice of McGowan's ear and came out the back of it." McGowan later claimed he had drawn a "fine bead" on Cunningham but was surprised by the speed of his adversary. He also discharged his rifle, but the shot went harmlessly over Cunningham's head.

Seriously injured, McGowan was taken to nearby Hamburg, South Carolina. He was back at his law practice in a few months, however, with an unchallenged reputation for bravery. His wound also left him with the uncanny ability to make a clicking sound with his ear when he moved his jaw, a feat that caused his grandchildren considerable amusement in later years. Cunningham, along with Yancey, who served as his second, was indicted for the shooting and stood trial in Abbeville in October. After a raucous proceeding involving the county's distinguished legal lights—a local newspaper called it "a red letter day in the history of Abbeville"—the jury convicted Cunningham, and the judge sentenced him to a year in prison. Miss Harrison married a local lawyer named Dennis Jones and devoted her remaining years to running a popular school.

Three years after the duel, McGowan volunteered as a private in the Palmetto regiment, and Miss Harrison, a gifted musician, composed a march dedicated to the outfit as the soldiers left to fight in the Mexican War. Promoted to captain on the quartermaster's staff, McGowan served as aide-de-camp to Brigadier General John A. Quitman, assisting the general during the storming of Chapultepec and the capture of the Belen Gate into Mexico City. Quitman complimented him in writing for gallantry in action, and he returned to Abbeville a war hero. He resumed his practice with Perrin and achieved his long-standing ambition of marrying Judge Wardlaw's daughter Susan. He also embarked on a political career and represented Abbeville for the next twelve years in the South Carolina House of Representatives, where he chaired committees on education and military affairs and championed the South Carolina Military Academy.

Like many Southerners, McGowan opposed secession. Passage of the Ordinance of Secession, however, persuaded him that resistance was futile, and he reluctantly went along with his home state. Die-hard secessionists opposed McGowan's request for a military appointment, but Governor Francis Pickens backed him, and in April 1861, he became assistant to the quartermaster general of South Carolina's provisional forces and served in that capacity during the firing on Fort Sumter.

With the transfer of South Carolina's state militia to the Confederate army, McGowan joined the staff of General Milledge Bonham. He saw action in the First Battle of Manassas, returned home to recruit the 14th South Carolina Infantry, and in the spring of 1862 became colonel of the regiment, leading several daring charges and gaining recognition as one of Powell Hill's most courageous officers. Wounded in the abdomen during the battles around Richmond in late June, he returned home to recuperate and rejoined Lee in time to mastermind another attack at the Second Battle of Manassas two months later, where he gained more praise and sustained a second debilitating wound, this time in the forearm. He was strong enough to fight again by December 1862, at Fredericksburg, taking charge of the South Carolina brigade when its commander Maxcy Gregg was killed. He escaped injury at Fredericksburg—although just barely, as a shell apparently knocked off the sole of his boot—and his presence of mind won him promotion to brigadier general. He confirmed his capacity for elevated command in the spring of 1863 with another blistering attack, this time against federal forces at Chancellorsville. There he received his third wound when a Union bullet hit his left leg below the kneecap, leaving him with a permanent limp.

During McGowan's latest disability, Lee placed the South Carolina brigade under Abner M. Perrin, a relative of McGowan's law partner Thomas Perrin. By early February 1864—the same month that Charles reached Virginia—McGowan had mended sufficiently to rejoin his troops at their Rapidan encampment. He had grown shockingly fat during his convalescence and walked with the aid of a cane, but he still exercised a powerful presence. His speeches, veterans noted, stirred even timid men to bravery. James F. J. Caldwell, who began a history of the brigade at McGowan's urging while it was still in the field, remembered that the general's discipline, "though not severe, was firm and consistent; his energy in battle was great; his courage was of a high order; his fortitude under reverses was indomitable and inspiring. And best of all, perhaps, he loved and trusted his officers and his men; and they fully reciprocated his confidences and his affections."

A successful lawyer, politician, and war hero, McGowan was everything that Charles was not. The charismatic general was brave and ruthless in combat (he had three wounds to prove it), and he expected no less of his men—all his men, even new recruits such as Charles.

★ ★ ★

Shortly after South Carolina left the Union in 1860, the state legislature authorized the raising of a six-month regiment, and volunteers assembled in Charleston under the leadership of the prominent lawyer and outspoken secessionist Maxcy Gregg. The regiment, designated as the 1st South Carolina, transferred to Confederate service and traveled to Virginia in June of that year. When its six-month term expired in July, the regiment was reorganized under the same name and colonel. It had been in the Old Dominion ever since.

McGowan's Brigade contained five regiments—the 1st, 12th, 13th, and 14th South Carolina, and Orr's Regiment of Rifles. The 1st South Carolina was the oldest regiment in the brigade and perhaps the oldest in Confederate service. It was a combat force par excellence, accustomed to attacking with abandon and charging into places where no other unit dared go. This was the regiment to which Charles was assigned.

The commander of the 1st South Carolina and Charles's immediate superior was an energetic young bachelor named Comillus

Wickliffe McCreary. Nicknamed Wick, McCreary was born in June 1836 in Williston, South Carolina, the eldest of eight children, and grew up in the first painted house on the forty-odd-mile stretch of road between Barnwell and Augusta. He enrolled in the Arsenal Academy in Columbia in 1854, where first-year cadets at the South Carolina Military Academy were educated, and transferred to the Citadel in Charleston the next year, where cadets spent their final three years, graduating in 1857. He was a "paid" student, meaning that his family financed his tuition, and he showed no particular promise, graduating thirteen out a class of twenty. After leaving the Citadel, he served as a professor and assistant principal of Aiken Classical and Military Academy in Aiken, South Carolina.

Answering his state's call for volunteers early in 1861, McCreary was commissioned a captain and raised a company from the rural district between Barnwell and Aiken. Before heading off to war, McCreary and his men enjoyed a raucous send-off at Hickson's Mill on Tinker's Creek. Festivities often degenerated into brawls in this part of South Carolina, and the barbecue at Hickson's Mill was no exception. Attendees later reported that elderly Mr. Hickson strung a rope barricade around the fire pit and stationed three stalwart guards to keep out the throng until the meat was cooked. Several unruly onlookers, however, refused to wait. "Crapt Moody stepped over the guarding rope and Mr. Buns Billy Woodward gave him a severe blow on the head," young Fred Hickson reminisced years later. "Then followed a general fight. I remember Mr. Nish Moody gashed the big fat ear of Mr. Josh Tyler and Captain Jim Harley drew a bowie knife. My father Ruben Hickson ran behind Mr. Billy Woodward and threw his arms around him and carried him across the creek through the water. He kicked like a mule," reminisced Hickson, "but my father had the advantage of him and locked him up in the grist mill house, some two hundred yards away. There were threats of breaking the mill door down, but my father persuaded them not to do so."

When the melee quieted, McCreary, who had retained his composure throughout the uproar, made a brief speech. "Fellow citizens and soldiers," his brother Richard, writing from memory forty-five years later, recalled him saying, "in the name of my comrades, I promise you that whether on the mountain tops of Old Virginia, or on the plains of South Carolina, the Palmetto Flag shall never fall, lest it be trailed in a sea of blood." And off the clamorous assemblage went, ultimately to become Company A of the 1st South Carolina.

Wick's bravery was legendary. In one battle, a bullet struck him in the chest and knocked him from his horse. Fearing that he was seriously wounded, he felt for blood but could find none. When he pulled a Bible from his shirt pocket, he discovered a lead ball buried three-quarters of the way into the book. Stories about a Bible saving a soldier's life are commonplace in Civil War literature, and serious scholars are understandably skeptical about them. In this instance, however, McCreary's Bible remained with his family as proof of the tale. A descendant, Leila McCreary Dixon, claimed to still have the book when her dwelling, along with the artifact, burned in 1946.

Absent the later part of 1863 because of illness, McCreary was promoted to colonel of the 1st South Carolina in January 1864. He was twenty-seven years old. Lieutenant Colonel Washington Pinckney Shooter, only a year younger, became his second in command. A short man, Shooter was also a graduate of the Citadel, a lawyer, and a newspaper editor in Marion, South Carolina. Volunteering at the outset of hostilities, he fought in all the regiment's battles, save at Sharpsburg. "He was a most gallant and efficient officer," a soldier wrote of Shooter. "He drilled accurately, disciplined carefully, fought obstinately and coolly." Two of his brothers served in the regiment with him.

Only 425 men strong, the 1st South Carolina was the smallest of McGowan's five regiments. Although most of its companies came from the interior of the state, Companies I, K, and L were recruited almost entirely from Charleston.

Charles found himself in Company I, headed by Captain Brailsford, who had enrolled him at Orange Court House. The company claimed a distinguished lineage. A few weeks after South Carolina seceded, a group of wealthy Charlestonians organized a military company called the Richardson Guards, named after F. D. Richardson, a signer of the Ordinance of Secession. The guards enjoyed parading around the city displaying a colorful hand-painted flag presented to them by the local ladies. When fighting started in earnest, they were mustered into Confederate service and sent to Virginia soon afterward. Their six-month terms expired in July 1861, but most of the guards reenlisted in Company I of the reorganized 1st South Carolina for the duration of the war.

Still called the Richardson Guards, the 1st South Carolina's Company I sustained massive casualties during the battles of 1862 and 1863, and its officers were seasoned veterans. Captain Brailsford, commanding the company, had been with the outfit since its formation. First Lieutenant Wallace Delph was wounded at Fredericksburg, and Andrew O'Brien, the company's first sergeant, carried a wound from Gettysburg. But the men who would be called on to do the fighting in the spring of 1864 were mostly novices. Of Company I's twenty-eight privates, only nine had ever seen combat; the remaining nineteen men had joined since Gettysburg. No one, of course, could know it at the time, but more than half of the men in Company I would be killed, wounded, or captured during their first week fighting Grant in the upcoming campaign.

★ ★ ★

Charles settled into the humdrum routine of winter camp. Lee's headquarters was a mile and a half east of Orange Court House in the shadow of Clark's Mountain, on Erasmus Taylor's farm. Powell Hill occupied a three-story mansion named Mayhurst, where his wife and children—including the infant Lucy Lee, named after the army's venerable commander—had joined him for the winter. Charles and his new companions contented themselves with humbler quarters. McGowan's troops initially camped on high ground in a stand of trees near Burnett's Ford on the Rapidan, but by February they had exhausted the wood supply and moved to a new camp half a mile upriver, close to a shallow river crossing known as Caves Ford.

The new camp sprawled across part of Montpelier, a plantation formerly owned by President James Madison. A grand mansion stood south of the plank road from Orange Court House to Liberty Mills; McGowan's regiments camped north of the road, across from the plantation house. Each regiment made its own camp, laid out like a small city with ten short streets lined with huts, each holding several men. The soldiers excavated shallow basements two or three feet into the ground and threw up walls of logs and planks pilfered from fences. The more industrious men plastered the chinks in their walls with mud and dug ditches around the dwellings to keep rainwater from draining in. Tarps and tent cloths passed for doors and sometimes as roofs, and soldiers built chimneys and fireplaces from stones and stacked open-ended barrels to serve as flues. Inside were beds made from elevated platforms covered with pine boughs for mattresses. "The camps were kept very cleanly," one of Mc-Gowan's officers remembered, "and the health of the command was as good as could be desired."

Food was scarce. A South Carolinian later recalled that he had too much cornmeal and far too little bacon, and that beef had become a remote memory. As a substitute for coffee, men ground parched corn, wheat, or rye, and mixed the concoction with hot water. Dinner, even at brigade headquarters, consisted of corn bread and soup made from mashed potatoes, cornmeal, and water. On good days, soldiers added meat for flavoring. As spring approached, dandelions and poke leaves peeked through the snow along the river flats, and men collected the sprouts to vary their diet. "This hunger was much the hardest trial we had to bear," a Confederate reminisced. "Going along all day with a gnawing at your insides, of which you were always conscious, was not pleasant. We had more appetite than anything else, and never got enough to satisfy it—even for a time."

No one expected the enemy to venture active operations until spring, so the troops whiled away their time talking, playing cards, and attending revival meetings. McGowan required two roll calls a day, at reveille and tattoo, and the exercises invariably provoked grumbling from the soldiers. "To be waked up and hauled out about dawn on a cold, wet, dismal morning, and to have to hustle out and stand shivering at roll call, was about the most exasperating item of a soldier's life," a rebel recalled. To keep his men occupied, McGowan had them fell trees and haul the timber to repair the road from Orange Court House to Liberty Mills, on the west end of the army's line. Soldiers "corduroyed" a five-mile stretch of mud by hewing the timber into planks and arranging the boards side by side in the roadbed. Other brigades passed the days breaking stones to pave the streets of Orange Court House.

The Confederate entrenchments began at Liberty Mills on the west end of Lee's defensive line and extended more than twenty-five miles east along the river to Sisson's Ford. High ridges dominated the southern shore, giving the Confederates a natural advantage, and soldiers strengthened the position still more by digging elaborate infantry trenches and artillery placements. The western half of the river line fell to Hill's Corps, and McGowan's Brigade was responsible for watching the banks from Caves Ford to Burnett's Ford, a little more than three miles of shoreline. McGowan initially assigned each of his five regiments a day of picket duty at a time. By February, however, it was apparent that a few men could do the job, so only five companies were posted each time. A company's rotation came up every ten days.

Patrolling the river was onerous work. The winter of 1863–1864 was especially harsh, and the Confederates were poorly clad. Many lacked shoes and had to make do by wrapping their feet with rags. Overcoats, other than those taken from dead Yankees in earlier battles, were in short supply, and snow swirled for days at a time, alternating with icy rainstorms. In February, parts of the river froze, and a rapid current swept huge chunks of ice past pickets shivering in lean-tos of sticks and pine boughs. "It is a great wonder," a Confederate wrote, "that these men did not freeze to death these terribly cold nights." In an attempt to minimize their misery, the men of both armies observed informal truces. In places, particularly at the fords, a lively black market sprang up in Yankee coffee, Confederate tobacco, and newspapers. Officers winked at the fraternization, respecting the code of honor between men who would be trying their best to kill one another when spring opened the season for active campaigning.

Charles and his new companions got to know one another. By day, they held races, wrestling matches, and snowball fights. Religious revivals enjoyed a widespread resurgence. And huddled around campfires at night, soldiers whiled away the time playing chess, dominoes, and cards. "When everything was frozen hard the going was good, and we danced every night in the company street," a rebel recalled. "But when a thaw came, and the rain wet us all up, the mud balled up on our feet."

Almost forty years old, Charles was the old man of Company I. Most of his fellow soldiers were half his age, and he doubtless looked askance at their sophomoric antics. Not surprisingly, he sought the companionship of someone of his own station and gravitated toward James Armstrong, acting captain of the 1st South Carolina's Company K. Born in Pennsylvania, Armstrong grew up in Charleston and considered himself a South Carolinian. He was only twenty years old, but he and Charles became fast friends. It was unusual for a private to dine with a captain, but they ignored that convention—Charles's age and his long-time service for Colonel Grayson probably made the exception palatable.

★ ★ ★

Armstrong's Company K was the 1st South Carolina's color company—the men who carried the regiment's battle flag into combat. Armstrong had been with Company K almost from the start of the war, serving as second lieutenant until late in 1861, when he was promoted to first lieutenant, and finally to acting captain after the Battle of Sharpsburg in 1862. He was slightly wounded at Sharpsburg, wounded again at Fredericksburg, and injured once more at Gettysburg, where he carried the colors when the regular color bearer was shot. Renowned for bravery, Armstrong was responsible for selecting the regiment's color bearers, training them, and making sure that replacements were ready to step up if the bearer faltered.

Battle flags, Charles learned, were not just brightly colored rags. For soldiers, especially those fighting far from home, the banners held deep emotional meaning, serving as tangible reminders of their communities and families. Attachments to these pieces of cloth were fierce, and men treated their flags with reverence. Soldiers who bore the banners never let them touch the ground, even in battle. No greater disgrace could befall a regiment than permitting the enemy to capture its colors.

Southerners marched off to war in 1861 under a hodgepodge of banners. The flag bearer for the 1st South Carolina, for example, initially carried the blue silk state flag supplied by William Whilden's firm of Hayden and Whilden. Each of the 1st South Carolina's ten companies also bore its own flag. The Richardson Guards sported a handmade banner with a palmetto palm wrapped in a ribbon proclaiming, "Always Ready."

In the fall of 1861, General Beauregard approved a standard design for a battle flag for the Confederate army in Virginia: a blue St. Andrew's cross bearing twelve stars—the number was later increased to thirteen—representing the states of the Confederacy, crisscrossing a red background. The clothing depot in Richmond issued several renderings of the battle flag, all made from wool but varying in dimension and in the color of the border. In the summer of 1862, the depot manufactured a version that historians have come to call the third bunting issue. This was a square battle flag with a white border bearing the familiar St. Andrew's cross.

During 1863, the 1st South Carolina went into battle bearing two flags. The regiment's color sergeant carried the blue silk state flag made by Hayden and Whilden, and a corporal carried the Confederate battle flag with its distinctive blue cross against a field of red. After the Battle of Gettysburg, the regiment's state colors were sent back to South Carolina for display at the state capitol in

Columbia. By the time that Charles joined the regiment, only the battle flag was carried in battle.

It was common practice for regiments to inscribe on their flags the names of the battles in which they had fought, and in January 1863, McGowan issued General Order No. 12 addressing that practice. "The campaign of the year 1862 is now ended," the general proclaimed, "and no soldier engaged in it will ever be ashamed to have it compared with any in history. This now veteran brigade has made many forced marches, suffered many privations, and fought many battles. In the cause of the country they have done much to be proud of, but in the same cause they may be called upon to do much more. Therefore, as an evidence of past and at the same time an incentive to future glory, the Brigadier General commanding directs that the following names of battles be entered in some conspicuous place on the standards of the respective regiments of the brigade:

1st South Carolina Regiment S. C. Vols.: Fort Sumter—Vienna— Mechanicsville—Cold Harbor—Frasier's Farm—2d Manassas—Ox Hill—Harper's Ferry—Sharpsburg—Shepherdstown—and Fredericksburg

The names of these battles were emblazoned onto the 1st South Carolina's battle flag, and new designations might have been added as the list of battles lengthened. By the winter of 1863–1864, it is possible that Chancellorsville, Gettysburg, Falling Waters, and Mine Run had also been inscribed on the regiment's banner.

The head of a regiment's color company exercised great care in selecting the soldiers who would carry the battle flag. The post of flag bearer was important, not only for sentimental reasons but for practical ones as well. When soldiers marched into combat, they looked to the flag bearer to guide them. Their eyes always sought the flag, floating above the smoke and confusion of battle, to signal where they were to go, when they were to press on, and when they were to fall back. Color bearers had to be tall and strong, able to hold the flag high in the thick of combat. Above all, they had to be fearless. Carrying the flag was an honor reserved for the regiment's best and bravest men.

Serving as a color bearer was also a deadly job. In the heat of battle, enemy troops invariably concentrated their fire toward the flags and the men who carried them in an attempt to bring down the colors to disrupt and discourage the foe. The 1st South Carolina habitually found itself in the thick of combat and served as a prime example of the risks of carrying the colors. During a single day's fight near Richmond in the summer of 1862, for example, the regiment lost five flag bearers. On that day, the 1st South Carolina started forward with Color Sergeant James Taylor carrying the large blue state flag with the palmetto on it. Three bullets tore into Taylor's body, killing him. Then Corporal Shubrick Hayne, the Color Corporal from Company L, picked up the flag, only to be mortally wounded; Private Alfred Pinckney, also of Company L, retrieved the banner and was shot to death with the flag in his hands; and Private Philip Gadsden Holmes was shot seven times as he tried to clasp the colors. Private Dominick Spellman finally seized the tattered rag and survived to carry it for the rest of the battle. He was promoted to color sergeant but was shot to death two months later at the Second Battle of Manassas. His successor, Color Sergeant James Larkin, was shot down the next year at Gettysburg, where Charles's friend Armstrong had carried the colors only to be wounded himself.

In 1864, Armstrong selected Corporal Andrew M. Chapman of the Butler Sentinels Company to carry the 1st South Carolina's battle flag in the impending campaign against Grant. He also des-ignated Chapman's successors, down through Private William Bunch of the Carolina Light Infantry Company. In the event that Bunch also fell—a remote possibility, considering that he stood third or fourth in line of succession—Armstrong would simply have to choose the best man available. The off chance that his choice might be Charles Whilden could not possibly have crossed his mind.

6

AN EERIE, INHOSPITABLE REGION

Several miles north of the Rapidan, in a home by the railroad tracks in Culpeper Court House, Grant was pondering the thorny question of how to defeat Lee. Charles was but a private and knew nothing of the designs of his own generals, of course, much less those of the enemy. But the plan of campaign evolving under Grant's scrutiny would determine his future in important ways.

Grant finally settled on a plan that made impressive use of his massive edge in numbers and materiel. The Army of the Potomac, facing Lee across the Rapidan, was to attack the Army of Northern Virginia and engage it in battle. At the same time a second Union army was to start south through the Shenandoah Valley west of Lee, depriving the Confederates of food and forage from the rich valley farms and threatening the rebel army's western flank. Simultaneously, a third Union army was to move against Richmond from the south and sever Lee's supply lines. Battered in front by the massive Potomac army, denied supplies by the Valley incursion, and harassed in the rear, Lee would be cornered and brought to bay. Grant's plan was a thoughtful exercise, carefully drawn to bring the war in the east to a swift conclusion.

Recognizing that the strong rebel earthworks lining the south bank of the Rapidan ruled out a frontal assault, Grant decided to send the Army of the Potomac across the river downstream from Lee, then swing back toward the Confederates, nullifying their advantage of position. Grant anticipated that Lee's army, routed out of its strong fortifications, would have no choice but to flee or turn to face the attackers. In either event, the movement was perfectly designed to flush Lee into open country and secure Grant the fight that he was seeking.

But the Union high command's strategy contained a fatal flaw. After crossing the Rapidan, the Northerners would find themselves in an eerie, inhospitable region of tangled second growth. In colonial times, large deposits of iron were discovered in the area, and the lieutenant governor of the Virginia Colony, Alexander Spotswood, had embarked enthusiastically on a smelting business. His first furnace, a contrivance with two stacks, began operation in 1724, and a quarter of a century later, six blast furnaces lit the sky, consuming by one estimate more than two acres of woods a day. By the early 1800s, most of the ore had been mined, but gold was discovered, and the smelting continued, devouring the rest of the trees. Planks had to be cut also to pave the two main roads through the dismal wasteland—one crossing at Germanna Ford and the other linking Fredericksburg and Orange Court House—as a hedge against the Virginia mud.

By 1864, a dense mat of brush and chinquapin, so thick in places as to blot out the sun, had grown up where forest once stood. Streams meandered in unexpected directions and serpentine foliage blocked the view, making it difficult for travelers to find their way. The region was virtually uninhabited except for a few weed-filled clearings and hardscrabble farms that dotted the suffocating landscape. Roads were scarce, and trails knifed through the green expanse to destinations known only to the locals.

Union planners recognized that this dreary forest of second growth was the worst place imaginable for fighting Lee. As soon as troops advanced, the skein of branches and saplings would swallow them up, and field commanders would lose sight of neighboring outfits. Grand maneuvers were impossible, and combat would degenerate into localized brawls. Grant held an impressive edge in artillery, but his cannon would be useless against an unseen enemy, and federal cavalry would be limited to a few roads and blind trails, unable to assist the infantrymen in any meaningful way. The Confederates, on the other hand, would benefit tremendously from their intimate knowledge of the obscure trails and byways of the Wilderness.

Yet astoundingly, the federal commanders decided to bring the Army of the Potomac into the Wilderness and to stay there for a night, exposing themselves to the risk of battle in the very forest that they had hoped to avoid. General George Meade, the Army of the Potomac's titular head, was concerned that his ponderous supply wagons might fall behind. Sensing endless possibilities for mischief, he directed his infantry to end its first day's march in the Wilderness to give the wagons time to catch up. His assumption that Lee could not move quickly enough to catch the Union army in the dark forest—the "first misfortune of the campaign," a Union officer called it—ranks among the most egregious command errors of the Civil War. And thus it happened that Grant opened his campaign by giving Lee a windfall, halting his army at the best location Lee could have imagined for his smaller force to give battle.

Lee, of course, had no way of knowing the precise route that Grant would take against him, but he suspected that the Northern commander would try crossing downriver though the Wilderness. Uncertain about Grant's plan, however, he felt compelled to keep his army dispersed across a broad area. Here was another paradox of the campaign. Lee could have invented no better place to confront Grant than the Wilderness, but he was reluctant to withdraw troops from his defensive line and send them into the Wilderness to intercept the federal army. In short, Lee did nothing to ensure a battle in the Wilderness, thereby forfeiting the initiative to his enemy.

★ ★ ★

The privates of both armies had no hint of the blunders their commanders were committing—Grant was offering Lee one of his best opportunities of the war, and Lee was ignoring it. They did understand, however, that hard marching and fighting were imminent. The weather had warmed, but smoke still billowed from fires on the Union side, alerting the Confederates that the Federals were burning items accumulated during the winter that might impede their march. At night, rebel scouts detected lights moving in the enemy camps. "Everybody knew what all this meant," a Southerner later explained.

In preparation for the campaign, Charles and his companions sorted through their possessions. Veterans knew from experience to take only what was absolutely necessary and to avoid extra weight at all cost. The rule was to start light, and men bid farewell to fiddles, chessboards, extra blankets, and shoes, all of which they loaded onto wagons bound for Richmond for safekeeping. "This meant that each man had left one blanket, one small haversack, one change of underclothes, a canteen, cup and plate of tin, a knife and fork, and the clothes in which he stood," a Southerner recalled. "When ready to march, the blanket, rolled lengthwise, the ends brought together and strapped, hung from left shoulder across under right arm, the haversack—furnished with towel, soap, comb, knife and fork in various pockets, a change of under-clothes in one main division, and whatever rations we happened to have, in the other—hung on the left hip; the canteen, cup, and plate, tied together, hung on the right; toothbrush 'at will' stuck in two button holes of jacket, or in haversack; tobacco bag hung to a breast button, pipe in pocket." In all, blanket, haversack, and con-tents weighed no more than ten pounds.

It rained hard the night of May 2, and a windstorm blew through the valley of the Rapidan, wrecking tents and sending tree limbs crashing through the camps of both armies. The next day, Charles and his fellow Confederates watched dust clouds gather over the Union side of the river. Wagons were moving, and the glint of rifle barrels disclosed troops marching downriver from the federal encampment.

After dark, a Confederate sergeant atop Clark's Mountain looked for signs that the Federals were beginning their campaign. Fires winked on the plain below, and flickers seemed to indicate the passage of troops. The sergeant strained to make out the direc-tion of march but could not tell which way the soldiers were head-ing. He alerted Lee's headquarters to the movement, and a query came back. Were the troops sidling to the east, toward Germanna and Ely's Fords, or to the west, toward Liberty Mills? The sergeant answered that he still could not tell. Lee ordered his corps com-manders to prepare to advance by daylight. Then he waited.

★ ★ ★

Near dawn on May 4, cavalrymen from Indiana ventured into the chill water at Germanna Ford, traded sporadic fire with North

Carolina troopers picketing the far bank, and drove them back. Then trained bridge builders floated pontoons into the river, spaced them fifteen feet apart, attached them with wooden stringers, and lay boards crosswise to make bridges capable of supporting troop columns, artillery, and wagons bulging with supplies. Five miles downriver, horsemen from New Jersey waded across the Rapidan and secured another crossing at Ely's Ford. Soon two unbroken lines of Union infantry were tramping onto Lee's side of the river.

May 4 was a spectacular spring day, bright with sunshine. Purple violets dotted lush green fields, lined with blankets and overcoats discarded by soldiers to lighten their march, and sunlight glinted from bayonets and musket barrels. Blue-clad soldiers filled the roads, and canvas wagon tops threaded sinuous white lines across the fields north of the river. The Army of the Potomac was on the move, and it was heading directly into the Wilderness.

Grant reached Germanna Ford midmorning and set up headquarters near Meade's tent. He could not help noticing Meade's new flag, a lavender, swallow-tailed affair sporting a golden eagle inside a silver wreath. "What's this?" Grant jocularly asked a staffer. "Is imperial Caesar anywhere about here?" Grant's aides also had something to laugh about. Their boss usually avoided finery, but this day he donned a black slouch hat with a gold cord and yellow-brown thread gloves that his wife had bought for him. Accompanying him was a congressman dressed in black, looking very much like an undertaker dressed to preside over the Confederacy's funeral.

Sifting through reports from scouts and from cavalry probes south of the river, Grant concluded that Lee had started toward the Wilderness, but that he was moving sluggishly. Grant could have hoped for no better development. The Army of the Potomac could continue its movement as planned and spend the night in a cleared portion of the forest around Wilderness Tavern. The next day—after the footsore federal troops had recuperated—the Union force would march out of the Wilderness refreshed and come to grips with Lee. "The crossing of the Rapidan effected," Grant wrote Washington. "Forty-eight hours now will demonstrate whether the enemy intends giving battle this side of Richmond."

★ ★ ★

As signal flags atop Clark's Mountain alerted Lee to the magnitude and direction of the Union army's advance, the Virginian faced one of the most difficult decisions of his military career. Grant was coming by the route that he had predicted, crossing downriver to avoid the impregnable Rapidan fortifications. Remaining dormant would forfeit the initiative to Grant and render the Rapidan defenses useless; falling back would only move the inevitable battle closer to Richmond and diminish the Confederate army's room to maneuver.

After weighing his choices—and after giving due deference to his uncertainty about Grant's intentions—the rebel commander decided to advance toward Grant and the Wilderness. From Lee's position at Orange Court House, two roads headed directly toward the Union army. The northernmost route was the Orange Turnpike, and immediately to its south was the Orange Plank Road, a rambling, winding way covered on one side with planks to provide travelers firm footing during rainy weather.

Lee ordered Richard Ewell's Corps to head toward the Wilderness along the Orange Turnpike and issued companion orders to Hill, who was to pass through Orange Court House and continue east along the Orange Plank Road, advancing more or less in tandem with Ewell so that each column could support the other. Hill left one division—six thousand men under the mild-mannered South Carolinian Richard Heron Anderson—to serve as a rear guard and directed his other two divisions under Henry Heth and Cadmus Wilcox to set off. The waiting was over, and Charles Whilden's Civil War was about to begin.

McGowan's camps buzzed with excitement. Neither soldiers nor officers knew where they were going or how long it would take to get there. Veterans threw wood on their campfires and began cooking rations, understanding from hard experience that food was scarce on the march and that supply wagons could take days or even weeks to catch up. Campaigning with Lee was an arduous affair, and a few days of tramping along dusty roads baked by a ruthless spring sun could transform a morsel of charred meat or moldy bread into a welcome banquet. The rules for survival were simple, and veterans of both armies followed them assiduously. "Get ahold of all the food you can," a mentor advised a greenhorn. "Cut haversacks from dead men. Steal them from infantrymen if you can. Let your aim be to secure food and food and still more food, and keep your eyes open for tobacco." Other points were also important. Canteens had to be filled at every stream, or anywhere else water could be found, and blisters must be prevented at all cost. It was folly for men to wash their feet before the day's march was finished, as that would only make them raw. One rule was paramount. "Get hold of food," veterans stressed, "and hang onto it; you will need it."

The Carolinians had no time to finish cooking their bread. "A universal stir ensued," one of McGowan's officers recalled. "In pursuance of a previous order, the officers' tents were torn down and cut up for distribution among the men. Knapsacks were packed, blankets rolled up, half-cooked dough or raw meal thrown into haversacks, the accumulated plunder of nine months thrown into the streets, accoutrements girded on, arms taken, and in half an hour we were on the march."

Charles and his companions filed onto the plank road running from Liberty Mills to Orange Court House. Other soldiers already packed the way. Leading the procession was Henry Heth's division, a mixed outfit containing men from Alabama, Mississippi, Tennessee, and North Carolina. Wilcox's division followed with two brigades of Tar Heels, a brigade of Georgians, and McGowan's troops from the Palmetto State.

Taking their place near the rear of the line, McGowan's soldiers felt exhilarated to be moving after the long winter encampment, and a sense of adventure prevailed. "Away slid the rattling, shuffling, close-jointed column," a South Carolina man remembered, "through camp after camp deserted, out into the high road, through Orange and beyond." The threadbare men chattered, sang, and called out greetings to children, women, and old men gathered by the roadside to watch the spectacle. They strode past scenes familiar from their winter's sojourn—past the overgrown fields of Montpelier and the stately home where Madison and his wife Dolley had once held court, a reminder of bygone times.

The Army of Northern Virginia was marching to battle, and Charles was proud to be part of it. On they trod, some men barefoot, some with rags tied around their feet, but all under the spell of the day. "It was very pleasant for us to get into the stir of the moving army again," a Virginian recalled. A popular topic was the disparity in numbers between their own army and the Northern force invading their soil. "And yet," recollected a Confederate who marched in the ranks, "knowing all this, these lunatics were sweeping along to that appallingly unequal fight, cracking jokes, laughing, and with not the least idea in the world of anything else but victory."

Cheering faces lined the streets of Orange Court House as Hill's men passed through. A few blocks of houses blurred by, then the courthouse, then the railroad station, and in a blink they were through the town and onto the open road. As the Third Corps approached the Taylor farm, Lee and his aides rode out. The general's place was at the head of his troops, near the evolving battlefront. Timing would be everything once Grant's intentions became clear, and Lee would have to react to events quickly. Lee never commented on why he chose to travel with Hill rather than with Ewell, whose Second Corps was marching on the turnpike a few miles north. On balance, he probably judged Hill the more questionable of the two generals, and that is why he chose to ride with him.

★ ★ ★

Ewell, on the Orange Turnpike, crossed Mine Run early in the evening and camped for the night, two miles short of the Wilderness. Near dark, the head of Hill's column reached the settlement of Verdiersville, a mile from Mine Run. Many of the troops, Charles included, had covered twenty miles since noon. And several miles to the southwest, a good day's march from the Wilderness, Longstreet's soldiers were also on the move, winding along a maze of country roads.

As evening shadows spread across the landscape, rebel cavalrymen rode into Lee's Verdiersville headquarters with tantalizing nuggets of information. Grant, they reported, had stopped in the Wilderness, and his overall direction of advance was toward the Confederate army. Grasping the opportunity that Grant had given him, Lee decided to attack immediately.

The risks were tremendous. By Lee's own estimation, he could muster a slim 35,000 infantrymen to throw against Grant's 120,000. His answer was to venture a gamble, breathtaking in scope and extraordinarily dangerous. Early in the morning, Ewell was to press east along the Orange Turnpike, engage the federal troops encamped around Wilderness Tavern, and fasten them in place. Hill meanwhile was to advance along the Orange Plank Road and lock horns with the enemy in his sector. While Ewell and Hill detained the huge Union host in the Wilderness, Longstreet was to slip below the forest's southern fringe and veer north into the exposed end of the Union army. If all went as Lee planned—and if the Union generals panicked when Lee's veterans appeared unexpectedly on their flank—Grant would be driven back across the Rapidan to share the fate of his predecessor, Joseph Hooker, who suffered defeat on this same ground almost exactly a year earlier.

For a day at least, Ewell and Hill would be locked in mortal combat with a foe that outnumbered them almost four-to-one. Each corps would have to wage its own battle, one on the turnpike and the other on the plank road, separated by three or more miles of intractable woodland, with no hope of reinforcements. If Grant discovered that Lee had divided his army, he could focus irresistible pressure against one rebel wing, defeat it, and then turn to destroy the other wing. Under that grim scenario—a possibility by no means far-fetched—the Army of Northern Virginia would cease to function, Richmond would fall, and the Confederacy would be doomed.

In fields and woods around Verdiersville, the soldiers of Hill's Corps, Charles among them, lay on blankets under a starry sky. Charles knew nothing of Lee's great gamble, or of the part he and his companions were to play in it. His thoughts, as he gazed into the black Virginia night smoking his meerschaum, must have wandered over the day's events, pausing occasionally to imagine what the morning might bring.

★ ★ ★

A few miles away, snug in their Wilderness camps, Grant's men were also reflecting on their situation. Many soldiers had fought on this very ground the previous spring, and the comparisons were unsettling. Union veterans combed through debris from their former battle for mementos. One man found the remains of a horse that had been shot from under him, and another located a comrade's skull, pierced through the head. Sitting on low mounds where their friends had been buried the year before, everyone felt uneasy. Veterans related that the Wilderness had caught fire, and wounded men had burned to death in flaming underbrush. "I am willing to take my chances of getting killed," a soldier experienced in such matters opined, "but I dread to have a leg broken and then to be burned slowly; and these woods will surely be burned if we fight here." A man who had been stabbing a shallow grave with a bayonet pried out a skull and rolled it across the ground. "That is what you are all coming to," he predicted, "and some of you will start toward it tomorrow." Lee, the veterans thought, would attack Grant in the Wilderness. And Lee, they agreed, would hold the advantage.

In tents near a gabled farmhouse by Germanna Ford, Grant, Meade, and their staffs were preparing to retire, ignorant of the fact that Lee had advanced within striking distance of the Union army. There was nothing less than a complete breakdown in the Potomac army's intelligence-gathering capacity, and the cavalry had neglected to guard the approaches from Lee's direction. Near nightfall, a soldier from Michigan saw puffs of smoke on the western horizon but erroneously surmised that they came from Union outposts. The evening, one of Grant's generals recalled, seemed "quiet and peaceful, as if there was not a reb within a hundred miles, or ever had been."

Meeting around a campfire, Grant and Meade congratulated themselves on having crossed the Rapidan under the very nose of the enemy. Feeling no urgency—they had, after all, received no reports that Lee might be near—they decided to use the next morning to regroup and start their movement toward the Confederates. By their reckoning, a great victory was in the making.

★ ★ ★

Charles and his companions were up before daylight on May 5. The camps around Verdiersville hummed with activity as Hill's soldiers made ready to resume their march toward certain battle. Lee was in an expansive mood and eager to exploit the opportunity Grant had given him by stopping in the Wilderness. Mounting Traveller, he joined Hill at the head of the troops, and soon the column spread out snakelike along the dusty road. A few miles to the north and east, Ewell's men trod along the Orange Turnpike. As the army advanced, the turnpike and the plank road diverged, increasing the distance between the two Confederate wings. Couriers rode back and forth on trails across the widening cleft, keeping Lee posted on developments.

A short way past Verdiersville, the Orange Plank Road began a gentle descent to Mine Run. Some of Hill's veterans thought they were going to entrench behind the creek and began loosening their knapsacks, but Lee and Hill kept on, riding across Mine Run and up the rise on the far side. Understanding that Lee intended to attack Grant in the Wilderness, the troops cheered and passed the news back through the ranks.

As a precaution, Hill spread a cloud of skirmishers in front of his column. Spaced several feet apart, the soldiers sifted through the woods and fields in front of the marching troops, looking for signs of the enemy. A short distance east of Mine Run, they ran into a regiment of New York cavalrymen, and rattling sounds of gunfire reverberated through the Wilderness as the Union troopers began shooting at the rebels with their seven-shot carbines. Pressed by superior numbers—a single regiment could do little to detain a corps—the New Yorkers reluctantly fell back along the plank road, firing as they retired.

From his position near the rear of Hill's column, Charles could hear muffled pops from the firefight. Shortly after crossing Mine Run, he began passing signs of the heated little fray. "We came to a dead Yankee in the road, lying flat on his back, his arms thrown out, his head turned back, showing a gray beard, his boots and pants taken off, his features and limbs rigid in death," a Confederate remembered. "Soon we came to another, shot through both legs below the knee, and yet alive." Charles and his fellow marchers quieted. Here was death and mutilation, stark portents of events to come.

A few miles north, the Orange Turnpike formed a leafy trough as it cleaved through the forest. Less than two miles from their night's camp, the soldiers at the head of Ewell's advance came to a stubble-filled clearing called Saunders Field, named after the family that had formerly farmed the place. Eight hundred yards away, on the field's far side, they spotted a scattering of blue-clad troops. Surprised by the appearance of rebels—the Union cavalry, after all, were supposed to be guarding the road—the Federals melted into the woods.

Ewell sized up the situation with an experienced eye. He had reached the Union picket line, a sure sign that Grant's army was close by, and Saunders Field offered him an excellent place to post his troops for the inevitable fight. The western edge of the field was elevated, providing the Confederates an unobstructed view across the clearing. And immediately in front, the ground dropped sharply into a deep swale, then leveled to form a flat expanse extending across to where the Yankees had been spied. If the enemy tried to attack, they would have to charge across half a mile of open ground under the muzzles of Ewell's veterans.

Cutting cross-country, a courier from Ewell located Lee on the Orange Plank Road. Ewell, he reported, had met only a few enemy pickets and planned to push ahead until he encountered the enemy in strength. Concerned about being pulled into a fight that he could not win, Lee advised against hazarding a battle just yet. He did not want to provoke a "general engagement" until Longstreet arrived, he stressed, which could not happen before dark.

It was not readily apparent to Ewell how to pin Grant in the Wilderness while avoiding battle, but preparing a strong defensive line struck him as a good way to start. Deploying his soldiers along the western margin of Saunders Field, he began extending his line into the woods on each side of the clearing. His Confederates stacked logs and tree limbs into low barricades and piled dirt against the front, facing across the field where they had last seen the enemy. The next move would be up to Grant.

★ ★ ★

Lee would have been pleased to learn that Grant and his generals were having a morning every bit as busy as his own.

Shortly after sunrise, Grant's subordinate on the Orange Turnpike—an ambitious, gangly New Yorker named Gouverneur Warren—began moving out his troops on a wagon road that angled cross-country to the south. Warren had just mounted his dappled-gray horse when a courier galloped up and announced that rebels were materializing at Saunders Field. Clouds of dust were boiling up behind them, suggesting that large numbers of enemy troops were approaching. Concerned, Warren forwarded the information to Meade.

Ordinarily Meade was cautious, but his desire to please Grant made him unusually aggressive this clear spring morning. After sending a note to Grant alerting him that rebels had appeared unexpectedly on the turnpike, he directed Warren to prepare to attack. "If any opportunity presents itself of pitching into a part of Lee's army," Grant urged, "do so without giving time for disposition."

Time for deploying his soldiers, however, was precisely what Warren needed. Most of his troops had already started off along the wagon road, and turning them around and bringing them back by the same route risked an impossible traffic jam. Instead, Warren tried to rearrange his corps into a coherent battle line across the eastern edge of Saunders Field and through the woods south of the clearing, facing Ewell's improvised barricades. The task verged on impossible because the Wilderness swallowed up troops as soon as they left the trails. Companies and regiments lost contact with units on either side, thick foliage obscured the sun, and groups of men wandered through twisting mazes of ravines, veering in different directions and unable to get their bearings. Officers tried to restore order by shouting at the top of their lungs, but their efforts only added to the confusion. Resorting to compasses to maintain a consistent direction of advance, some troops attempted to navigate the Wilderness like mariners on a choppy sea. The precise location of Ewell's line remained a mystery. Rebels were plainly visible across Saunders Field pitching up barricades, but there was no telling how far their formation extended into the woods.

His attention fixed on the Orange Turnpike, Meade had forgotten all about the Orange Plank Road. Around nine o'clock, he received a disturbing dispatch reporting sporadic firing from the south, and the true state of affairs became painfully clear. Lee was advancing on at least two fronts, one on the turnpike and the other on the plank road, and the Federals were poorly situated to counter. Beset by rebel columns popping up phantomlike, the Union offensive that had started with so much promise the day before was quickly unraveling.

Pitching his camp next to Meade on a knoll near the turnpike, Grant directed Meade to rush soldiers toward the Orange Plank Road to intercept Hill. Their objective was a remote intersection in the Wilderness where the plank road, running west to east, crossed a north-south route called the Brock Road. The dense forest around the obscure road junction would soon gain notoriety in the annals of American military history. It would also figure prominently in Charles Whilden's baptism of fire.

As aides dashed off with this latest spate of orders, Grant sat on a stump and lit a cigar. There was nothing more that he could do to prepare for the fight, and the forest prevented him from seeing what was happening. Taking out a penknife, he picked up a stick and began whittling. Absentmindedly, he shredded his new cloth gloves along with the stick. He stayed on the knoll most of the day, whittling, smoking, and reviewing dispatches as they arrived from the battlefronts.

★ ★ ★

Hill's troops, Charles among them, were making good time along the Orange Plank Road when ten or so Yankee horsemen—a courier and his escorts trying to get information back to Meade—galloped into a clearing near the road. To the startled Carolinians, all of Grant's cavalry seemed to have descended on them. "Yankee cavalry," a Southerner cried, and the greenhorns in McGowan's Brigade darted from the ranks and began running for the cover of a nearby stand of trees. There ensued a "general scramble, most provoking and foolish," a sheepish participant later admitted.

Scarcely breaking their stride, McGowan's veterans faced toward the interlopers, fired a few shots, and sent the Yankees wheeling their horses back the way they had come. Relieving their tension with a few belly laughs at their comical overreaction to a handful of enemy riders, McGowan's new men filtered back onto the plank road and resumed their march, casting nervous glances at the neighboring woods and fields.

Two miles farther on, in the heart of the Wilderness, the plank road passed along the southern edge of another ragged clearing. The property of a wealthy local landowner, the field had lain fallow for years. It was presently home to Catherine Tapp, a fifty-nine-year-old widow who lived there with several children, a granddaughter, and a white laborer. Overgrown with broom grass and saplings, the forty-acre meadow was known locally as Widow Tapp's field.

Lee chose Widow Tapp's field for his headquarters. The clearing was three miles due south of Saunders Field, where Ewell was girding to do battle with Warren's thousands, and it was about a mile shy of the intersection where the Orange Plank Road and Brock Road crossed. Hill's lead elements under Heth had not yet reached the crossroads, and Lee doubted that the enemy would relinquish the critical road junction without a fight. Simply put, Widow Tapp's field gave the Confederate commander an ideal location for monitoring developments on both emerging battlefronts.

While the troops of Heth's division continued east toward Brock Road, Lee, Hill, and the rebel cavalry commander Jeb Stuart sat under a tree near Mrs. Tapp's cabin and discussed the day's developments. Without warning, a line of Union soldiers stepped from the woods and strode into the field, their muskets leveled. "Get out of here!" a Southern soldier cried to the generals. "You will be killed!" Lee walked calmly toward the plank road; calling for his adjutant, Stuart stood and stared at the intruders, and Hill remained transfixed, an aide by his side. Unknown to the Northerners, the cream of the Confederate army's high command lay within their grasp.

The enemy visitors, however, were as surprised as their quarry. "Right about," a Union officer shouted, uncertain of the strength of the rebels he had stumbled upon and unaware of the identities of the figures unceremoniously evacuating the field.

The dramatic appearance of Union troops at Widow Tapp's farm underscored the danger that the gap between Ewell and Hill posed for Lee's venture. A few Federals—no more than a squad—had infiltrated the unguarded three-mile interval and almost captured the Army of Northern Virginia's commander and two of his chief subordinates. What if Grant sent into the breach a division, or even worse, a corps? The gap had to be plugged, Lee concluded, and he gave the assignment to Charles's division commander, Cadmus Wilcox.

Meanwhile, Hill's other division, under Heth, continued east, unaware that Grant had dispatched a sizable force toward the Brock Road–Plank Road intersection to intercept them. As the first of the winded Federals reached the road junction, their commander, Brigadier General George Getty, directed them into a north-south line along the Brock Road to hold the Southerners in check. Discovering Federals in front of them, Heth's troops spread into the forest on both sides of the Orange Plank Road, forming a line facing Getty's, and began digging in along a low ridge cut by gullies. Only a few hundred yards of saplings and undergrowth separated the opposing lines, and Union and Confederate pickets shot at the slightest flicker of movement.

A mile back at Widow Tapp's field, Lee felt relieved. Half the daylight hours had passed, and his plan seemed to be working.

Ewell and Hill had pinned Grant in the Wilderness, and if the Northern generals continued to dawdle, Lee would have time to wedge Wilcox into the gap between the divided portions of his army and unite it in a continuous line. But if Grant threw his weight against either wing of Lee's force, a Confederate collapse would be inevitable. Not since Sharpsburg had the Army of Northern Virginia faced a comparable risk of disaster.

★ ★ ★

Whittling and stewing at his knoll on the Orange Turnpike, Grant was nearing the end of his patience. The two armies were squaring off on two separate fronts, one at Saunders Field on the turnpike and the other at the Brock Road–Plank Road intersection. It was now early afternoon, and Meade's field commanders in both sectors still had not attacked.

Grant was particularly miffed at Warren. Taking advantage of the delay, Ewell's Confederates were now firmly ensconced behind log-and-earthen barricades, and their artillery was rolling into place. In the six hours that had passed since Ewell's unexpected appearance, the Confederates had made Saunders Field a death trap. Predicting a disaster if he tried to advance, Warren beseeched his superiors to let him stay put until reinforcements could be brought up.

Pressured by Grant and Meade, Warren finally ordered his men to attack. A bugle sounded, and the Northerners instinctively leaned forward as though preparing to step into a storm of bullets. With a shout, they strode into Saunders Field, forming neat lines of blue across the yellow-brown stubble. Shots rang out, men began falling, but the line pressed on, soldiers shifting to close the gaps. When they reached the swale midfield, rebel artillery chimed in, and sheets of fire exploded in the Union men's faces. A second line pressed on, stepping over corpses and injured soldiers and opening to let hollow-eyed troops from the first line stumble back. A regiment from New York, resplendent in colorful sashes and leggings, crossed the swale and started up the slope toward the Confederates. Blasts poured down from the ridge, and the air seemed filled with bodies and screaming forms. "The regiment melted away like the snow," a New Yorker reported in disbelief. "Men disappeared as if the earth had swallowed them up."

Saunders Field became the slaughter pen of Warren's prediction. Northerners hunkered in the swale, where the roll of ground afforded protection so long as they stayed down, and bodies dotted the slope from the ravine to Ewell's line. Some Northern units, their ranks thinned during the charge, managed to crest the ridge, but the rebels dropped back into the woods, firing at the Union men silhouetted against the sky. A few Federals made it into the woods, where gun smoke floated through the underbrush and the constant rattle of musketry amplified the forest's disorienting effect. Men would scream out, clutch a wound, and fall to the ground writhing in agony. All semblance of order evaporated as the battle dissolved into desperate fights at close quarters between clusters of men.

The rebels counterattacked, ramming into pockets of disheartened troops and driving them back. Men yelled, groaned, and swore as they forced their way through the tangled mass of briers and brush, lacerating their flesh and tearing their clothes. The receding blue wave gave Ewell's marksmen excellent targets, making the retreat as deadly as the advance. As the rebels pursued the stampeding Yankees into Saunders Field, volleys of musketry from Union soldiers in the far woods tore into them, forcing them into the narrow ditch with Northerners who had sought protection there during their own charge. The steady patter of rifle shots reminded one man of the sound a stick makes when it rasps against a picket fence. A few troops tried to dash to their respective sides of the field and were shot down. Injured men called for water, but no one dared to try and rescue them.

In the woods south of Saunders Field, Yankees and Confederates groped through impossibly dense undergrowth looking for vulnerable points in opposing battle lines. Regiments and companies lost sight of one another in patches of dwarf pine and matted undergrowth, colliding in tangled heaps with other outfits or heading off on tangents. Men stumbled into thorns and briers and slogged through gullies and swamps knee-deep in mud. In places, officers rallied their soldiers, and deadly stand-up fights between isolated bands of armed figures swayed back and forth in the foliage.

Then the dry stubble ignited, and thick black smoke rolled across Saunders Field. Patches of the clearing crackled in flame, creating a nightmarish scene as wounded men tried to hobble to safety, using their muskets as crutches or gouging their elbows into the ground to pull their bodies along. Soldiers burned to death, and others were killed when the flames reached the cartridge boxes at their waists, igniting the powder. A few soldiers too injured to escape chose to kill themselves rather than suffer death in the flames. Heaps the size of men lay charred beyond recognition in areas blackened by the conflagration.

In little more than an hour, the fighting—at least the organized part of it—was over. Repulsed in their attack at Saunders Field, Warren's men huddled in the tree line on the clearing's eastern edge, throwing up low mounds of dirt and logs in imitation of Ewell's troops on the field's far aide. Ambulances and wounded men on foot packed the Orange Turnpike all the way back to

Wilderness Tavern, where surgeons assembled under trees, hacking off arms and legs. Piles of severed limbs rose higher by the minute.

★ ★ ★

At about the same time that Warren was launching his ill-fated attack at Saunders Field, Wilcox's division strode through Widow Tapp's field and turned north to cement the junction of Hill and Ewell. Marching past Lee, Hill, and Stuart, Charles and the men of McGowan's Brigade trudged on for a mile or so to a broad field on top of a ridge. This was the Chewning farm, and Confederate scouts had already clambered onto the roof of the Chewning family's house to gain unobstructed views of the surrounding countryside. In the far distance, across the treetops, they could make out Horace Lacy's house and the sea of tents around it that made up the Union army's command center.

Two of Wilcox's brigades—McGowan's South Carolinians and a brigade of North Carolinians—settled down to rest on the Chewning plateau. The remainder of Wilcox's troops—better than half his division—continued north along a string of fields leading toward the lower end of Ewell's line.

Charles lounged in the fresh clover of the Chewning farm and followed the battle's progress. White smoke from gunfire mingled with billowy black clouds from burning stubble to mark the location of Saunders Field, where Ewell's fight against Warren was winding down. The sporadic discharge of muskets to the east designated the point where Heth and Getty confronted each other, at the junction of the Orange Plank Road and the Brock Road. Combat in that quarter seemed to be heating, and Charles paid it close attention. The chaplain of Orr's Rifles, resting near the 1st South Carolina, seized the occasion to lead the soldiers in prayers.

"It was one of the most impressive scenes I ever witnessed," one of Charles's officers remembered of the impromptu sermon on Mr. Chewning's hilltop. "On the left thundered the dull battle; on the right the sharp crack of rifles gradually swelled to equal importance; above was the blue, placid heavens; around us a varied landscape of forest and fields, green with the earliest foliage of spring; and here knelt hirsute and browned veterans shriving for another struggle with death."

★ ★ ★

As the combat at Saunders Field waned, Grant pestered Meade to launch an offensive along the plank road. Getty was in place at the Brock Road intersection, but he did not want to attack until supporting troops under General Winfield Scott Hancock arrived. At four o'clock, his patience exhausted, Meade ordered Getty to attack, with or without Hancock. The Vermont general protested, denouncing Meade's directive as poor strategy. But orders were orders, and perceiving no way out, Getty instructed his men to advance into the thickets toward Heth. The day's second battle—this one on the Orange Plank Road—was about to begin. And once more, the impatience of Union headquarters had concocted a recipe for disaster.

A brigade of Vermont soldiers waded into the Wilderness, brushing through branches and vines and stumbling over logs and stumps hidden in the undergrowth. Heth's pickets heard them coming and dropped back to low barricades of logs and dirt along the elevated ground that marked the main rebel line. The Vermonters marched on, twigs snapping underfoot. They could see only a few yards as they thrashed ahead, trying to push the mass of greenery aside like a curtain covering a window.

Muskets flashed, sheets of lead tore into the Union ranks, and the men from the Green Mountain State fell to the ground, shooting blindly back at the wall of fire and smoke in front of them. "Advance!" officers shouted, and soldiers instinctively rose, only to be riddled by bullets slamming into them at point-blank range. The blast blotted out all other sounds, and a thick, sulphurous smell of gunpowder rolled down from the Confederate ridge. Minié balls whistled through the branches, pinning the Yankees in place. Moving forward or back spelt immediate death, and lying still was little better.

Soldiers from Pennsylvania, Massachusetts, and Rhode Island pushed into the foliage to the right of the Vermonters. The rebel ridge was steeper there, and Heth's Confederates lay entrenched along the face of the slope in three lines, one above the other. As fresh waves of Union troops reached the base of the rise, the rebels opened fire so vigorously that the sound of their muskets discharging reminded one participant of an army of drummers beating the long roll. The Federals lay flat, hugging the ground and firing back through the haze at indistinct flashes, their lips black with powder from tearing open paper cartridges with their teeth.

Tramping feet heralded the approach of Hancock's Corps, and the tide of battle began to turn. Hancock—a handsome, imposing Pennsylvanian called the Superb for his striking presence and battlefield exploits—rode onto Brock Road and began barking orders, directing one of his divisions into the fray and calling for another. Fresh soldiers disappeared into the forest by the thousands, and shell-shocked men dragged wounded companions back as reinforcements took their places. Faced with overwhelming numbers, Heth urged his troops to redouble their efforts. Protected behind barricades, rebel marksmen fired into the mass of enemy soldiers huddled below and handed their smoking muskets to wounded men to reload.

As evening shadows stole over the Wilderness, the woods immediately west of the Brock Road intersection witnessed a scene of unrelieved slaughter. "There seemed to be as many dead men in our front as we had men engaged," a rebel soldier remarked. Reflected one witness: "A butchery plain and simple it was, unrelieved by any of the arts of war in which the exercise of military skill and tact robs the hour of some of its horrors. It was a mere slugging match in a dense thicket of small growth, where men but a few yards apart fired through the brushwood for hours."

Monitoring developments from Widow Tapp's farm a mile behind the front, Lee glanced nervously at his watch. It was a little after five. Night—and relief from Hancock's pounding—was fully three hours away. The pace of combat on the plank road escalated to a fever pitch as wave upon wave of Union soldiers pummeled Heth with mounting violence. More enemy were reportedly advancing through the forest to the south in an attempt to get into Heth's rear. With the numerical odds stacked more than five-to-one against him, Heth's thin line risked being swamped in a sea of blue uniforms.

The battle had reached its point of crisis. Heth had to be reinforced immediately. The fate of the Southern army depended on it. And therefore, as he had so often before, Lee dispatched a courier to Hill. Little Powell, he instructed, must bring up Wilcox—and with him his South Carolinians—and buttress Heth's beleaguered line until dark. Charles was about to receive his introduction to combat in one of the Civil War's nastiest fights.

7

Like a Saturday Evening Market in Augusta

Officers shouting orders roused Charles and his companions from their reveries on Mr. Chewning's hilltop. Heth was pressed to his limit and in desperate need of reinforcements.

Falling into rank, the South Carolinians retraced their way along the farm road to Widow Tapp's field and turned left onto the Orange Plank Road. Behind came the brigade of Tar Heels, trailed by the rest of Wilcox's troops. "The roar of muskets became continuous, augmented occasionally by the report of cannon, and always by the ringing rebel cheer," a man in the 1st South Carolina remembered of those moments.

Charles's regiment led the way through the pack of soldiers, artillery, and ordnance wagons that crowded the road. The situation was unsettling, even for veterans such as Captain Brailsford. Officers urged the men to hurry. Marching sometimes in quick time, sometimes at the double-quick, they pressed east along the plank road, the bone-jarring pounding of artillery fire and the crackle of musketry growing steadily louder.

Charles and the other greenhorns in Company I glanced uneasily about, buffeted by conflicting emotions. Fear was paramount. Stomachs tightened, time seemed to slow, and their surroundings—contorted corpses dotting the roadside, smoke curling through trees, marching lines of men—appeared as though etched in sharp relief. Frightened as the novice soldiers were, they kept their emotions to themselves, fighting down urges to panic. Their manhood was at stake, and any sign of alarm was certain to draw jeers from the veterans.

The road became more chaotic as the Carolinians advanced. Shadowy figures emerged from the woods. Here were broken and wounded men, some hobbling, some leaning on companions, nearly all showing ghastly wounds as they materialized from the smoke-filled forest like ghouls from a bad dream. The clatter of musketry, the cries of injured soldiers, and the frenzied shouts of combatants merged into a blur of noise. Bullets and fragments from exploding shells plowed the roadbed around them.

Wilcox, an incongruous figure astride a white pony, halted a hundred yards behind Heth's battle line. Striking a martial pose, he waved his troops into position. The 1st South Carolina and Orr's Rifles, he ordered, were to shift south of the plank road and form a line in the woods. Oriented perpendicularly to the plank road, Orr's Rifles would constitute the line's northern edge, brushing the roadway, and the 1st South Carolina was to trail south into the forest. The brigade's other regiments—the 12th, 13th, and 14th South Carolina—were to construct a companion line north of the plank road, their southern end anchored on the road next to Orr's Rifles and the rest of the line extending north toward a tributary of Wilderness Run.

The men of the 1st South Carolina left the plank road and disappeared into a dense growth of saplings and bushes. Creepers festooned with blossoms and fresh green tendrils lent a festive touch to the jungle. The soldiers could see only a few feet in any direction, but there was no question about the way to the front. To the east, the ruckus was deafening and the gun smoke was billowing. Forming a line in the matted tangle was a matter of feel and guesswork. The stifling forest suppressed any semblance of a breeze, and the air hung still and heavy, laced with the unmistakable stench of gunpowder. Gnats invaded everyone's eyes and ears and stuck to their skin, and woolen uniforms hung damp from perspiration.

Satisfied that the 1st South Carolina was tolerably in formation, Wick McCreary reported his regiment ready. Officers instructed the soldiers to advance at McCreary's and Lieutenant Colonel Shooter's command, guiding left to preserve the semblance of a unified line and to keep in contact with the units to their north. Charles and the rest of Company I's privates waited nervously, shifting from one foot to the other and swatting bugs.

"Charge!" McCreary shouted, and the men of the 1st South Carolina jolted forward, brushing aside thickly matted tangles of branches. The soldiers of Orr's Rifles, to their left, also stepped off, trying to keep apace, but second growth interlaced with vines played havoc with the alignment. Gaps opened as men detoured around stumps and bogs, crowding soldiers into the men next to them and jumbling the formation. Straining to see in front, Charles and his fellow Carolinians caught a glimpse of the rear of Heth's battle line. The soldiers there had stacked logs and branches and heaped dirt against the side facing the enemy. Forms in homespun uniforms knelt behind the makeshift barricades, firing as rapidly as possible at unseen foes. Orderlies scurried about crablike as they distributed boxes of ammunition, bent over to avoid being hit. Flecks of dirt and wood spit skyward from the top of the barricades where bullets struck.

Caught up in the excitement of the moment and determined to set an example, McGowan spurred his horse, leapt over Heth's barrier, and rode toward the enemy, brandishing his sword overhead. The portly general's dramatic gesture had the desired effect, and the men of the 1st South Carolina and Orr's Rifles cheered and ran forward, elbowing through Heth's thinning ranks and vaulting over the barricades in a wild burst of energy. Frightened out of his wits, Charles charged with them.

The battle cry turned out to be a mistake. "We should have charged without uttering a word until within a few yards of the Federal line," an officer in the 1st South Carolina ruefully conceded after the dust settled. Alerted by the ruckus that the rebels were attacking, the Federals—they were now throwing up barricades of their own less than a hundred yards away—loosed a volley. Dull thuds followed by anguished cries told of bullets penetrating flesh and splintering bones. But the Carolinians kept on, leaving a trail of dead and wounded men in their wake. Tangled branches and vines held some corpses almost erect.

The 1st South Carolina, on the extreme right of McGowan's advancing line, was especially hard hit. Union troops occupied the woods south of the regiment, overlapping the end of the line. Exposed to fire from in front and from their right, Charles and the rest of McGowan's Southerners dropped to the ground and began shooting back at invisible targets. Then bullets began tearing into them from behind. Heth's men were shooting again, and their "friendly fire" was hitting the Carolinians from the rear. A Confederate who lived through the ordeal later described the regiment's predicament. "All idea of a charge had to be abandoned," he explained, "for, in addition to the worst conceivable ground for marching, and the demoralizing spectacle of [Heth's] division lying down, and, after we had passed them, firing through our ranks, the enemy's line extended far to the right of ours."

Just when it seemed that the situation could not get worse, it did. Orr's Rifles, immediately north of the 1st South Carolina, advanced onto an exposed piece of high ground. Pelted by musketry from the Vermonters, the soldiers of the regiment rolled to the back side of their ridge. "The first regiment was now entirely alone," a man with the 1st South Carolina remembered. "There were no troops to the right of them on the same line, and on the left was the gap left by [the retreat of Orr's Rifles]—at least one hundred and fifty yards."

Charles's initiation into combat became a battle for survival. The 1st South Carolina had punched ahead of the rest of the Confederate army and was fighting virtually alone. The men lay in the woods, bereft of cover, shooting blindly in the direction where enemy fire seemed heaviest. At regular intervals, a soldier would groan and lie still, blood oozing from a wound. Casualties mounted, among them one of Washington Shooter's brothers, Benjamin Franklin Shooter. The only protection for the survivors was the foliage that screened their position and kept the enemy ignorant of their true numbers and situation. "I could not see anything distinctly," a man in the 1st regiment remembered, "on account of the bushes, the smoke of our line and that of the Federals." A panicked officer urged Shooter to pull the regiment back, but he refused. "I know we are all about to be destroyed," Shooter reportedly replied, "but I cannot consent to retire." Creeping into the underbrush for a better look, the officer discovered that Union troops were pounding the regiment on both of its exposed flanks. Returning to Shooter, he again urged the lieutenant colonel to withdraw the regiment. "I cannot, will not yield," Shooter insisted, and his men fought doggedly on.

When a lull in musketry from the Union side persuaded McGowan that the enemy might be weakening, he hurled his 12th, 13th, and 14th regiments forward north of the plank road. The attack ruptured the enemy line there and punched through almost to the Brock Road. At the sight of three regiments of screaming Southerners breaking their formation, the Union commanders shifted their attention north of the plank road, easing the pressure against the 1st South Carolina south of the road.

But McGowan's precipitous advance was short-lived. Discovering that the rebels had outdistanced their supporting units, the Yankees moved in from both sides, surrounding them. The 12th South Carolina managed to cut its way out of the pocket closing around it, but at a tremendous cost in lives, including the mortal wounding of its commander, Colonel John Miller, shot through the bowels with a minié ball. The 13th and 14th South Carolina, led by McGowan himself, continued toward the Brock Road.

The pressure of federal firepower became too concentrated for even McGowan to withstand. In a stroke of luck, he stumbled into a stretch of woods that the Yankees had left unguarded and in the confusion led his soldiers back to Wilcox's main line. "Our loss was very heavy," the brigade's historian reported. A Union officer described the ferocious pace of combat. "The musketry was terrific and continuous," he reminisced. "Usually when infantry meets infantry the clash of arms is brief," he added. "One side or the other speedily gives way. Here neither side would give way, and the steady firing rolled and crackled from end to end of the contending lines, as if it would never cease. But little could be seen of the enemy. Whenever any troops rose to their feet and attempted to press forward, they became a target for the half-hidden foe, and lost severely."

In an attempt to reunite his divided command, McGowan ordered the 1st South Carolina and Orr's Rifles to cross to the north side of the plank road. Union artillery complicated the movement, but the South Carolinians came up with an ingenious solution. A few men would dart across the road about a hundred yards from the enemy guns. The guns would then blast away at them, but always too late, and while the gunners reloaded, large numbers of soldiers would run across the road. "At length," a Union man wrote, "the object of the performance was seen; namely, to draw the fire of our guns."

Still in the fore of the Confederate force along the plank road, McGowan's Brigade fought on, virtually unaided. The Federals continued their pincer movement, attacking from in front and from both sides, compressing the brigade, a rebel later wrote, into "the shortest, most huddled, most ineffective line-of-battle I ever saw." The battle became a formless brawl in which men charged blindly through the darkening woodland, firing and stabbing. Soldiers lost their sense of direction and stumbled into enemy lines where they were captured or shot. Generalship meant little; this was a life-and-death grapple on a grand scale, a soldier's fight with bayonets and muskets wielded like clubs by desperate men. Death came unseen and unexpected in blazes of lead from the greenery, laced orange with muzzle flashes in the gathering dusk. On the portion of line manned by the 1st South Carolina, men faced south to ward off attacks from that direction. "But for the gallantry of our troops, which surpassed itself, all must have been lost," a South Carolinian later wrote of the affair. "Still they pressed us, filling the air with shouts and the roll of arms, and sweeping the woods with balls."

Veterans of Sharpsburg, Fredericksburg, Chancellorsville, and Gettysburg could recall nothing like this. "Such woods, if you have one line which is to remain stationary and on the defense, are an advantage," a Carolina man reminisced of the melee in the Wilderness. "But if you attack (as we always did by countercharge, if not by the first charge), or if you must relieve one line with another, it is the worst place in the world. It is impossible to keep even a regiment well dressed. Then the enemy open fire on you. Some men will invariably return this fire. Gradually all join in it; and once the whole roar of battle opens, there is an end of unison of action." McGowan's soldiers—Charles included—experienced all this and more. A South Carolina sharpshooter likened the confusion to a Saturday evening market in Augusta.

Attrition in flag bearers in the 1st South Carolina was tremendous. "As usual our color bearers and guards were nearly all shot down," Charles's friend Armstrong wrote home. A bullet clipped Corporal Andrew Chapman, carrying the battle flag, in the head. The flag passed through several hands, until only Private William Bunch, of the Carolina Light Infantry Company, was left.

★ ★ ★

It was almost dark before Wilcox could get the rest of his brigades to the battlefront. "The troops could not be seen," the general later wrote, "the rattle of musketry alone indicating where the struggle was severest, and the points to which the reinforcing brigades should be sent." Guiding by ear, Wilcox directed a North Carolina brigade into the woods south of McGowan. The infusion of fresh troops probably saved the 1st South Carolina, as the newcomers drove back the Unionists attacking from the south. Also under Wilcox's direction, a brigade of Georgia soldiers slipped into place on the north end of McGowan's line, where the South Carolinians had been barely able to hold on. Both ends of McGowan's formation were now secure.

Hill was feeling ill, but he rode into the battle to encourage McGowan's fought-out troops. On the way back to Widow Tapp's farm, one of Hill's aides met Jeb Stuart and Walter Taylor, a staff officer to General Lee. The three men studied the cacophony to the east with the practiced ears of experienced soldiers. Wilcox's reinforcements were going in, they observed, but so were more Yankees. Another hour of combat, and the fragile Confederate line faced collapse. "If only night would come!" one of them said, expressing the sentiment of all.

The fog of war—what military experts call the slippage that invariably attends combat—helped save the Confederates. Wilcox's bold stand, combined with the disorientation caused by the Wilderness, caught the Union generals by surprise. Victory was within the grasp of the federal commanders, but they were oblivious to their opportunity, and injured soldiers hobbling back to the Brock Road intersection created the illusion of defeat. "The wounded stream out, and fresh troops pour in," a Northern newspaperman wrote in his account of the battle. "Stretchers pass out with ghastly burdens, and go back reeking with blood for more. Word is brought that the ammunition is failing. Sixty rounds [per man] fired in one steady, stand-up fight, and that fight not fought out. Boxes of cartridges are placed on the returning stretchers, and the struggle shall not cease for want of ball and powder." Unable to gauge the damage he was inflicting on the rebels but painfully aware of his own losses, Hancock thought only of surviving. "We barely hold our own," Meade's emissary informed headquarters as the carnage mounted. "Fresh troops would be most advisable."

But Grant was beginning to understand Lee's game. The Confederate army, he recognized, was divided into at least two parts, one on the turnpike and another on the plank road, and neither portion could be very large. Ewell, firmly entrenched along Saunders Field, seemed well neigh invulnerable, but Hill, on the plank road, made an inviting target. Hancock and Getty fastened Little Powell in place, like a butterfly pinned to a board. Why not forward troops from the turnpike sector to strike the exposed northern end of Hill's line?

The Union brass chose General James Wadsworth to lead the new attack. An unabashed patriot, Wadsworth was reputedly the wealthiest man in Grant's army and certainly the oldest general to hold elevated command. Lord of a princely estate at Geneseo, New York, he volunteered for military duty at the beginning of the war and served with distinction, interrupting his army stint to wage an unsuccessful bid for the governorship of New York. Wadsworth had seen his division badly mauled during Warren's afternoon offensive along the Orange Turnpike, and he was anxious for revenge.

Leaving his encampment near Wilderness Run, Wadsworth headed south with his troops, burrowing through a mile of intractable wilderness. At the same time—none of this was orchestrated; it was pure happenstance—Hancock launched his best division under his most aggressive commander, Francis Channing Barlow, against the front of Hill's line. A dour twenty-nine-year-old New York lawyer, Barlow liked to wear a checkered flannel shirt and faded blue trousers that made him resemble, as one of Meade's aides put it, a highly independent newsboy. Barlow was also a firm disciplinarian, and his division numbered among the Potomac army's finest combat elements. Flailing into the woods near the south end of Wilcox's line, Barlow's soldiers bogged down in a nasty scuffle with a nest of North Carolinians arranged behind a swamp.

Just as the full weight of Barlow's attack began to register against the southern end of Hill's line, word reached the Confederate commanders of Wadsworth's approach from the north. Here was Lee's worst scenario coming to pass. Blue-clad soldiers were streaming into the void between Ewell and Hill to overwhelm the unprotected northern end of Hill's line. Hill's only reserves were some 150 Alabama troops guarding prisoners in the rear, and having no other choice, Little Powell sent the Alabamians to attack the head of Wadsworth's column and fight it to a halt. Astoundingly, the gambit worked. It was nearly dark, Wadsworth's men were thoroughly jaded from thrashing about in the blackening woods, and a mob of frenzied Alabamians was the last thing they wanted to contend with. Wadsworth's movement ground to a halt a short distance from Hill's thinly guarded flank, and Barlow's offensive ran out of steam at the same time. It was simply too dark for anyone to see what he was doing. "Night came at last," one of McGowan's soldiers remembered with relief, "putting an end to actual battle." It was a close call for Hill, but fortunately for the Confederates, the Federals had no idea how near to victory they had come.

For Charles, May 5 was a memorable day. He had been afraid and had stared death in the face, but he had not run. He had stood by his companions and endured the worst that Grant could throw at him. "Though but a new member of the regiment," Charles's friend Armstrong wrote home, "he behaved in a manner worthy of a veteran." And because of his bravery—and also, one must assume, because of his friendship with Armstrong—Charles received a special honor. Private Bunch had been wounded, and Armstrong had selected Charles to carry the battle flag at the head of the regiment.

★ ★ ★

The night of May 5–6 was a scene of horror. Hostile lines stood less than a hundred yards apart in places. Stabs of flame from skirmish fire periodically lit the darkness, cries from wounded men made sleep impossible, and sharpshooters in the no-man's-land between the armies kept everyone on edge. "There was no moon to light the clearing," a Union man by Saunders Field remembered. "Only dim stars, and the air was hazy and pungent with the smoke and smell of fires yet smoldering. We couldn't see the wounded and dying, whose cries we heard all too clearly; nor could our stretcher bearers go out and find them and bring them in; the opposing lines were near, and the rebels were fidgety, and quick to shoot." A soldier from Pennsylvania penned a vivid recollection. "As the fires," he wrote, "which had blazed since the early afternoon, drew nearer and nearer to the poor unfortunates who lay between the lines, their shrieks, cries and groans, loud, piercing, penetrating, rent the air, until death relieved the sufferer."

The situation on the Orange Plank Road was chaotic. Darkness ended active combat, and soldiers of both armies entrenched where they stood. Little effort was made to straighten the lines or to bring order out of the tangle of barricades. One of Hill's aides thought that Heth's and Wilcox's layout resembled a worm fence. Earthen mounds followed every twist and turn of the Wilderness's low ridges, facing wherever the enemy had been last seen.

Little more than a biscuit's throw separated Hill's frazzled soldiers from Hancock's, Getty's, and Wadsworth's thousands. Neither army had shovels or digging utensils, so soldiers improvised, gouging the soft earth with bayonets, cups, spoons, and even their hands. The lines of the hostile forces were so intertwined that soldiers could hear enemy troops digging and talking, and men shot at anything that moved in the darkness, igniting flurries of musketry. Cooking was impossible, as the slightest flicker drew hostile fire. Soldiers dragged wounded comrades back to the roadway, where ambulances carried them to the rear.

Charles and his fellow soldiers huddled low in entrenchments north of the Orange Plank Road, the right end of their formation touching the roadway and the rest of the line angling northwest, following the terrain. Pickets knelt in rifle pits in front of the line, ready to sound the alarm if the enemy came. Rations of bacon and hardtack were brought up and distributed among the troops.

One of the unfortunates lying wounded in the burning woods was Joseph Brunson, a twenty-four-year-old sergeant from South Carolina. Unable to crawl, he was saved from the fusillades of musketry by another injured soldier who dragged him into a ditch. Bleeding to death, Brunson had all but given up hope when he heard a familiar voice exclaim, "Boys, they have got poor little Joe." Pick Posey, a friend of Brunson, had gone in search of the sergeant and had seen his friend's form lying motionless in the ditch. "No, they haven't, Pick, come and get me," Brunson managed to cry out. Braving the bullets, Posey scooped up his wounded friend and carried him back into Confederate lines, where a surgeon extracted the ball.

Berry Benson, a sharpshooter with the 1st South Carolina, left a vivid account of conditions along the plank road front that night. Returning from a reconnaissance after dark, Benson found the men lying awake in expectation of an attack at any moment. Feeling his way along the earthworks, he stumbled into an unoccupied gap. Concerned that he might have blundered into enemy lines, he called out, "First South Carolina?" and a voice whispered back, "Here! This way!" Another voice, from the opposite direction, piped up. "Don't go that way. That's a Yankee." Concluding that the last speaker sounded more like a Southerner than the first, Benson cocked his rifle and walked toward the sound of the voice. He guessed correctly, but his near capture underscored how closely the opposing troops lay.

★ ★ ★

Three-quarters of a mile west of McGowan's improvised line, in Catherine Tapp's field, Lee was reconsidering his plans. Ewell had performed as well as the rebel commander had dared hope, but Hill's situation was far different. His men had fought every bit as heroically as Ewell's, but they lacked Ewell's commanding advantage of ground, and the Federals in their sector had seemed more determined. Another hour of daylight, and they would have broken Hill's formation.

Lee had begun the day hoping that Ewell and Hill could pin Grant in the Wilderness, and they had not disappointed him. He had also expected that Longstreet would arrive by the next morning and swing into the Union army's vulnerable southern flank. The Federals, however, were bound to renew their assaults, and if Hill collapsed, the entire Confederate army would be endangered. Reluctant to risk the entire venture, Lee revised his grand strategy and directed the War Horse to shift north onto the plank road and come up in support of Hill.

Riding cross-country, Lee's aide Charles Venable located Longstreet at Richard's Shop, ten miles away, and delivered Lee's orders to reach the battlefront by daylight. Calculating his marching distance, Longstreet decided to let his men rest until one in the morning before setting out for the Wilderness.

Acting on assurances that Longstreet would arrive by morning, Lee firmed his new plans. Ewell was to keep the Federals busy on the Orange Turnpike, he instructed, and as soon as Longstreet appeared, Hill was to pull back to Catherine Tapp's farm and reach north, filling the void between the Confederate force's two wings. With his army united and fighting defensively, Lee hoped to complete his stalemate of Grant in the Wilderness.

Concerned that their troops were too exhausted to withstand a concerted attack, Heth and Wilcox made their way to Widow Tapp's field and found Hill sitting on a camp stool by a fire. "Your division has done splendidly today," he congratulated Heth, senior of his two subordinates. "Its magnificent fighting is the theme of the entire army."

"Yes, the division has done splendid fighting," Heth replied, "but we have other matters to attend to just now." He and Wilcox explained that their lines were in disarray and could not be defended. "Let me take one side of the road and form [a] line of battle," Heth suggested, "and Wilcox the other side and do the same. We are so mixed, and lying at every conceivable angle, that we cannot fire a shot without firing into each other. A skirmish line could drive both my division and Wilcox's, situated as we are now. We shall certainly be attacked early in the morning," he added.

Hill admonished Heth and Wilcox not to worry, because Lee had assured him that Longstreet's fresh troops would arrive well before dawn. By sunrise, Longstreet would be in the front line, with Hill's reunited Third Corps behind him, and all would be well. Heth was still worried and repeated his concern to Hill. "Longstreet will be up in a few hours," Hill replied, this time a little testily. "He will form in your front. I don't propose that your division will do any more fighting tomorrow. The men have been marching and fighting all day and are tired. I do not wish them disturbed."

Lee's headquarters tent was a few hundred yards away, and Wilcox walked over to talk with the army commander. As Wilcox entered the tent, Lee announced that he had just finished a report praising Wilcox's and Heth's masterful defense on the plank road. He added that Hill's other division under Richard Anderson was on its way, as was Longstreet's entire corps. "The two divisions that have been so actively engaged will be relieved before day," Lee assured Wilcox. Hearing from Lee essentially the same information that he had already received from Hill, Wilcox decided not to repeat his suggestions about changing his line.

Later that evening, Heth and Wilcox pestered Hill again for permission to rectify their lines, and again he refused. When Heth piped up a third time, the ailing corps commander lost his temper. "Damn it, Heth, I don't want to hear any more about it," he exploded. "The men shall not be disturbed!"

"The only excuse I make for Hill," Heth later wrote, "was that he was sick."

But Heth's and Wilcox's persistence did not fall on deaf ears. After midnight, Hill paid a visit to Lee. The army commander, according to an aide who accompanied Hill, repeated his orders that Little Powell was to keep his men in place until Longstreet arrived. "We could not sleep," the aide remembered, "but waited for news of Longstreet; for we knew that at the first blush of the morning the turning attack on our right would open with overwhelming numbers, and, unsupported, the men must give way."

★ ★ ★

From their knoll near Wilderness Tavern, Grant and Meade gazed out over the dark woodland. Less than a mile west, an orange glow marked the site of Saunders Field. Barely visible was a section of the turnpike, where wagons rumbled toward the front carrying food and ammunition and returning with wounded men. Eastward spread the Union encampments, dotted with flickering campfires. At Grant's feet lay a jumble of cigar butts, wood shavings, and remnants of the cloth gloves his wife Julia had given him.

The generals gathered around a campfire to discuss the day's events. Grant expressed his opinion that the fight had involved little more than jockeying for position, but that he now understood the gamble that Lee had taken. From prisoners, Grant realized that he was fighting Ewell on the turnpike and Hill on the plank road.

Longstreet remained a wild card, as his whereabouts were as yet unknown to the Union generals.

Meade's inability to mount a coherent offensive perplexed Grant, and he voiced strong ideas about what to be do. Henceforth, there must be no more random attacks with isolated brigades, divisions, and corps. Part of the army would remain on the Orange Turnpike, attacking Ewell at Saunders Field to hold him in place and prevent him from sending reinforcements to Hill's wing. The main attack would take place on the Orange Plank Road, where Hancock would wield temporary command over nearly half the Union army, fully seven divisions of infantry. His assignment was to crush Hill's two divisions under Heth and Wilcox with overwhelming numbers.

The weight of the blow would fall on the front of Hill's Corps, held by McGowan's Brigade. Charles's luck was holding true to form.

★ ★ ★

Near midnight, Longstreet's officers roused the men from their slumber at Richard's Shop, and they were on their way within the hour. Longstreet, however, was unfamiliar with the road, and everything that could go wrong did. A guide sent by Lee attempted a shortcut and lost his way. In places, the route was so overgrown that the path seemed invisible, and where the road crossed fields, wagon tracks became so faint that the lead elements strayed and could not find where to enter the woods on the far edge. "Such a march, and under such conditions, was never before experienced by the troops," a soldier remembered. "Along blind roads, overgrown by underbrush, through fields that had lain fallow for years, now studded with bushes and briars, and the night being exceedingly dark, the men floundered and fell as they marched." Trying to make up for lost time, Longstreet ordered his divisions to double up and march abreast.

At Widow Tapp's farm, a sleepless Hill and his division commanders waited for signs of Longstreet. "Twelve, two, three o'clock came, and half-past three, and no reinforcements," Wilcox remembered of his vigil. "I walked the road all night," recollected Heth. Still no sign of Longstreet.

Shortly after four o'clock, the first blush of dawn appeared. Hill was beside himself with anxiety. Exhausted and in the throes of his sickness, he mounted his horse and rode off to inspect the gap between his own troops and Ewell's. Wilcox could stand the waiting no longer. He needed workers, he stressed, with axes and shovels to throw up a new line of entrenchments for Longstreet's men, assuming they ever appeared. The workers arrived, but the Federal line was so close that they could not begin digging. Heth rode west along the plank road for two or three miles, looking for the promised reinforcements. Seeing no sign of Longstreet, he returned to his division.

Charles and his fellow Confederates were of a single mind. "All were praying for the arrival of Longstreet," a soldier recalled.

A Confederate artillerist walked from Widow Tapp's field to the front. Sunlight was beginning to filter through the trees. The enemy assault could come at any moment, but no one seemed concerned, and soldiers dozed with their muskets stacked in neat rows along the roadside. Spying an officer, the artillerist asked why no one was preparing for the inevitable attack. Hill's troops, the officer answered, had been told that fresh men would relieve them before daylight, and they expected reinforcements any minute. Where, the artillerist inquired, were the Yankees? The officer was unsure, but he ventured a guess that they were in the woods in front. "He struck me as being very indifferent and not at all concerned about the situation," the artillerist wrote. "I could not help feeling troubled, although I supposed somebody knew how things stood."

General Wilcox was well aware of the state of his lines, and he was sick with apprehension. "The tree tops were already tinged with the early rays of the rising sun, but the enemy lay quiet," he wrote years later of that fateful morning. "At length the sun itself was seen between the boughs and foliage of the heavy forest, and on the plank road the Confederates, eager to catch at straws in their unprepared state, began to have hopes that the Federals would not advance."

Five o'clock approached, and Wilcox's troops listened intently to small arms fire bristling to the north, in Ewell's direction. The battle was starting along Saunders Field. Straining toward the woods in front, Charles could hear occasional cracks of rifle shots as Union skirmishers started through the forest on both sides of the plank road. The firing grew heavy, signaling that thousands of soldiers were tramping through the woods, shooting as they came. The Union offensive had begun.

Charles and his companions looked back, hoping to see the promised reinforcements. The Orange Plank Road lay empty under the soft morning light. Lee had gambled everything on the timely arrival of his War Horse, and his War Horse had not come.

8

A MORTIFYING DISASTER

As the blast from a signal cannon reverberated through the forest, a huge force—nearly half the Union army—closed in on Hill's entrenched formation. The Union commanders used the lull in combat during the night to their advantage and organized for a concentrated, irresistible push, while the Southerners frittered away the time waiting in vain for Longstreet. "We had reckoned too confidently on the coming of the War Horse," a South Carolinian ruefully admitted.

McGowan's line of troops slanted back from the roadway along the crest of a low ridge. The 1st South Carolina was posted near the center of the position, waiting behind stacks of logs, rocks, and dirt. During the winter, McGowan had organized his best marksmen into a special battalion of sharpshooters who could hit a bull's-eye at a hundred yards, and they were on picket duty this morning a few hundred yards in front of his main position, spread thinly along the length of a ravine. Hidden behind trees, they watched as the mass of enemy soldiers started toward them.

The foremost Union troops picked their way down a gentle slope into the ravine, forcing McGowan's sharpshooters to turn and fall back, firing blindly into the thickets behind them. Charles, grasping the flagstaff, could gauge the enemy's approach by the volume of fire. Aiming into the ravine, the South Carolinians fired volley after volley in hopes that they might somehow halt Grant's monolith. But the Confederates posted south of McGowan faltered, and enemy troops overran the lower end of the rebel line, seizing flags and clusters of bewildered prisoners. Rendered helpless by the collapse of the adjoining units, Charles and his compatriots abandoned their barricades and fled back toward Widow Tapp's field.

Writing later, a South Carolina officer tried to put a positive face on the retreat. "The men seemed to fall back [out of] a deliberate conviction that it was impossible to hold the ground, and, of course, foolish to attempt it," he explained. "It was mortifying, but it was only what every veteran has experienced." Most participants, however, admitted that they offered no organized opposition. The Confederate line, a Tar Heel reported, simply "rolled up as a sheet of paper would be rolled without the power of effective resistance." Another Southerner termed the collapse "perfectly disgraceful" and confessed that he and his companions "ran like deer through the woods, leaving the enemy far behind." Yet another Confederate pronounced the fiasco "one of the worst stampedes I ever saw." Concluded a witness: "In effect, the men were ordered to run, and the signs are they obeyed, with all the means which God and nature had put into their feet."

Fear drove some Southerners to desperate acts, such as propping injured Yankees against trees and stumps and using them like human shields. But nothing could stop Hancock's juggernaut, and demoralized rebels surrendered by the score to the approaching Federals, hands raised high, imploring their captors not to shoot. "They were evidently badly frightened," a Northerner recalled, "as well they might be." Charles's career as a color bearer was off to a bad start.

* * *

From his headquarters at Widow Tapp's field, Lee could tell that things were going terribly wrong. The explosion of artillery fire and musketry in Hill's direction had the earmarks of a major enemy offensive. Smoke was boiling up from the forest, and Hill's soldiers—some wounded, nearly all visibly panicked—began dribbling into the clearing from the front. The Army of Northern Virginia was accustomed to tight scrapes, but here in Catherine Tapp's pasture it faced its most serious crisis yet. Longstreet had not arrived, Hill's troops were manifestly unable to hold their ground, and no organized body of Confederate infantry was in the clearing. The last line of resistance was a stand of sixteen artillery pieces under Lieutenant Colonel William T. Poague, a twenty-eight-year-old Virginian. At Poague's direction, the gunners loaded their cannon with charges of canister capable of inflicting tremendous carnage against troops at close range.

The trickle of retreating soldiers became a flood, and Widow Tapp's field was soon awash with Hill's men, preventing Poague from firing without hitting Confederates. Lee sat astride Traveller near Poague's guns, an island of resolve in a sea of soldiers flowing rearward. The Confederate commander took pride in his capacity to remain calm in a crisis, but this time he was visibly shaken. Unwilling to watch passively while his army disintegrated, Lee rode into the mob of soldiers and called on them to rally. "Go back, men! You can beat those people," an onlooker remembered him shouting. Deeply distraught, Hill abandoned any pretext of command; having served as an artillery officer before the war, he dismounted and began helping the gunners load their weapons.

Wilcox materialized in the swirling vortex of troops, nosed his pony through the press of soldiers, and rode close to Lee. His division, he shouted, was in shambles. "Longstreet must be here," Lee insisted. "Go bring him up." Reduced to the status of a courier, Wilcox rode off on his white pony, searching for signs of the War Horse.

McGowan's troops, Charles among them, scrambled past Lee and his aides. Mounted, McGowan stood out above the press of butternut and gray uniforms. "My God!" Lee shouted as he spied the rotund figure, his urgent voice piercing the din. "General McGowan, is this splendid brigade of yours running like a flock of geese!"

Lee's gibe cut deeply, largely because it was true. The army's premier combat element was fleeing like a frightened assemblage of barnyard fowl, and the men were mortified. "General," McGowan called back, hoping to salvage a vestige of his brigade's honor, "the men are not whipped. They only want a place to form, and they will fight as well as they did."

Extricating themselves from the crush of panicked Confederates, Charles and his compatriots gathered behind Poague's line of guns. The battle flag, still in Charles's grasp, hung limply in the still air. Hill, an officer recalled, "expressed himself rather roughly to us, especially to us unfortunate file-closers; but I am not sure but his anger implied a sort of compliment to our past performances." For the time, McGowan's crestfallen warriors were reduced to little more than observers.

Looking east, Lee could see Yankees edging into the clearing and more enemy soldiers working through the woods south of the plank road, fighting their way from tree to tree. Bullets kicked up dust around Traveller's hooves, and Poague's artillerists bent low behind rough barricades of fence rails and logs, waiting for the last of Hill's soldiers to move out of their line of fire. One of McGowan's men noticed Lee wiping his eyes with a white hand-kerchief, and a staff officer reflected that he had never seen the general so disturbed.

Rising sounds of musketry to the south alerted Lee and Hill that Union troops had penetrated the woods on their right. Hill directed Poague to fire obliquely across the field into the trees, but an aide protested that canister would hit Confederate soldiers still in the clearing. The general refused to wait. The guns, he insisted, must open immediately. At Poague's direction, the artillerists pulled their lanyards, and tongues of flame spit from sixteen cannon, sending fistfuls of iron balls into the approaching Northerners. Smoke drifted across Widow Tapp's field, obscuring the view, but the gunners kept firing—fifty discharges by one estimate, whirring some three thousand iron slugs across the clearing.

But sixteen guns could not hold back an army. As Lee waited in silence on Traveller, peering into the smoke and chaos, a single thought dominated his mind. "Why does not Longstreet come?" an aide heard him ask. If help did not appear soon, Lee would be killed or captured, dooming his army and his cause. "This was one of the most anxious times I felt during the war," one of Hill's staffers admitted. "The minutes seemed like hours, and the musketry was getting uncomfortably near and everything looked like disaster."

★ ★ ★

Shortly after sunup, the head of Longstreet's marching column broke onto the Orange Plank Road at Parker's Store. Five miles east, Hill's hard-pressed battle line was crumbling under the relentless Union onslaught.

Longstreet's First Corps, ten thousand men strong, hit a rapid stride. Conscious that the fate of the army depended on them, the soldiers hurried forward, eight men abreast. They were exhausted, having covered some thirty-five miles in the past forty hours with only five hours rest, but the distant growl of artillery served as a potent antidote to weariness. One man remembered the march as a race and a run. Glancing up from the dusty road, an Alabamian noticed the sun rising above the Wilderness, blood red from battle smoke.

Pressing east, Longstreet's troops passed the site of a field hospital where stacks of arms and legs amputated after the previous day's fight lined the roadside. Then came the camps of an artillery reserve. The gunners were listening to the escalating musketry with apprehension, casting anxious glances in the direction where Longstreet was expected to appear. "Look out down the road!" a cannoneer shouted. "Here they come!"

The head of Longstreet's column emerged from a cloud of dust, and the gunners broke into wild yells at the sight of the gaunt figures striding purposefully toward the front. "Here's Longstreet!" they cried. "The old War Horse is up at last! It's all right now." When the general himself rode past, the artillerists broke loose with their loudest yells. "Like a fine lady at a party," a witness wrote years later, "Longstreet was often late in his arrival at the ball, but he always made a sensation and that of delight, when he got in, with the grand old First Corps, sweeping behind him, as a train."

Nearing Widow Tapp's field, Longstreet's veterans encountered the remnants of Hill's broken division tumbling rearward. Panicked soldiers were darting everywhere, pursued by officers attempting to get them to stop. "Do you belong to General Lee's army?" Longstreet's troops scolded the retreating Confederates. Through it all, the men of the First Corps never slowed their pace. One of Lee's aides, sent back to look for Longstreet, recorded his impression of their approach more than fifteen years later. "It was superb, and my heart beats quicker to think about it even at this distance of time."

A brigade of South Carolinians in Longstreet's vanguard reached the edge of Catherine Tapp's field, and aides directed them into woods south of the road. Next came Longstreet's premier brigade. Composed of three Texas regiments and a regiment from Arkansas, the so-called Texas Brigade had earned laurels in the war's early years. This day it was commanded by John Gregg, a thirty-five-year-old Alabama lawyer who had adopted Texas as his home. Still suffering from a serious neck wound inflicted the previous year at Chickamauga, this was Gregg's first time commanding the Texas Brigade in combat. He and General Lee had never met.

Riding into the clearing, Longstreet immediately sized up the situation. A Union skirmish line was advancing from the opposite direction, followed by troops arrayed in a line of battle. A counter-attack had to be made at once, and the War Horse acted decisively, passing among his soldiers as they pulled up and steadying them.

Soldiers from Texas and Arkansas began lining up behind Poague's cannon, where a gentle roll of ground sheltered them from the enemy's view. "Keep cool, men, we will straighten this out in a short time—keep cool," Longstreet admonished. McGowan's men had taken cover behind the same rise and looked on as the Texas Brigade prepared to charge. Their disgrace was complete. Not only had they dishonored themselves in front of Lee, but they now had to watch while another brigade ventured a daring attack to recover the ground they had lost.

★ ★ ★

Intent on the enemy troops advancing into the field, Lee took no notice of the Texans and Arkansans until Gregg rode up. Spying the figure on horseback, he turned to Gregg, who was obviously in charge of the fresh troops.

"General," Lee asked, "what brigade is this?"

"The Texas Brigade," Gregg answered.

Relief swept over Lee. Longstreet was up at last, and he was preparing his best men for a counterattack. The Virginian, usually reserved, was beside himself with excitement. "Hurrah for Texas!" he shouted. "Hurrah for Texas!"

Regaining his composure, Lee leaned in his saddle toward Gregg. "When you go in there, I wish you to give those men the cold steel," a soldier heard him say. "They will stand and fight all day, unless you charge," the general added, his eyes narrowing as he studied the distant troops in blue. "The Texas Brigade has always driven the enemy, and I want them to do it now," he said to Gregg. "And tell them, general, that they will fight today under my eye," he stressed by way of encouragement. "I want every man of them to know I am here with them."

Gregg turned to his troops. "Attention Texas Brigade," he boomed out. "The eyes of General Lee are upon you." Pointing across the field, he shouted in his best command voice. "Forward, march."

Lee could no longer contain his excitement. He stood high in his stirrups, emotion contorting his face. Lifting his hat and swinging it wide, he cried out, "Texans always move them!"

A Texan near Lee summed up the men's feelings. "A yell rent the air that must have been heard for miles around," he remembered, "and but few eyes in that old brigade of veterans and heroes of many a bloody field was undimmed by honest, heartfelt tears." One of Gregg's couriers swore in a voice choked with emotion: "I would charge hell itself for that old man."

At Gregg's order, the brigade started forward, and Poague's artillery fell silent, permitting the troops to pass through the guns.

To the men's surprise, Lee turned Traveller toward the enemy and started riding with them. Some of Gregg's troops close by later recalled him announcing that he would lead them. Those farther away could not hear what he said, but it was apparent to all that he meant to head the charge. The soldiers were horrified. Mounted high on Traveller, Lee faced certain death.

The response of the soldiers was immediate. "Go back, General Lee, go back!" men shouted, but Lee continued on, eyes to the front, determined to set an example.

"Lee to the rear!" someone cried, and more soldiers took up the refrain. "Lee to the rear!" they chanted, slowing their pace. "Lee to the rear!"

Still Lee continued on. "We won't go on unless you come back," men called, determined to stop their beloved commander's folly, but still he ignored their pleas. Some of Lee's staff officers gathered around the general. One of them grasped his arm, and another reached for Traveller's reins. Irritated, Lee shook them off and kept riding into the field.

Finally the Texans took matters into their own hands. A tall, bearded officer firmly seized Traveller's bridle, and several of his companions stood in front of the animal, forming a human barricade. Gregg rode over to the general with Lee's trusted aide Venable, and together they urged Lee to turn around. Their words were not recorded, but whatever they said had the desired effect. "Well then, I will go back," Lee agreed, and he turned Traveller toward Poague's artillery line. "Can't I, too, die for my country?" a staffer heard him mutter under his breath.

Longstreet greeted Lee by the line of guns. "I never was so glad to see you," Lee assured his War Horse. Observing from Lee's demeanor that the army commander was off balance, Longstreet urged Lee to stay out of harm's way. He could restore the Confederate battle line if given a free hand, he promised, but if Lee did not need him, he would like to leave because it was "not quite comfortable where we are," he announced. Lee got the hint, and riding past McGowan's huddled soldiers, he set up headquarters in a protected hollow well to the rear.

His horse at a walk, Longstreet arrayed the rest of his brigades in support of the Texans and Arkansans. To maximize his striking power, he formed the soldiers in compact columns along each side of the Orange Plank Road, creating a narrow front with plenty of punch. If all went as planned, Longstreet's assault would tear through the Union line, clearing the enemy from the Tapp farm and restoring the initiative to the Confederates. "Load and cap your pieces, men!" officers shouted. Recollected a Southerner: "The jingle of the hundreds of iron ramrods up and down the line denoted that something horrible was about to take place."

★ ★ ★

With piercing yells, Gregg's troops charged across Widow Tapp's field. Skirmishers in the fore of the Union line scattered, clearing the way for the soldiers coming behind them to open fire on the Confederates. Gregg's men kept on, determined to drive back the invaders. Another volley sounded, bringing down more figures in gray, but the survivors only tightened their line to close the new gaps and kept marching, straight into the enemy. "There was a terrible crash," a Texan recalled, "which settled down into a tremendous roar of musketry."

For half an hour, soldiers from Texas and Arkansas—approximately eight hundred men—grappled face-to-face with Hancock's thousands. Longstreet pumped fresh brigades from Georgia and Alabama into the fray, and finally, imperceptibly at first, and then in a rout, the Unionists gave way. Still harder the War Horse pounded, sending more soldiers south of the plank road to drive the enemy from the woods. Grit and determination won the day, and when the musketry finally abated, Longstreet's victorious Confederates found that they had driven the Federals several hundred yards back from Widow Tapp's field. They immediately began throwing up log-and-fence-rail barricades to consolidate their gains and to protect against a counterattack by the enemy.

This was Longstreet's proudest hour. Through an impressive feat of arms, he had reversed the battle's momentum and broken the Union offensive. The price in blood, however, was high. The Texans and Arkansans were worst hit; more than five hundred of their eight hundred combatants were killed, wounded, or captured. In one company, a single soldier survived to answer roll call the next day.

While Longstreet's men dug trenches and stacked logs to consolidate their gains, Hill arranged his fought-out soldiers in a reserve line designed to plug the gap between the two Confederate wings on the turnpike and the plank road. McGowan's Brigade returned to the Chewning clearing, where the soldiers had listened the previous afternoon to the good reverend's absolutions. Encountering a thin line of Union skirmishers at the edge of the field, they drove back the paltry enemy force, dashed to the ridge top, and stacked fence rails for protection. Union artillerists blindly fired a few long-range shells at them but inflicted no discernable damage. Still smarting from their humiliation earlier in the day, the South Carolinians waited hopefully for an attack, but none came. "It would have been a great relief to chastise someone in reparation of our morning's misfortune," one of Charles's officers wrote. "This disaster to their prestige was mortifying in the extreme to our brave soldiers," another man remembered, "and their minds were well prepared to retrieve it at the next opportunity."

Little did Charles and his companions suspect how soon the chance would come to redeem their standing, or how terrible the occasion would be.

Charles and his fellow greenhorns were initiated into combat in one of the war's most intense bouts of fighting. The battle cost their brigade 481 soldiers, including 55 men killed, 383 wounded, and 43 missing. Heaviest hit was the 1st South Carolina, which sustained 137 casualties—more than a quarter of the brigade's losses.

★ ★ ★

While Charles and his companions reclined behind their rails and tree limbs on Mr. Chewning's farm, Lee sought to exploit the initiative that Longstreet's counterattack had gained him. As the War Horse's troops drove back the disordered Union lines, Lee's chief engineer, Martin Luther Smith, made an important discovery. Reconnoitering south of the Orange Plank Road, Smith stumbled onto the trace of an unfinished railroad. Planned before the war as a rail line between Orange Court House and Fredericksburg, the corridor had been cleared, but no tracks had been laid. By 1864, the unfinished railway grade was little more than a path through the forest.

Generals in the Union and Confederate armies were well aware of the unfinished railroad grade, but no one had considered using the route until Smith's exploration. Around ten in the morning, the engineer approached Longstreet with a plan. The lower end of the Union army had come to rest in woods a few hundred yards north of the unfinished railroad grade, he explained, and the Confederates could achieve a remarkable surprise by advancing troops along the jungle path until they reached a point near the unprotected end of the Union force and then charging into the unsuspecting invaders.

Longstreet saw the merits of the scheme at once and added a wrinkle to increase the damage. As soon as his hidden troops struck the flank of the Union line, he would launch a major attack against the front of the Federal formation, assaulting along the axis of the Orange Plank Road. Hit by Confederates from in front and from the lower end of their line, the Union force was bound to collapse. A vigorous pursuit, predicted Longstreet, might well drive the invaders back across the Rapidan and give Lee the victory he sought.

Lee immediately approved the plan and left Longstreet to execute it. Assembling a handful of brigades, Longstreet sent them through the jungle to the point designated by Smith and thrust them north. In an astounding oversight, the Federal commanders had neglected to strengthen their exposed flank or to post pickets, and the Confederate attack came as a complete surprise. Then Longstreet hurled the rest of his corps into the front of the Union formation, and the result was precisely as he desired. "You rolled me up like a wet blanket," Hancock admitted to Longstreet after the war.

The morning's despair turned to jubilation as Longstreet rode onto the Orange Plank Road, accompanied by his headquarters cavalcade, several generals, and fresh troops from South Carolina under young Micah Jenkins, one of Lee's most promising brigade commanders. Someone jokingly remarked that the uniforms of the new men were so dark that they looked like the garb that Federal soldiers wore.

Everywhere the enemy seemed in retreat. Jenkins, who had recently returned to the army following an illness, was giddy over the success. "We shall smash them now!" he gushed. "We will put the enemy back across the Rapidan by night."

Just ahead, a cluster of Virginians in the fore of the flanking party crossed the plank road, realized they had outdistanced their supporting units, and circled back. Moving into the roadway, they spied a large body of troops approaching. Leading were several men on horseback, accompanied by soldiers wearing what appeared to be enemy uniforms. Fearing that Federals had slipped into their rear, the Virginians opened fire. "Steady men, for God's sake steady," Jenkins hollered and tumbled from his mount, a ball through his brain. Realizing that a mistake had been made, Longstreet spurred his horse forward. A minié ball tore through his neck and came out his right shoulder. Dazed, the War Horse turned and tried to ride back, flopping from side to side as though about to fall. His aides dismounted, quieted his horse, and lifted him to the ground. Laying him under a tree, they called for Dr. Dorsey Cullen, the corps medical director.

Longstreet's wounding seemed like an ill omen. Almost precisely a year before and within this same wilderness, Stonewall Jackson was mortally wounded in an accidental shooting by his own soldiers. The parallel with Longstreet's shooting was uncanny, because Jackson, like the War Horse, was cut down while executing a brilliant turning movement. "A strange fatality attended us!" one of General Lee's aides later observed. "Jackson killed in the zenith of a successful career; Longstreet wounded when in the act of striking a blow that would have rivaled Jackson's at Chancellorsville in its results; and in each case, the fire was from our own men. A blunder! Call it so; the old deacon would say that God willed it thus."

With the mastermind of the movement incapacitated—Longstreet was seriously injured, Dr. Cullen decided, but he would not die—the Confederate counterattack ground to a halt, and an unaccustomed quiet settled over the woodland while Hancock pulled his forces back to the Brock Road and reorganized them in a line along the roadway, facing west. Anticipating that Lee might attack, the Northerners cleared the land a hundred yards or so in front of their position and stacked the felled trees into chest-high barricades. All afternoon, Hancock's troops prepared for the expected onslaught.

Lee did not disappoint them. Ever aggressive and hoping to capitalize on Longstreet's feats of the morning, the Confederate general spent the afternoon arranging his First Corps to assail Hancock's Brock Road entrenchments. Jenkins's South Carolinians, anxious to avenge their dead commander, were to spearhead the attack.

At quarter after four, Jenkins's troops drove back Hancock's pickets and burst into the cleared killing zone in front of the Federal barricades. Union muskets unleashed a volley at close range— "heavy fire that made the bark fly from the saplings," a participant recalled. Jenkins's front rank was obliterated, but the next line of attackers dropped to their knees not thirty yards from the Federals and began shooting back. Secure behind their barricades, the Northerners took few losses; the rebels, fully exposed in the cleared swath, were slaughtered in droves. Near the plank road, the barricades caught fire and spewed thick, resinous pine smoke into the defenders. With a determined yell, Jenkins's soldiers catapulted over the smoldering barriers, appearing, a Northern man thought, like devils leaping through the flames. The breach was in front of a massed stand of Union artillery, and the gunners opened at close range with double-shotted canister. Pellets hissed into the attackers, reddening the air with flesh, and Union reinforcements rushed in from other parts of the line, closing the break almost as quickly as it had opened. The artillery fell silent, and with a shout, Hancock's men vaulted over their wooden fortifications and charged into the demoralized Confederates, driving them back through the woods.

While Lee's men fell back from the Brock Road and its flaming barricades, his generals on the Orange Turnpike initiated yet another offensive. Near dark, General John Gordon, one of Ewell's most aggressive subordinates, quietly moved troops near the far northern end of the Union line. It just so happened that the Yankees occupying this important piece of real estate were novices from New York who had spent most of the war manning the forts at Washington. They had just stacked their muskets and started cooking when Gordon's men descended on them like a pack of wild dogs.

Couriers rushed to Grant's headquarters with news of the disaster, but Grant refused to succumb to panic. Pulling up a camp stool in front of his tent, he lit a cigar and directed that reinforcements be sent to the endangered point. "General Grant, this is a crisis that cannot be looked upon too seriously," a frenzied officer warned, obviously unnerved by Grant's calm demeanor. "I know Lee's methods well by past experience," the man continued. "He will throw his army between us and the Rapidan, and cut us off completely from our communications." Standing, Grant removed the cigar from his mouth and spoke his mind. "Oh, I am heartily tired of hearing about what Lee is going to do," he said. "Some of you seem to think he is suddenly going to turn a double somersault, and land in our rear and on both of our flanks at the same time. Go back to your command, and try to think what we are going to do ourselves, instead of what Lee is going to do."

The danger had indeed been greatly exaggerated, and spreading darkness and the disorienting effect of the Wilderness took the steam out of Gordon's attack. Union reinforcements soon expelled the attackers, and the crisis was over.

★ ★ ★

Two days of combat in the Wilderness exacted a shocking toll. Grant lost some eighteen thousand soldiers, and Lee's subtractions were about eleven thousand. All told, more people than had lived in Detroit during the years that Charles resided there had become casualties in the battle.

Those close to Grant saw that the battle affected him deeply. Lee proved to be a more cunning adversary than Grant had expected. Aides noted that Grant whittled incessantly, absent-mindedly carving twigs to sharp points and snapping them in half. He also completed the destruction of his cloth gloves. A staffer counted Grant as smoking twenty cigars that day, a record that he never again equaled, and a secondhand report had the general throwing himself onto his cot and giving vent to his feelings "in a way which left no room to doubt that he was deeply moved."

Lee was grimly satisfied. His aggressiveness had cost him close to 20 percent of his army, but he had stopped Grant. In narrow terms, the Wilderness was a Confederate victory, but the longer outlook was disturbing. Grant had fought with persistence unusual for Union generals in Virginia. A few more battles like the Wilderness, and Lee's army would be whittled away like one of Grant's sticks. And Grant still held the strategic edge; locked in place by the larger Union force, Lee was unable to launch the grand maneuvers that characterized his warring in the past. The next move was up to Grant, and Lee could only trust that his own reflexes and the sturdiness of his men would enable him to counter.

While the generals laid their plans, the soldiers suffered through another grueling night. Wounded men called from between the lines, and sharpshooters fired at dark forms moving in the blackness. Undergrowth burst into flame, and blazes crackled through the pines. One of Grant's aides summed up the feeling of the men of both armies. "It seemed," he wrote of those two terrible days in the Wilderness, "as though Christian men had turned to fiends, and hell itself had usurped the place of earth."

9

DEATH WAS
ALWAYS PRESENT

Grant rose early on May 7 and strode briskly from his tent near the Lacy house, looking not at all like a general who had just lost a battle. He seemed a little rumpled but otherwise showed no signs that he had spent the night agonizing about his campaign against Lee. After a light breakfast, he discussed his latest plans with an aide. There was no point, he concluded, in continuing to butt heads with Lee in the Wilderness. The rebels were firmly entrenched, and resuming the previous two days' program of attacks would result only in a senseless repetition of a failed strategy. Better, Grant had decided, to give up any hope of victory in this hostile woodland and to focus instead on maneuvering Lee onto ground more favorable to the Union army.

After consulting his maps, Grant decided to leave the Wilderness and head south, slipping his force between Lee's army and Richmond. His immediate objective was Spotsylvania Court House, an important road junction ten miles below the Wilderness. After the federal army seized the hamlet, Grant predicted that Lee would have no choice but to follow to protect his capital. If all went according to Grant's plan, Lee would come out and fight him on open ground.

All day, the Union army prepared to march, but details of the move were kept secret from the men. Some soldiers speculated that Grant intended to retreat, following the example set by his predecessors. Others predicted that he would head off under cover of darkness to steal a march on Lee.

At his headquarters in Catherine Tapp's field, Lee worked to divine Grant's intentions from scattered bits of intelligence, much like a soothsayer studying a goat's entrails. Taking a cautious approach, Lee decided to hedge his bets and hold most of his troops in the Wilderness until Grant showed his hand. The Union army already controlled the main north-south artery—the Brock Road—and Lee ordered his artillerists to hack a new road through the woods a mile west, as an alternative route for the rebel army. Late in the day he directed Longstreet's successor—the meerschaum-smoking South Carolinian Richard Anderson—to start the Confederate First Corps out on the freshly cut path.

Charles and the men of the 1st South Carolina, unaware of the grand strategies that were keeping Lee's headquarters buzzing, spent a miserable day, sweltering in the heat, swatting flies, and finishing off their last morsels of dried beef and hardtack. "Fires swept the forest for miles around," one of Charles's officers recalled, "obscuring the sun with smoke, and filling the air with stench."

★ ★ ★

The Army of the Potomac began threading out of the Wilderness at eight-thirty that evening with Grant, Meade, and their staffs at the head of the column. The commander in chief had dressed for business, discarding his fancy uniform in favor of a regulation army hat, a plain blouse and trousers, and a pair of muddy cavalry boots that looked incongruous for a man of his rank.

Grant turned his horse onto the Brock Road, and the men understood that they were going to continue south; the night march was not a retreat, but a triumphal procession. "On to Richmond!" soldiers cried, clapping and throwing their hats into the air. In the minds of many men who were there that night, the turning point of the American Civil War was not Gettysburg. Union victory became inevitable only that fateful moment in the Wilderness when Grant turned his army toward Spotsylvania Court House, signaling that he meant to prosecute the war to conclusion. "Afterwards," an officer reminisced, "in hours of disappointment, anxiety, and doubt, when the country seemed distrustful and success far distant, those nearest the chief were wont to recall this midnight ride in the Wilderness, and the verdict of the Army of the Potomac after Grant."

Not long after Grant set off, Anderson began withdrawing his Confederates from the Wilderness and shuttling them along the narrow trail carved through the forest. Far off on the right of the Confederate line, someone raised a shout—whether signaling a charge or simply hollering in good cheer was not readily apparent —and soldiers to the left took up the call, passing it man to man to the line's far end, five miles away. The chorus of voices had no sooner died than another shout rippled along the Confederate line, and then a third. "The effect was beyond expression," a Carolinian remembered. "It seemed to fill every heart with new life, to inspire every nerve with might never known before; and I believe that if at that instant the advance of the whole army upon Grant could have been ordered, we should have swept it into the very [Rapidan]."

The vast Union host jostled south all night along the Brock Road, heading for Spotsylvania Court House. Two days of fighting had left everyone exhausted. Wagons and artillery caissons clogged the roads, churning up blinding clouds of dust, and men marked time for hours waiting for the procession to move on. At the same time, on a parallel route a mile to the west, Anderson's soldiers were pursuing back roads and trails toward Spotsylvania Court House, putting as much distance as possible between them and the smoke and reek of the Wilderness. Shortly before daybreak, the Confederates reached the Po River, a narrow stream a short way from the court house town. In one of the campaign's most fateful decisions, Anderson decided to stop and rest his men.

Meanwhile Confederate cavalrymen waged a determined action to delay Grant's advance, piling fence rails and logs across the Brock Road and fighting on foot. Despairing that his cavalry would never push the rebels aside, Grant gave the job of clearing the road to his infantry. The foremost Union troops were commanded by General Warren, who had initiated the Battle of the Wilderness with the disastrous assault at Saunders Field. Still smarting from Grant's and Meade's complaint that he had moved too cautiously, Warren resolved to press aggressively on this time. "Go on, boys, you'll soon find them," dust-caked Union horsemen chided Warren's men as they marched to the front. "They are just ahead."

Determined to make a good impression, Warren's soldiers battered their way south, overrunning by sheer weight of numbers the obstacles thrown up by the Southern cavalrymen. About a mile and a half north of Spotsylvania Court House, the hard-pressed rebels, now led by Jeb Stuart himself, prepared to make a final desperate stand. Retreating across the farm of the Spindle family— Sarah Spindle was eating breakfast in her house, along with several of her children—the Confederate troopers lined up along a low ridge called Laurel Hill. Stuart, resplendent in his plumage and theatrical garb, helped stake out the position, and he chose the ground well. From Laurel Hill, the rebel cavalrymen had an unobstructed view across Mrs. Spindle's field, in the direction of the Yankees.

From their bivouac a mile and a half away, Anderson's soldiers could hear the din from Warren's and Stuart's fight. Suddenly couriers pounded up from Stuart requesting reinforcements and artillery support, and Anderson directed his troops closest to the action to hurry to the cavalryman's assistance. The Confederate First Corps was the outfit that had reached Widow Tapp's farm in the nick of time to save Lee; now it was embarked on another spectacular last-minute rescue. Clambering up the back side of Laurel Hill just as Warren's Federals were preparing to march across Mrs. Spindle's field, Anderson's lead elements piled behind the makeshift barricades tossed up only moments before by the cavalrymen. Stuart directed them into place—"cool as a piece of ice, though all the time laughing," an observer recalled.

Watches read eight-thirty, but already the air felt unseasonably oppressive, as though it were midsummer. Blue battle lines snaked into Mrs. Spindle's field, brittle cornstalks crunching underfoot. A brigade from Maryland had just reached an elevated stretch of ground near Mrs. Spindle's wood-frame house when the Confederates opened fire. The volley was horrific, slaughtering the first line of Marylanders. A second line took the place of the first, fired a round at the rebels and then began reloading, a costly mistake that left them fully exposed to the Southern marksmen. More white smoke puffed up from Laurel Hill, and lead tore into the Yankees, who had no place to hide. A bullet sent shards of bone and gristle through the leg of General John Robinson, heading the Union attack, and the Maryland Brigade lost three successive commanders in as many minutes. "At points where the enemy's fire was most concentrated," a Union man recollected, "the drone of bullets blended into a throbbing wail, like that of a sonorous telegraph wire pulsing in a strong wind, punctuated by the pert *zip* of the closer shots." The Spindle farm became a place where no one could expect to survive.

Desperate to gain the ridge, Warren pumped more troops into the field, seemingly oblivious to the advantage that the rebels held over his men. The infusion of soldiers only provided denser targets for the rebel riflemen, and a battery of Confederate artillery jangled up a short distance in front of Stuart's line and began spewing canister into Warren's ranks. Stuart was in his element, "sitting on his horse amidst a storm of bullets," a Southerner recalled, "laughing and joking with the men and commending them highly for their courage and for the rapidity and accuracy of their fire." Horrified at the turn of events—his corps was being annihilated before his very eyes—Warren seized a flagstaff and rode into the field, vainly attempting to rally his shattered ranks as his soldiers stampeded back.

Federal sharpshooters took cover in Mrs. Spindle's house and outbuildings and began picking off the Confederates posted on Laurel Hill. Anderson's artillery was now in place, and the Confederates responded by lobbing an incendiary shell into the house, catching it on fire. "And then I saw a sight I never wanted to see again," a Southerner recounted. Sarah Spindle, her hair streaming behind her, ran from the burning structure with her children, seeking shelter in the Confederate lines.

While Anderson hurried the rest of his troops onto Laurel Hill, Lee began forwarding the remainder of his army toward the emerging battlefront. On their way out of the Wilderness, McGowan's soldiers passed over the ground where they had fought on May 5 and 6. "Every tree seemed to be riddled with balls," an officer remembered. "Small arms, mostly broken or bent, strewed the ground, with every conceivable damaged article of accoutrement or clothing, and graves, filled with the dead of both armies, were fearfully frequent." Everything reeked of smoke and death. "The gases steaming up through the thin covering of the graves," one of Charles's officers remembered, "almost suffocated me in the hot, close air of the forest."

Grant was determined to keep hammering, and during the hot and sultry afternoon, he brought the rest of the Union army up. Toward evening he sent more troops forward, hoping to slip them past the eastern end of Anderson's position. But just as the Federals started to charge, Ewell's Corps arrived from the Wilderness, glided into place next to Anderson, and repulsed the enemy with ease, securing Lee's hold on Spotsylvania Court House. Everything had gone right for the Confederates this bloody May 8.

★ ★ ★

Lee's engineers labored all night to lay out a defensive line along high ground facing Grant. Anderson's Corps held Laurel Hill, on the Confederate left; Ewell's Corps fastened onto the right end of Anderson's formation and extended the line eastward; and early on the morning of May 9, Hill's troops tramped in from the Wilderness and tacked onto the east end of Ewell's entrenchments, digging a line of fortifications dipping to the south. By the end of the day, the Army of Northern Virginia occupied a continuous six-mile line covering Grant's possible approaches to Spotsylvania Court House.

The earthworks that Lee's men erected along their Spotsylvania line were a huge leap in sophistication from the rough fence-rail barriers in the Wilderness. Here the rebels cut down trees, drove the trunks into the ground, and stacked logs to form upright frames. Then they carved trenches behind the wooden forms, pitching dirt between the uprights, and piling soil against the front of the frames. The resulting battlements stood breast high and were several feet thick, adequate for stopping bullets and even artillery projectiles. To protect their heads while they fired, the rebels lay heavy logs, elevated with chinks of wood, along the top of the barriers. They also constructed short, stubby mounds called traverses every fifteen feet or so to provide places to rally in case the enemy breached their defenses. Viewed from above, the earthworks with their traverses and back walls resembled a line of square pens, each occupied by several soldiers.

Lee's engineers made ingenious use of the terrain in laying out the defensive lines, configuring them so that enemy troops would have to cross open ground, usually uphill. To slow the attacking force, they heaped tangled mounds of trees and brush against the face of the fortifications with their pointed ends facing toward the enemy. And rather than arranging the entrenchments in straight lines, they wove them back and forth, following the ground's contours to create angles and pockets that subjected the attackers to overlapping fire from several directions at a time.

While the confederates dug, Grant's men dug as well, constructing their own fortifications facing the rebel line. The armies pressed close against one another, like antagonists in a death grip, bent on squeezing the life from their foe. "If anyone got any sleep," a Union man remembered of his sojourn near Spotsylvania Court House, "it was in very short naps in line on the ground with their guns by their sides, or in their grasp, ready to meet threatened attacks which came almost hourly." Wounded men lying in Mrs. Spindle's farm cried piteously for water, but no one called a truce, and the field remained a killing zone. Sharpshooters made life miserable for everyone, hiding behind logs, in trees, and behind rolls of ground in wait for a head to show above the ramparts. Soldiers generally honored an unwritten code that forbade firing on a man who was relieving himself, but not the sharpshooters. "I hated sharpshooters, both Confederate and Union," a soldier remembered, "and I was always glad to see them killed."

★ ★ ★

The armies spent May 9 jockeying for position. McGowan's troops deployed along a ridge half a mile east of Spotsylvania Court House, guarding a road that slanted over from Fredericksburg. The ridge looked across fields sloping gently down to the Ni River, and on the far side of the creek—the Ni was little more than a trickle—Charles and his companions could make out the forms of Union soldiers throwing up earthworks and moving artillery into place. The South Carolinians immediately followed suit. "The neighboring fences were robbed, and the rails piled up before us," one of McGowan's officers recorded. "Earth was then thrown over these, from the inner side, so that by night we had a pretty good trench and breastwork to cover us."

Grant spent the next three days launching a flurry of attacks in the hope of breaking through Lee's battlements. The scheme, however, failed to reckon with Lee's phenomenal audacity and with the propensity for slippage in the ability of the Potomac army to execute Grant's plans. An attempt by Hancock to slip around the western end of the rebel line almost ended in disaster when Lee unexpectedly assailed the detached Union force, seriously mauling it. More attacks were also launched against Laurel Hill, but the rebel stronghold there was manifestly unassailable, leaving the attackers no choice but to wriggle into hollows and depressions for shelter from the searing volleys churning the sandy soil.

The men of both armies were relieved to get out of the Wilderness, with its horrors of deep-woods combat and consuming fires. At Spotsylvania Court House, they were initiated into the dark, numbing hell of trench warfare. Charles Whilden's world had become a grim place indeed.

One attack in this otherwise dismal pattern of assaults held a gleam of hope for the Union commander. A major component of Grant's offensive on the afternoon of May 10 was an assault led by young Emory Upton, a fiery colonel from upstate New York. Upton had studied the layout of Lee's line at Spotsylvania and thought he understood why the Union attacks were failing. The soldiers, he argued, were charging in a manner that forced them to spend too much time under fire, and he had a plan to solve that problem.

Upton's superiors gave him twelve hand-picked regiments to demonstrate whether his idea could work. Examining the front, Upton found a finger of woods that reached within two hundred yards of a part of the Confederate line and quietly arranged his troops into a compact formation. The men in the first line were to charge across the clearing without pausing to fire, and when they reached the rebel works, they were to leap onto them, shoot and bayonet the defenders, and spread out along the battlements, pushing left and right to widen their lodgment. The second line was then to pile in, followed by the third line, while the fourth line remained in the woods, awaiting developments. After Upton cleared the enemy troops from the breach, an entire division was to charge into the opening and complete the business of ripping Lee's army in half.

Shortly after six o'clock, Upton's troops, tightly packed and marching quickly as instructed, stepped into the field and started running toward the rebel works. Few of his men expected to come back alive. "I felt my gorge rise, and my stomach and intestines shrink together in a knot, and a thousand things rushed through my mind," a New Yorker remembered of those moments. Bursts of smoke dotted the earthworks ahead, and dirt puffed up where bullets struck the ground, but Upton's front line did not stop. "Forward!" cried Upton, who was running with his soldiers. Men clawed their way up the face of the ramparts and leaped onto the battlements, stabbing with their bayonets and swinging their muskets like clubs.

Spreading quickly to the left and right, Upton's troops widened the cleft, allowing the second line to pour in, and then the third. Georgians defending the broken segment of works fought back viciously but were overwhelmed by the weight of Upton's numbers. Slowly, however, the Confederates began rallying to expel the invaders. Ewell rode toward the tumult, excitedly barking orders and pulling on his moustache. "Don't run, boys," he called to some troops who started falling back. "I will have enough men here in five minutes to eat up every damn one of them!" Mounting Traveller, Lee also started toward the fight, turning back only when his aides promised to make sure the ground was recovered.

Upton's success depended on reinforcements, but fresh troops, due to a mix-up, were no longer available, and the assault faltered. Overpowered, Upton's soldiers climbed back over the rebel earthworks and sought shelter against the outer face of the barricades, where they contemplated the unpleasant choice of surrendering or fleeing across the field now swept by Confederate guns. As darkness fell, many chose to run the gauntlet of enemy fire, dragging wounded comrades with them. Of the nearly five thousand soldiers who made the charge with Upton, more than a thousand did not return. The grand venture was a failure, through no fault of Upton's. "I cried like a whipped spaniel," a participant admitted.

★ ★ ★

While battles raged on other fronts, McGowan's troops kept close watch of the enemy soldiers camped across the Ni. Toward dark— Upton's charge was petering out a few miles away—Federal troops flying banners from Michigan, Pennsylvania, and New York splashed across the stream and into the field in front of the South Carolinians. Confederate artillery opened, and shells burst above the deep green carpet to form white, cloudlike designs that floated above the field. Fully protected behind earthworks, Charles and his companions sighted down their muskets, waiting for the enemy to come within range and give them an opportunity to make amends for their embarrassing flight in front of General Lee.

But the Northerners had no stomach for attacking: Much of the rebel line was hidden in the woods, it was getting dark, and the Confederates seemed well entrenched. Easing to within a few hundred yards of McGowan's works, the Yankees stopped. Skirmishers probed the contours of the Confederate position but found it "so bewildering," a Union officer later put it, "and the enemy completely concealed from view, that it was impossible for the time to know the exact relative positions of the contending forces." The Federal troops breathed sighs of relief as their superiors ordered them to fall back to the river. Disappointed, the South Carolinians relaxed their trigger fingers and watched the enemy go.

Night came, and sounds of suffering engulfed the battlefield. At the home of the Harris family, across the Ni from McGowan, wounded soldiers filled the outbuildings and the neatly manicured lawn. "One by one the poor groaning fellows would be laid upon a table," a visitor remembered, "chloroform would be administered, a surgeon would wield his glinting knife and saw, and, in a few moments, a severed and ghastly limb as white as snow but spattered with blood would drop to the floor, one more added to the terrible pile." Miles away at Laurel Hill, Confederates listened to the wails of soldiers injured in Warren's latest attack. "The cry of the wounded for help, which would not come," a Mississippian remembered, "was something heart rending."

Grant thought over the day's failed offensives as he nursed a cigar and studied the embers in his campfire. Once more, as in the Wilderness, the Army of the Potomac had let him down. Generals had bickered, orders had gone astray, and Meade had failed to achieve even the semblance of coordination.

Upton's attack, however, raised a glimmer of hope. The New Yorker had demonstrated conclusively that Lee's line could be broken if an assault was pressed swiftly. If reinforcements had appeared at the right time to exploit Upton's initial success, it seemed to Grant that the outcome would have been vastly different.

The prospects set Grant to thinking. What if the assaulting force were larger? What if he sent in not merely a brigade but an entire army corps? What if he magnified the element of surprise and attacked just before sunrise, taking advantage of the darkness? And what if the reserve force consisted of not a division but rather the remaining three corps of Grant's entire army?

Here, concluded Grant, was a recipe for success. A cavalryman at headquarters claimed to have heard the Union commander discussing the possibilities with his aides. "A brigade today," he heard Grant emphasized. "Will try a corps tomorrow."

The stage was set for Charles's moment of glory.

THE MULE SHOE

Grant was a picky eater. His breakfast on the morning of May 11 was a cup of coffee and a morsel of beef charred black. Lighting his ever-present cigar, he began a letter to Washington, noting that after six days of very heavy fighting the result was "much in our favor." Losses were severe—Grant estimated twenty thousand Union casualties, five thousand shy of the actual mark—and he requested reinforcements, quickly and in "great numbers." Whatever the cost, Grant promised to remain true to his initial assurances to Lincoln. "I propose to fight it out on this line if it takes all summer," he wrote in a sentence that was soon to dominate the headlines in Northern newspapers.

Where and how to launch the next attack was very much on Grant's mind, and as the morning progressed, intelligence arrived about the configuration of Lee's line that went far toward answering his questions. The Confederates had constructed their defensive line on the spur of the moment. Near the center, the engineers had bent the line to the north, jogged it eastward, and then headed it off to the south, following the contour of the terrain. The result was a large bulge about half a mile wide and half a mile deep, pointing toward the Federals and occupied by Ewell's Corps. The protuberance resembled a mule shoe, and the soldiers began calling it by that name.

The Mule Shoe was a salient, in military parlance, and the formation was notoriously difficult to defend. If enemy troops attacked the head of the salient, defenders along the two legs were in no position to help; and similarly, defenders holding the salient's head were helpless to fend off attacks against the legs. Salients also ran the risk of being pinched off by attacks against both legs at once, dooming the defenders and creating a large gap in the defensive line. As one rebel put it, the Mule Shoe would be "a dangerous trap to be caught in should the line be broken on the right or left." All told, salients were nasty business for an army on the defensive.

Lee and his chief engineer Martin Smith—the mastermind of Longstreet's flank attack of May 6—were well aware of the problems inherent in salients. After inspecting the Mule Shoe, however, they decided to leave this particular salient alone. The Mule Shoe ran along high ground, and Lee and his advisors were loath to relinquish the position to the enemy. If the Federals held the ridge, Lee feared that they could more easily shell whatever line he took up farther back.

In Lee's judgment, two factors made the Mule Shoe defensible. The flat head of the salient was the most vulnerable part of the formation. Broad fields, however, extended north from the Mule Shoe's head, and if the Federals attempted to attack there, they would be exposed to fire from the defenders. To make sure that no troops could make it across the fields, Lee directed Ewell to pack the Mule Shoe with artillery, thirty pieces in all. That accomplished, Lee rested easy about the salient, although some of his subordinates remained concerned. "It was a bad piece of engineering and certain to invite an attack as soon as the enemy understood it," a Confederate gunner fretted.

By May 11, Grant had learned about the Mule Shoe and concluded that it was the ideal spot for his next attack. After four days of fruitless hammering against Lee's Spotsylvania line, he finally found the weak spot that he had been seeking.

This time, there would be no generalized offensive across Lee's entire front. Instead, Grant would focus his overwhelming resources against a discrete part of the Confederate position, and he would hold nothing back. Half a mile north of the Mule Shoe stood the ramshackle wooden home of the Brown family, and Union commanders identified the fields around the house as ideal staging grounds for the attack. Just before sunrise on the morning of May 12, Grant planned to send Hancock's entire corps—a force some twenty thousand soldiers strong, nearly double the number of men involved in General George E. Pickett's famous charge at Gettysburg ten months before—charging against the head of the Mule Shoe. At the same time, two more corps containing a total of forty thousand or so soldiers would plow into the Mule Shoe's eastern and western legs, and another corps would pin down the rebels at Laurel Hill. Crushed by irresistible numbers, the Mule Shoe's defenders would be driven out and the rebel army split in half, leaving Lee's troops no choice but to scatter or face destruction.

★ ★ ★

The sky darkened on the afternoon of May 11, and rain pounded down in torrents, extinguishing campfires and flooding the trenches. Soldiers from both armies sat in mud, unable to even brew coffee. In places, troops stretched tent flies over sticks for shelter, but the efforts afforded scant relief. "The wind was raw and sharp, our clothing wet, and we were just about as disconsolate and miserable a set of men as ever were seen," a waterlogged warrior reported.

The weather worked to Grant's advantage. In preparation for the massive assault the next morning, Hancock's troops shifted from the western end of the Union line to the center, a march of about three miles, taking with them their guns, wagons, and other military gear. Late in the day, rebel scouts heard the sounds of men marching and wagons moving, but the Southerners were unable to penetrate the Union picket lines and discover precisely what the enemy was doing.

Meeting with his generals near dark, Lee reviewed the mounting reports of enemy activity. Lee was generally an astute judge of his opponent's intentions, but this time he misread the evidence and concluded that signs of increased activity in the Union rear indicated that Grant was preparing to retreat, probably in the direction of Fredericksburg.

Aggressive as ever, Lee wanted his army poised to follow the foe and harass him during his expected withdrawal. But much of Lee's artillery was in the Mule Shoe, where the roads and paths were quickly turning into streambeds. With Grant apparently in retreat, Lee threw caution to the winds. To facilitate his pursuit, he ordered the cannon extracted from the Mule Shoe and brought back nearly two miles to main roads at Spotsylvania Court House.

And so, as night descended over the rain-scoured fields of Spotsylvania County, Grant's massive force began concentrating for a strike against the Mule Shoe. At the same time, rebel gunners began removing their pieces from the salient. Acting on a fatal misapprehension of Grant's intentions, Lee was weakening the very sector of his line that the Union commander had targeted for a massive offensive.

★ ★ ★

The night was pitch black and rainy as the weary soldiers of Hancock's Corps wound along a labyrinth of country roads and trails. The route to the Brown house ran through fields, forests, and swamps, and crossed streams swollen by the spring downpour. The marching column kept breaking in the darkness, and officers flailed about, cursing as they tried to reunite the pieces. One man later swore that he was able to follow the figure in front of him "not by sight or touch, but by hearing him growl and swear, as he slipped, splashed, and tried to pull his 'pontoons' out of the mud."

Grant selected Hancock, his most aggressive general, to lead the main assault force, but the striking Pennsylvanian had grave reservations about the assignment. Riding at the fore of the troops feeling their way along the sodden trails, Hancock's subordinates spoke freely about their concerns. Union scouts had teased out the general shape of the Mule Shoe, but rebel pickets had prevented them from conducting detailed surveillances, and no one on the Union side knew how strongly the earthworks were manned or how much artillery the Confederates had placed there. In fact, even the half-mile stretch of ground between Hancock's assigned staging area at the Brown house and his objective at the Mule Shoe remained a mystery. One of Hancock's generals sarcastically inquired whether he might encounter a thousand-foot ravine that would swallow up his troops, and no one knew the answer. Another frustrated general denounced the undertaking as madness, and another added his voice against it. Finally Francis Channing Barlow, one of Hancock's senior commanders, became so concerned about the effect the grumbling might have on morale that he ordered his fellow generals to keep quiet.

But soon even the tight-lipped Barlow succumbed to the prevailing mood. "As we staggered and stumbled along in the mud and the intense darkness," the young general remembered of the nighttime ride, "and I vainly sought for information, the absurdity of our position—that we were proceeding to attack the enemy when nobody even knew his direction, and we could hardly keep on our own legs—appealed to me strongly." Soon Barlow was cracking jokes along with the rest of the party. "It was an exquisitely ludicrous scene," he later wrote, "and I could hardly sit on my horse for laughter." Turning to an aide, he requested: "For heaven's sake, at least face us in the right direction so that we shall not march away from the enemy and have to go round the world and come up in their rear."

Mud-spattered soldiers filed into the Brown house fields all night. The men now had no doubts about their mission. They were fodder, it seemed, for another blind, futile charge against strongly fortified Confederate earthworks.

Hancock commandeered the Brown place as his headquarters and took a short nap on Mr. Brown's couch. Barlow slept on the floor, in front of the fireplace. Soldiers crammed the neighboring fields, waiting in the dark, their woolen uniforms heavy with dampness. Most men stood quietly, staring into blackness and thinking of home. Some shifted pensively from foot to foot, absentmindedly sloshing back and forth in the syrupy ooze. Dawn—and with it death—was but a few hours away.

★ ★ ★

A little over half a mile to the south, Confederate pickets stationed in the fields in front of the Mule Shoe listened attentively to the muffled sounds floating through the rain from the north. A Confederate staffer likened the noise to the sound made by water falling in the distance or by machinery. A few scouts worked their way north and returned with tales of troops marching and of workers clearing brush, as though opening the way for an attack.

The head of the Mule Shoe was manned by General Edward "Allegheny" Johnson, whose division contained about forty-five hundred troops. An irascible, colorful figure, Johnson was known also as Clubby for the stout wooden cane that he carried to help compensate for an ankle wound inflicted earlier in the war. By midnight, persistent reports from his outposts convinced Johnson that Grant was preparing to attack the Mule Shoe. Worried about the absence of his artillery, he sent an aide to Ewell, asking to have the guns sent back. Ewell declined Johnson's request, noting that Lee had "positive information" that Grant was pulling out in the morning, but Johnson was not accustomed to taking no for an answer. Riding in the dark to Ewell's headquarters, the cane-wielding subordinate made a personal appeal to his corps commander. Persuaded by Johnson's urgent air that he might be correct, Ewell sent a dispatch ordering the guns returned and a companion message to Lee informing him of Johnson's misgivings. Satisfied, Johnson returned to his headquarters at the home of the McCoull family. Located in a clearing some four hundred yards behind the apex of the Mule Shoe, the dwelling afforded Johnson ready access to all parts of his line. There he stretched out fully clothed for a short rest.

Lee rose as usual around three and was informed of Ewell's note. Reading it, he expressed puzzlement. He still believed that Grant intended to retreat, but Ewell's warning could not be ignored. If the general was correct, the Mule Shoe's defenders were dangerously vulnerable. Out of caution, Lee also ordered the artillery to be returned to the salient by daylight.

But the couriers bearing Ewell's and Lee's messages had difficulty locating the guns, and it was near four before a rider sloshed into the artillery camps near Spotsylvania Court House and handed a note to Colonel Thomas Carter, of Ewell's artillery. "Striking a light," Carter recalled, "I indorsed on the order that it was then twenty minutes to daybreak, and the men all asleep, but the artillery would be in place as soon as possible."

Getting the artillery under way was an agonizing process. Men had to be awakened, limbers checked, and horses hitched. The road was only faintly illuminated by the first glow of dawn as the guns started back toward the front, horses straining and wheels slipping in muddy ruts.

★ ★ ★

At three-thirty in the morning, an aide woke Hancock. An officer had been found who knew something of the area, and he sketched the rebel position on Mr. Brown's living room wall. He understood that a home owned by the McCoull family lay within the center of the rebel salient, he explained, and he added a mark on the drawing for the house. As a way to orient his troops for the charge, Hancock drew a line on the wall from the Brown house to the McCoull place. The compass bearing would serve as the axis for the attack.

Barlow and another of Hancock's generals, David Bell Birney, debated how best to arrange the soldiers for the assault. Barlow insisted that he mass his division into a compact body, but Birney disagreed, maintaining that Confederate artillery would slaughter the troops if they were tightly formed. "If I am to lead this assault," Barlow announced, "I propose to have enough men when I reach the objective point to charge through hell itself." Depressed over the prospect of commanding an attack that he considered hopeless, Barlow went into the yard to brief his subordinates. Gathering his generals around him, he traced in the dirt the map he had seen on the Brown house wall. His division was to form with the men tightly massed, like the head of a sledgehammer. Birney's division would extend to the west in two parallel lines, forming the hammer's handle, and two more divisions would gather behind, adding weight to the charge. At the signal, some twenty thousand men were to hurl toward the Confederate fortifications, reputedly half a mile south. Having explained the plan, Barlow stood to go. "Make your peace with God and mount, gentlemen," a staffer recalled him saying. "I have a hot place picked out for some of you today."

The downpour slowed to a drizzle shortly before dawn, and a fine mist drifted over the fields around Mr. Brown's home, collecting as pockets of fog in low-lying hollows. A fringe of dense woods was scarcely visible a few hundred yards away, where soldiers designated as skirmishers spread out three feet apart, forming a line. Rainwater dripping through leaves, men breathing, and the occasional crack of branches underfoot were the only sounds that disturbed the silence. The figures waited anxiously, anticipating orders to start south. Surprise was the watchword, and the success of the venture depended on it.

Hancock peered out Mr. Brown's window. His watch read four o'clock, and he could barely make out the forms of his troops in the field. Back home, these men were farmers and shopkeepers, bosses and laborers. They should be getting out of their beds, eating their breakfasts, and kissing their wives good-bye as they hurried off to work. Instead they stood lined up in Mr. Brown's field, waiting for the order—his order—to charge. The deadly frontal assaults at Spotsylvania Court House had all failed, and the odds were stacked against success this time also.

Hancock conferred with Barlow. "It's too dark," the young general urged. "I think it would be better to wait half an hour." Hancock agreed. Outside, the men remained in ranks, swaying restlessly, waiting for the word.

Four-thirty arrived. The sun struggled to peer through the swirling, clinging mist. Across the fields and woods, reflected Hancock, the Confederates would be rising and manning their battlements. The time for the charge was now or never. "To your commands," Hancock softly told his division heads, and orderlies brushed swiftly through Mr. Brown's door into the yard. The charge—the grand offensive aimed at bringing three years of war to a close—was to begin.

Half a mile south, aides roused Clubby Johnson from his sleep and warned that they could hear the sound of troops approaching from the north. Riding to the battlements lining the broad head of the Mule Shoe, Johnson mounted the earthen walls and strained to see across the fields. The rain had lessened, and mist rose from the ground like steam. Confederate pickets were running back, shouting and firing sporadically behind them. Johnson struck an impressive figure, striding back and forth atop the earthworks at the Mule Shoe, exhorting his men to get ready. Some soldiers stood on their firing steps, squinting beneath the head logs at the misty field in front. Others crawled groggily from their tents. "The fog was so dense we could not see in any direction," a Confederate remembered of those tense moments, "but soon we could hear the commands of officers to the men, and the buzz and hum of moving troops."

★ ★ ★

Hancock's soldiers started forward. Neither they nor their commanders had seen the ground where they were heading, but they all knew from experience exactly what was there. "It is a rule that, when the rebels halt, the first day gives them a good rifle pit," a Yankee observed. "The second, a regular infantry parapet with artillery in position; and the third a parapet with abatis in front and entrenched batteries behind." Sometimes, he reflected, the rebels were able to finish this three days' work in the first twenty-four hours. Lee's troops had occupied their line in front of Spotsylvania Court House for three days. By any reckoning, they had been granted ample time to construct earthworks of the most deadly fashion.

Soldiers in blue thrashed through underbrush and foundered in marshes, but the main portion of the Union force marched on, skirmishers in the fore, listening for the scream of projectiles tearing through the air. "Not a sound disturbed the moving line," a Union officer recalled. "Instinctively every man knew the importance of covering as much ground as possible before being discovered." Suddenly the land in their front rose slightly, and the lead troops emerged onto a farm road pocked with rifle pits. It was the rebel picket line. Taken by surprise, the gray-clad pickets fired a few hurried shots to warn the main body of troops in the earthworks and began running to the rear. With a mad rush, Federal soldiers jumped into the pits, stabbing with their bayonets and scooping up as many rebels as possible to keep them from sounding the alarm. In the confusion, a few Southerners got away. Sprinting back, one Virginian looked behind him and saw the captured picket line "perfectly blue with Yankees."

Some Northerners mistook the picket line for the main rebel position and concluded that they had won a quick and relatively bloodless victory. Glancing south through the ground fog, they saw a chilling sight. The terrain dropped off into a maze of gullies and then rose across open ground cleared of brush and trees. On the far side of the field were entanglements, sharpened branches facing outward, and atop the far ridge ran a raw mound of red dirt several feet high, surmounted by head logs. The report of a cannon broke the quiet, and a ball winged over the men in blue. "It did not require anyone to tell us what to do," a Union man remembered. "Everyone seemed to catch the inspiration that his safety depended on getting to those works." Hancock's thousands began running forward, pouring down the slope, into the swale, and up the far side toward the entanglements. Specks of smoke dotted the tops of the earthworks, and minié balls struck among the Union ranks. On the men pressed, a wave of blue uniforms. In the high pitch of fear and enthusiasm, soldiers ripped into the obstacles, clawing the branches aside.

The attack caught the Confederates unprepared. Only a few of the artillery pieces had returned, and Clubby Johnson's men were still waking up and taking their places at the firing slits. Pounding hooves and screeching wagon wheels announced the approach of the rest of the guns from the rear, but the pieces had arrived too late. The rebels who had clambered onto the ramparts aimed their muskets at the sea of blue uniforms and pulled the triggers. Percussion caps exploded in a flurry of pops, but the powder in many muskets was too wet to ignite. The devastating volley that Hancock's troops feared never came; the best the rebels could manage was sporadic bursts of firing. One of Johnson's generals remembered the frustration years later. "I saw Federal officers ride up to the lines and step from their stirrups onto our breastworks without harm to themselves or their horses," he wrote.

Form and order dissolved as Hancock's compact mass of troops swarmed through the entanglements and onto the earthworks. Confederates met them at the parapets, shooting and stabbing. Men shouted and muskets exploded in flame as the foremost Union soldiers leaped onto the head logs and emptied their weapons into the defenders. A New Jersey man remembered vaulting into the rebel works with his companions, "yelling and firing like a pack of demons, with our guns right in their faces." Pushed from behind by the press of troops in their rear, the Union soldiers piled into the pens formed by the traverses on the rebel side of the works. Jammed tightly together, the antagonists waged brutal, individual fights with bayonets and muskets swung like bats. One participant recalled a scene of "blood and death, an indescribable pandemonium."

Clubby Johnson cut a stirring figure, limping atop the breastworks, clothes torn, ferociously brandishing his walking stick as though his willpower alone could stem the Union onslaught. A Pennsylvanian finally persuaded him to surrender and led him back to the Union side of the field. In parts of the salient, the stunned defenders gave up with scarcely a fight. Other sectors witnessed terrific hand-to-hand combat as Federals battered their way along the trench line behind the works, fighting from traverse to traverse. Most fighting was over in minutes, and some three thousand Confederates found themselves prisoners. The guns that had rolled in from Spotsylvania Court House fell to the Yankees.

Hancock won a spectacular victory, breaching the rebel defenses precisely as Grant wished. So unexpected was his triumph, however, that it quickly became apparent that no one had made plans for exploiting the breakthrough. It was as though the cat had finally caught the mouse and was so surprised by success that it could not decide what to do with its prize. Twenty thousand Federal troops were now shoehorned into the tip of the salient. Companies, regiments, and brigades were intermixed, and all semblance of organized command disappeared. Men milled about, seizing prisoners, collecting mementos from abandoned rebel camps, and tossing their hats into the air as they cheered their success.

Hancock rode to the front to try to get his troops moving. "Forward! Double-quick!" he shouted, urging his officers to regroup and pursue the defeated enemy. But the attack was stymied. "The enthusiasm of a broken line resulting from a victory is only a little more efficient than the despondency of one broken by defeat," a Northerner who witnessed the scene reflected. "The officers commanding the divisions were capable men and knew what the situation demanded," he noted, "but they were almost powerless."

★ ★ ★

Confederate leadership within the Mule Shoe was also in shambles. Johnson was a prisoner, and volatile Richard Ewell, his superior, seemed beside himself, cursing and calling the soldiers stampeding to the rear cowards. "Yes, goddamn you, run!" a man heard him exclaim. "The Yankees will catch you. That's right, go as fast as you can!" Lee rode into the Mule Shoe and found Ewell in the yard of the McCoull home whacking retreating soldiers across their backs with his sword. "How can you expect to control these men when you have lost control of yourself?" Lee demanded, adding, "If you cannot suppress your excitement, you had better retire."

It was Lee's good fortune that his reserve forces were in the hands of John Gordon, the lanky, thirty-two-year-old Georgian who had spearheaded the evening attack in the Wilderness against the northern end of the Union line. Gordon lacked formal military training but numbered among Lee's most aggressive subordinates. A born orator, he had a knack for inspiring men to do the impossible, and his bravery was legendary. "He's most the prettiest thing you ever did see on a field of fight," a soldier claimed, adding that just looking at him would "put fight into a whipped chicken."

Gordon was in top form this rain-soaked twelfth of May. Bringing up a brigade of North Carolina soldiers, he rushed them through a stand of woods toward the eastern leg of the Mule Shoe.

Union troops had already overrun that stretch of line and were starting to come Gordon's way. Seizing the initiative to surprise the attackers, Gordon ordered his men to charge. "It was still not light and the woods were dense and the morning rainy," Gordon later recalled. "You could not see a line of troops a hundred yards off." The sheer audacity of his plan worked. Caught unaware by a vicious counterattack and uncertain about how many rebels they faced, the Northerners gave up ground, dropping back to the Mule Shoe's eastern leg and seeking cover against the outer face of the earthworks.

Riding into the center of the Mule Shoe, Gordon began forming another line of battle with troops from Georgia and Virginia. Lee rode up and watched Gordon arraying the soldiers as minié balls from the approaching Federals struck the ground around Traveller. Riding to the center of Gordon's line, Lee turned his horse toward the enemy, intending to lead the charge as he had tried to do in the Wilderness. A murmur went through the line. "You must not expose yourself," Gordon insisted, speaking what was on everyone's mind. "Your life is too valuable to the army." Waving his hand toward the soldiers, Gordon assured Lee, "They will not fail you here." To underscore his point, he called out in his grandest voice, "Will you, boys?" And the men cried back, "No, we'll not fail him." Turning to Lee, Gordon insisted that he go to the rear. A sergeant took Traveller's bridle and began leading horse and rider through the troops. "Lee, Lee, Lee to the rear," the soldiers chanted.

Union troops could be seen approaching through the distant haze, perhaps no more than sixty yards away. "There was no shout, no rebel yell," a Virginian recalled. "But, as I looked down the line, I saw the stern faces and set teeth of men who have undertaken to do a desperate deed, and do not intend to fail." Gordon led the charge. "Forward, men. Forward!" he cried, and his example was contagious. On the Confederates swept, fighting like demons and overrunning the surprised Northerners in their front. In a swirling free-for-all involving pistols, muskets, bayonets, and swords, Gordon once again drove the attackers to the far side of the earthworks.

While Gordon struggled to rally the broken Confederate ranks, Lee considered his options. Grant had chosen the Mule Shoe as the focus of his attack. Hancock's entire army corps was engaged there, and fugitives from other sectors of the line reported still more Northern units converging on the salient. As Lee saw it, his only choice was to abandon the Mule Shoe and prepare a new line on high ground a mile to the rear.

Digging fresh fortifications, however, would take time, and to buy that time a portion of Lee's army would have to hold off the entire Union offensive. Gordon had performed a workmanlike job of driving the invaders out of the eastern portion of the Mule Shoe, and the battle in that sector was stabilized, with Confederates occupying trenches on their side of the earthworks and Union troops plastered against the outer face of the same earthen wall. Only a few feet of dirt separated the antagonists, but Gordon seemed confident that he could hold on. The situation on the Mule Shoe's western leg and across its apex, however, remained dangerous. Here massive numbers of Northern soldiers had overrun the heart of Clubby Johnson's line, and Grant had ordered up artillery.

Lee's task was clear. His army's survival required driving the enemy from the Mule Shoe's western leg and apex and holding them in check until he could construct a new line in the rear.

★ ★ ★

In past battles, Lee generally delegated responsibility to his subordinates and exercised only general supervision himself. Now all that had to change. Longstreet had been seriously wounded in the Wilderness, Hill was sick, Ewell seemed incapable of exerting intelligent leadership, and Johnson, whose division had occupied the Mule Shoe, was captured. It was up to Lee to select the units to send in and tell them where to go.

The point of danger now was the western leg, where waves of Union troops had routed the rebel defenders. Strikingly handsome Robert E. Rodes, one of Ewell's division commanders, rode among the soldiers on a black horse, trying to restore order. "Every now and then he would stop and attend to some detail of the arrangement of his line or his troops," an onlooker noticed, "and then ride on again, humming to himself and catching the ends of his long, tawny mustache between his lips." A determined stand by a small North Carolina brigade, supported by a brigade of Georgians, momentarily halted the progression of the Federal onslaught. The Tar Heels, however, were hard-pressed, and their commander was brought down by a minié ball through his bowels.

Lee called upon young Stephen Dodson Ramseur, commanding another North Carolina brigade, to expel the invaders. "Check the enemy's advance," Lee directed the youthful general, "and drive them back." Shifting into the McCoull's yard, where Lee had set up his command center, Ramseur's men looked across several hundred yards of open field to the interior wall of earthworks that belonged to the salient's western leg. Through the fog, the Tar Heels could see the Stars and Stripes floating over the captured fortifications. Halfway between the Federals in the works and Ramseur's staging area ran a stubby wall of reserve entrenchments, also held by enemy troops, and more Union soldiers packed the interval between the two sets of barricades. Ramseur's command numbered about a thousand men; marching across an open field against Grant's teeming force seemed a desperate act indeed.

Riding to the front of his brigade, Ramseur barked out orders to charge. As his troops stepped out, the Union lines erupted in fire. A bullet tore into Ramseur's right arm, but he kept on, blood spurting from a wound below his elbow. Pushing up a gentle rise, his soldiers captured the reserve line of works and hunkered low as bullets splattered against the far side. Ramseur's wound incapacitated him, and command of the brigade passed to his senior regimental commander, Bryan Grimes. Fearing that the low reserve works might become a death trap, Grimes ordered the soldiers to climb over them and charge on to the main entrenchments. In a remarkable act of bravery, a man named Tisdale Stepp struck up "The Bonnie Blue Flag" at the top of his lungs, leapt over the reserve works into the open field, and started marching toward the Yankees, loading and firing as he sang. A Confederate marching behind Stepp accidentally dropped his musket, and the weapon discharged into the back of Stepp's head, killing him. Advancing through a veritable blizzard of musketry, the North Carolinians drove the Northerners from the earthworks in front of them and regained a segment of the Mule Shoe's western leg.

Ramseur's soldiers had leaped from the frying pan into the fire. They were now wedged into a short sector of trenches, and hordes of Union soldiers pressed against the other side of the same earthworks, only a few feet away. Thousands more enemy troops occupied the trenches to their right. Receiving killing fire from two directions, the North Carolinians huddled low in the pens formed by the main line of works and the traverses. So close were the Yankees that one of them pulled a rebel adjutant over the earthworks by his hair, and another Yankee reached over and tore a flag from its staff. Grimes launched a charge along the trenches to his right, and his men battered their way from traverse to traverse, driving the enemy back to gain a brief respite. Conspicuous in the fight was an elderly conscript bent over with rheumatism who insisted on leading the charge, exhorting his comrades, "Strike home!" while he wielded a ramrod.

Terrain governed what happened next. To the right of Ramseur's troops, the line of entrenchments—formerly held by rebels, but now brimming with Yankees—dipped gently downhill for about a hundred yards and then rose another hundred yards or so to a slight crest. It just so happened that the crest represented the point where the Mule Shoe's western leg started to bend east, marking the beginning of the broad, flat apex. From this point of high ground, later designated as the west angle on battlefield maps, Union troops could fire down into the length of the western leg. The only protection for the Confederates trying to reoccupy the trenches there was the scant cover provided by the traverses. The low earthen walls, however, were of little use against the enemy troops holding the angle because the Yankees were higher than the defenders and could fire down into them. Simply put, whoever controlled the elevated piece of land commanded the trench line that Lee so desperately needed to recapture.

Grimes's men hugged tightly against the traverses, seeking in vain to find shelter from the plunging fire. The whine of minié balls reminded one Southerner of musical instruments. "Some sounded like wounded men crying; some like humming of bees; some like cats in the depth of the night, while others cut through the air with only a 'Zip' like noise," he recalled. Thuds and groans signaled when men were hit. Unless the Confederates found a way to capture the angle, the brigade faced annihilation.

Lee summoned more troops to the McCoull house, intending to send them across the interval to occupy the few hundred yards of line between the exposed right end of Ramseur's position and the angle. First to arrive were Alabama troops commanded by Abner Perrin, the relative of McGowan's former law partner Thomas Perrin, who briefly commanded the South Carolina brigade during McGowan's most recent convalescence. A brigadier general, Perrin quipped that he would emerge from the battle as either a live major general or a dead brigadier. Leading his men across the open field a little to the right of where Ramseur crossed, Perrin came under intense musketry, and as he vaulted his horse over the reserve works, a bullet severed his femoral artery, making him the dead brigadier of his jest. As usual, the Yankees seemed intent on killing the men who carried the flags. An Alabama color bearer was shot near the McCoull house; his replacement fell a few yards farther on, and a third bearer made it only slightly farther. One Alabama man expressed thanks that the Yankees seemed to be shooting high. "If the bullets had been sweeping closer to the ground as thick as they were through the trees," he reminisced, "I don't see how many of us could have gotten through."

Buffeted by intense fire from straight ahead and from the right, the Alabama troops dispersed into scattered clusters. Some men piled into the fortifications to the right of Ramseur and found themselves in an even worse predicament than the Tar Heels, because they were closer by yards to the foot of the high ground at the angle and even more vulnerable to the deadly fire. Yankees pressing against the other side of the earthen wall seemed especially aggressive. Worked into a frenzy, Federals kept jumping onto the top of the barricade and shooting into the Alabamians huddled against the inner side. "Now you stand here," one of Perrin's lieutenants ordered his men, "and as you see them come I will run the bayonet through them and pitch them over to you and you catch them."

Mississippians commanded by Nathaniel Harris filed by the McCoull house and prepared to go in next. The grimy soldiers were resting in a field—General Harris reminded one observer of a bundle of dirty rags—when the call to combat arrived. Lee watched Harris's ragamuffins line up near the McCoull house, staring periodically across the clearing through his glasses. Two shells exploded near him, and a projectile passed under Traveller's stirrup. Unable to spot Harris, Lee once more started to lead the soldiers himself. Then he spotted Harris emerging from the fog and gun smoke. "If you promise to drive these people from our works, I will go back," Lee demanded, now fully aware of what to expect. "We will, we will, General Lee," the soldiers cried. One warrior, less respectful than the others, was heard to shout: "Won't someone take that damn fool away from there!"

Harris led his brigade along a wagon road that ran from the McCoull house to a point some fifty yards short of the angle. Musketry ripped into the soldiers as they advanced, and the column almost went astray when a staff officer sent to guide Harris lost his nerve and ran off. Uncertain precisely where he was supposed to go, Harris continued his men straight ahead at a run. Hitting the segment of works occupied by Perrin, they swung around so as to lap slightly to the right of the Alabamians, extending the segment of captured earthworks closer to the critical west angle. Federals blazed back from adjacent traverses and from the other side of the works, and flag bearers still seemed to be their favorite targets. Alexander Mixon of the 16th Mississippi jammed his flagstaff into the ramparts and was shot through the head; two other members of his color detachment were also killed. But the banner flying from the recaptured works provided a rallying point for the Mississippians.

Now Harris was trapped in the same killing field that held Perrin and Ramseur in its deadly grip. In places, the combatants pressed so close that their flagstaffs crossed, and wave after wave of Union assaults battered Harris's troops. "The powder smoke settled on us while the rain trickled down our faces from the rims of our caps like buttermilk on the inside of a tumbler," penned a survivor. "We could hardly tell one another apart. No Mardi Gras Carnival ever devised such a diabolical looking set of devils as we were. It was no imitation affair of red paint and burnt cork, but genuine human gore and gun powder smoke that came from guns belching death at close range."

Frantic to capture the high ground on his right, Harris leapt up and faced toward the angle. "Charge!" he hollered, calling on his men by name to follow him. Spurred by Harris's example, the Mississippians began overrunning the traverses on their right, beating their way up the slope under a hail of musketry. The battle, Harris later wrote, "became a hand to hand conflict, the bayonet and the butt of the musket being freely used; the Union troops contesting the possession of each traverse stubbornly." A few traverses short of the crest, Harris's advance ground to a halt. Union soldiers packing the angle and firing down into the Confederates were simply too numerous and too well positioned to be driven from the high ground.

The stretch of earthworks adjacent to the angle had become the focal point of the combat. The scene was chaotic, made more so by the heavy rain that lashed the combatants. Determined to hold the ground, Grant ordered another corps into the fight. Three Union brigades, three thousand men strong, pounded across the field and crammed against the north side of the works across from Ramseur, Perrin, and Harris. Massachusetts and Rhode Island troops moved onto the ground directly in front of Harris and along the works to his right to reinforce Hancock's soldiers already holding that important sector.

Now rank upon rank of Union soldiers stood plastered against the outer face of the earthworks, and more Yankees crouched behind traverses near the critical bend in the line. A few feet away, separated from the enemy by low walls of earth and timber, huddled the beleaguered rebels, bullets slamming into them seemingly from all directions. "The breastworks were slippery with blood and rain, dead bodies lying underneath half trampled out of sight," a Southerner recalled. Artillery shells whined in, and the air pulsed from the unbroken shriek of rifle balls and exploding projectiles. Between charges, Confederates pried muskets from the hands of dead men, pitched the corpses from the trenches, and stacked the rifles in preparation for the next onslaught. Soldiers jammed muskets through chinks in the earthworks and shot blindly into whoever happened to be on the other side. Troops jumped onto the parapets and fired into the enemy below while compatriots handed up loaded muskets. When a man fell, another would vault up and take his place. "The enemy seemed to have concentrated their whole engine of war at this point," claimed a Confederate who lived to tell the tale.

Newly arrived Union soldiers also found themselves in a nasty predicament. The field in front of the rebel position was so crammed with men that the rear ranks could not fire without hitting the soldiers in front of them. Tightly packed, the Yankees made easy targets for the Confederates, who poured lead into the field as fast as they could pull their triggers. One of Hancock's aides looked in horror as an officer waved to him just as a shell took off his entire head above the lower jaw. "As I passed he fell backward," the aide related, "and in looking down at him the tongue was moving in its socket as if in the act of speaking—a horrible sight I can never forget." Confirmed a Union man: "It was a saturnalia of blood."

The fate of the battle depended on which side could hold the elevated ground at the angle. If Southern troops failed to seize the high point, and quickly, the sheer weight of Union numbers would crush the three brigades Lee had thrown into the Mule Shoe's western leg. For the second time in a week, the Army of Northern Virginia faced an imminent risk of annihilation.

The crisis demanded the army's best combat unit, and Lee did not hesitate. Wheeling his mount in a spray of mud, a courier dashed off through the haze of rain and smoke in search of General McGowan.

11

A HUMAN FLAGPOLE

Receiving orders during the night to shift to a line of reserve
earthworks about a mile below the Mule Shoe, McGowan's
men trod through the dark gloom, grumbling all the way. Near
morning they could hear the staccato chatter of musketry and the
boom of artillery, but the uneven terrain and dense foliage made it
impossible for them to tell what was happening. The sound of
fighting seemed to be moving closer—a bad sign, the men concluded, because it probably meant that the Confederates were being driven back, and they waited anxiously, each absorbed in his
thoughts. "A feeling of unrest among officers of high rank indicated disaster," one of McGowan's colonels recalled.

Near nine o'clock, the courier from Lee splashed up on his lath-
ered mount. Charles's friend James Armstrong was nearby and
watched with interest as McGowan held a hurried conference with
the visitor and began shouting orders. Captain Langdon Haskell,
McGowan's adjutant, started purposefully toward the section of
works occupied by the 1st South Carolina. A soldier from the regiment who had collected water from a nearby spring sprinted past,
canteens jangling at his waist, and jumped into the trenches with

the rest of the men. Armstrong, writing years afterward, remembered the moment well. "Look out, boys!" the water carrier shouted, pointing to a neighboring regiment. "The Twelfth's falling in!"

"First regiment, fall in," Colonel McCreary shouted, and the cry rippled along the line as McGowan's five regiments moved into place. They were to march toward the sound of combat, led by the battalion of sharpshooters.

The troops stepped off, trudging along a farm road that jogged west and then veered north toward the fields of the McCoull farm. The 12th South Carolina was in front, followed by the 1st regiment. Rain lashed the marching figures, and men slogged in mud knee-deep in places, doing their best to hurry. Individual musket shots were now coming so quickly that they blended into a continuous sound, like sheets tearing, and the explosion of artillery projectiles was deafening. "Shells came thicker and nearer," a Carolina man remembered of their approach to the battlefront, "frequently striking close at our feet, and throwing mud and water high into the air." Minié balls, another man recalled, "whistled around us at a terrific rate."

In due course the outline of the McCoull house appeared, barely visible through the haze, on a slight eminence surrounded by fields. A farm road ran north from the house, descended into a thick forest of oak, crossed a little creek by the McCoull springhouse, and continued for a few hundred yards up a gentle incline to a line of reserve works held by elements from Harris's and Perrin's brigades. Another hundred yards farther north, the road reached the main fortifications of the Mule Shoe, near the right end of the sector held by Harris's Mississippians. From there, the critical piece of high ground at the angle was less than a hundred yards to the right.

Lee greeted McGowan as the corpulent general reached the edge of McCoull's fields. Enemy troops had broken into the Mule Shoe, Lee announced with concern in his voice, and he was counting on the South Carolinians to seal the breach. McGowan replied that his men were up to the task, and Lee looked visibly relived. "We will have it all right very soon," a witness heard the gray-haired Virginian say. Lee added that General Rodes, Ewell's division head who was trying to coordinate the Confederate attacks, would show McGowan where to go.

McGowan led his men into the clearing. Rodes, as promised, was waiting by the roadside. "What troops are these?" the general called, uncertain of the identity of the soldiers emerging from the mist. "McGowan's South Carolina Brigade," an officer shouted back. "There are no better soldiers in the world than these," Rodes replied loudly, hoping to stiffen their resolve, and the tactic worked. "We hurried on," a Carolinian recalled, "thinking more of him and more of ourselves than ever before."

As McGowan rode at the head of his strung-out brigade, Rodes indicated the general direction of the attack. Halting his brigade on high ground around the house, McGowan was to form a battle line facing north and charge into the oak woods, following the farm road. After passing over the reserve entrenchments, he was to continue to the main works and wrest the fortifications on Harris's right from the enemy. At any cost, he must take the high ground at the angle. There, Rodes stressed, was the key to the battle.

McGowan began arranging his troops facing north, under conditions that were far from ideal. Less than a hundred yards away, the road led into a dense stand of woods. Acrid clouds of gun smoke swirled in the rain-driven wind, and projectiles tore through the forest, showering the ground with tree limbs and confetti-like particles made of leaves and tree bark. "It was so desperate that staff officers would not go near enough to point out where we must enter," one of McGowan's colonels complained.

The veterans of the sharpshooter battalion were accustomed to this deadly business and formed a skirmish line along the northern edge of the McCoull clearing, facing into the woods in preparation to attacking down the farm road. The 12th South Carolina lined up on the right side of the road, next to the McCoull house. Colonel McCreary brought the 1st South Carolina up next and began placing the soldiers along the left side of the road.

In the front of McCreary's column came the stooped figure of Charles Whilden, panting heavily and in visible distress as he hefted the regiment's battle flag. He was already in fragile health when he joined the army, and the rigors of the campaign had taken a perceptible toll. An onlooker noticed him shaking uncontrollably as though gripped by an epileptic seizure. Armstrong was appalled at his friend's condition. "Feeble in health and totally unfitted for active service," was how he later described Charles. "In fact," Armstrong recalled, "he was stumbling at every step."

Armstrong was reluctant to let Charles continue. The flag bearer represented the regiment's emotional spirit and soul; if he faltered, so might the men. Fully aware of the importance of the task before him and his men—the army's fate depended on their success—Armstrong asked his ailing friend to give him the flag.

Charles at first resisted Armstrong's suggestion. The flag had been his since the first day's fight in the Wilderness, and he had borne it at Widow Tapp's farm, where the brigade had disgraced itself in front of General Lee. Now once again the army was in peril, and Lee had again asked the South Carolinians for help, giving them a chance to restore their reputation, and his as well.

There was no time to argue, and Armstrong settled on striking a deal with Charles. If the ailing Charlestonian would hand the flag over to him, Armstrong proposed to carry it through the woods to the battlefront. When the regiment halted to wage its fight, he promised to return the flag to Charles, assuming the sickly private was in any condition to take it back.

Armstrong's offer made sense to Charles. He wanted nothing more than to carry the flag, but he also recognized the difficulty of making the quarter-mile dash to the front, especially if he were burdened with the flag and its heavy staff. Letting Armstrong take the flag to the point of combat, Charles decided, would increase his chances for carrying it in battle.

And so Charles nodded, and the battle flag passed from his hands to the hands of his friend.

★ ★ ★

At McGowan's command, Charles and the rest of the brigade started down the slope toward the forest, each step bringing them deeper into the wooded interior of the Mule Shoe. Enemy fire poured in from the left, where Ramseur's men stood locked in mortal combat with enemy troops pressed against the outside of their entrenchments. More bullets whined in from in front, where thousands more Federals were focusing sheets of lead toward Harris. And still more fire angled in obliquely from the right, where the dense Union hordes who had crammed into the angle kept up a continuous stream of blind musketry into the oak forest.

Yelling loudly, McGowan's troops descended the remaining stretch of field to the small creek, splashed across, and disappeared into the woods. It seemed like the Wilderness all over again as minié balls fired by invisible foes tore indiscriminately through foliage and flesh. "There was a good deal of doubt as to how far we should go, or in what direction," a Southerner recalled of the confused advance.

McGowan's injunction was to plug the gap on Harris's right, a task that required him to orient his line somewhat to the right, in the direction of the heaviest fire from the angle, and to negotiate several hundred yards of forest. The easier course, the general decided, would be to follow the farm road; the danger was that he would arrive a little to the left of his objective and emerge in Harris's rear. But by McGowan's reckoning, the attack stood no chance of success unless he could hold his brigade together, so he ordered his regimental commanders to keep advancing along the axis of the road. "Forward, my brave boys!" he shouted, making a conspicuous figure on his large gray horse.

The South Carolinians kept up their double-quick pace. A "whirlwind of rifle balls," as one of their number described it, slammed into them, and their formation, untidy to start with, quickly unraveled. The road jogged somewhat left, changing part of the line's orientation, and regiments drifted apart. "The fire was too hot for us to wait for the long, loose column to close up, so as to make this an entirely orderly advance," an officer candidly reported. The 12th South Carolina, on the right end of the formation, found itself slightly ahead of the rest of the brigade. Subjected to galling enemy fire, the men of the 12th regiment sprinted straight through the foliage and piled in behind a mound of reserve works almost directly south of the angle. The 1st South Carolina, its right flank now exposed, halted briefly by the farm road to wait for the rest of the brigade. As his men began falling around him, McCreary changed his mind about waiting and gave the order to push on. With another shout, Charles and his companions left the road and crashed through the woods to the reserve works, where they burrowed in next to the 12th regiment. The angle was no more than 150 yards away.

For reasons that no one ever explained, Major Thomas F. Clyburn, commanding the 12th South Carolina since the Wilderness—today was his twenty-first birthday—ordered his regiment to charge. The command was sheer suicide, but the soldiers obeyed, and climbing over the reserve works, they started through the woods toward the angle, dodging from tree to tree. Musketry from the Federals holding the high ground hit them with such force that they were driven to the left, and unable to continue on, the men of the 12th sought cover behind the traverses on Harris's immediate right. Twice enemy bullets shattered the 12th South Carolina's flagstaff, but the flag bearer jammed the shredded piece of staff into the works as a place for the men to rally.

Flailing through the woods on his mount, McGowan rode to the reserve works and restored a semblance of order. The 12th South Carolina had disappeared into the gloom on its forlorn attack, leaving McCreary's 1st South Carolina as the right end of McGowan's line. Colonel Benjamin T. Brockman's 13th South Carolina pulled up on the left of McCreary's regiment; Orr's Rifles, under Colonel George Miller, formed on Brockman's left; and the 14th South Carolina under Colonel Joseph Newton Brown moved up to form the far left end of the line.

Bullets and fragments from exploding shells seemed to be flying everywhere. One ball ripped into McGowan's right arm, inflicting his fourth war wound. Aides escorted the stricken general to the rear, and command devolved on the brigade's senior colonel, Brockman of the 13th South Carolina. Brockman scarcely uttered the order to charge when enemy bullets struck his head and an arm, mortally wounding him, and the reins of brigade command passed to Colonel Brown of the 14th South Carolina, who was next in seniority. Brown, however, had no idea of his unexpected promotion because he was on the far left of the line with his regiment. But at this point it mattered little who was in charge; it was impossible to pass orders through the din and confusion. The men had to rely on their own resources to save themselves.

Acting almost on impulse, the rest of McGowan's soldiers scurried over the reserve works and started toward the angle, following the path that the 12th South Carolina had taken a few minutes before. Predictably, they met much the same fate as their sister regiment. As they emerged from the woods into the cleared area behind the main set of works, killing musketry from the angle battered them to the left. Seeking any cover they could find, the Southerners dove into the trenches next to the Mississippians and hid low behind the traverses to escape the surge of bullets from the angle. As usual, the enemy made special efforts to kill the color bearers. A bullet pierced the forehead of Calvin Galloway, carrying the flag of Orr's Rifles, blowing out fragments of brain. Armstrong, still waving the flag of the 1st South Carolina, managed to bolt across the short interval between the woods and the works without being hit. Charles, determined to hold Armstrong to his promise, stumbled along close behind.

The South Carolinians had failed to take the angle. In the confusion, soldiers took refuge in entrenchments already occupied by Harris's men, prompting South Carolinians and Mississippians to fire blindly into each other's ranks. "Go to the right!" the Mississippians shouted in an effort to untangle the overlapping units. After the troops repositioned, the rightmost elements of McGowan's Brigade—the 1st South Carolina and some of the 12th South Carolina's survivors—held the fortifications slightly to the right of the Mississippians, suffering much the same fate as the troops whom they had been sent to rescue. Federals rose ghostlike from the haze and fired into them from the other side of their barricade. And relentless fire pelted them from the high ground at the angle a hundred yards to their right.

Charles and his companions had no choice but to huddle in the pens formed by the main works and the traverses, stooping low to avoid the barrages. "The sight we encountered was not calculated to encourage us," a man in the 1st South Carolina remembered. "The trenches, dug on the inner side, were almost filled with water. Dead men lay on the surface of the ground and in the pools of water. The wounded bled and groaned, stretched or huddled in every attitude of pain. The water was crimsoned with blood." It was certain death, a survivor recalled, to attempt to peer over the main barricade or the traverses.

Colonel Brown, now commanding the brigade, recognized that his men's survival required them to capture the high ground and ordered the 1st and 12th South Carolina, which were closest to the angle, to face to the right and assail the angle, fighting from traverse to traverse. The high ground, he insisted, must be taken.

Colonel McCreary straightened from behind a traverse and pointed toward the angle. "Charge!" he cried, standing tall in the driving rain, attracting bullets the way a magnet attracts iron filings. The order scarcely left his lips when he fell back into the muck severely wounded.

In the confusion of the advance to the main works, the 13th South Carolina became intermixed with the 1st South Carolina. Isaac Hunt, commanding the 13th regiment since Brockman's death, looked for his superior officers only to learn that they were all dead or wounded. Working his way along the line, he found Lieutenant Colonel Shooter, who had succeeded McCreary and was now in charge of the 1st South Carolina. Low-lying battle smoke made it impossible for Hunt to see the enemy, but bullets slanting into the troops from the right indicated a heavy concentration of Federals in that direction. To get a better look, Hunt and Shooter climbed onto the top of the works. Now somewhat above the smoke, they could catch glimpses of the Yankees firing down on them from the angle.

"It was plainly a question of bravery and endurance now," a rebel recalled. Acting immediately, Hunt ordered his soldiers to charge, and Shooter did the same, leaping onto a traverse while he waved his sword and cheered loudly. A minié ball slashed into his breast and catapulted him into a water-filled pen. "Forward, men!" he called with his last breath. "I know that I am a dead man," Armstrong claimed to have heard Shooter rasp, "I die with my eyes fixed on victory." One of Shooter's brothers had died in the Wilderness. Another brother, Evander C. Shooter, stood up to charge and crumpled dead into the pen where his sibling lay, dead as well. Sergeant A. F. O'Brien of Company I leaped onto the embankment only to fall wounded as a bullet shattered a bone in his right arm.

More men stood only to be cut down. The momentum that Shooter's bold example had inspired seemed about to die. Someone had to take the initiative, or they would all be killed.

Charles understood the situation with stark clarity. Crammed tightly against the side of a muddy traverse, he could hear the splats of bullets fired from the angle flattening against the other side of the wall, a foot from his head. Spray from the impacts misted onto his side of the low barrier. Squatting in a viscous ooze of blood and mud, Charles realized what he must do. Armstrong was next to him, and he reached for the flagstaff.

Whether the two men spoke was never recorded. But Charles's intentions were clear. The overaged epileptic from Charleston—the man whose endeavors throughout his life had been singularly marked with failure—wanted to carry the flag. We can only speculate about what motivated him. Perhaps he was driven by personal concerns, by a desire to atone for the disappointments of his past. Perhaps his decision was an altruistic act, spontaneously provoked by the realization that someone had to set the brigade in motion, and that he was that man. Raw fear doubtless played a part. And he may also have been inspired by the thought that dying while carrying the flag had more to recommend it than dying while burrowed behind a mud heap.

We do know that Charles and Armstrong's eyes met, and that Armstrong handed the flag back to his friend.

* * *

Charles's moment had come. Grasping the staff firmly in both hands, he stood, planted a foot firmly on the traverse, and began waving the banner, swinging it from side to side. The effect was electrifying. Here, floating in the vapor above this unimaginable scene of death and horror, was a symbol of hope to the men of the 1st South Carolina. The flag still flew, and the battle was not lost! Soldiers began running toward the banner and the improbable figure who held it aloft.

Hefting himself onto the traverse, Charles stepped onto the head log that ran along the top of the earthworks. Deliberately, slowly, he started in a halting gait toward the angle, fully exposed to the blaze of musketry cascading down from the high ground in front of him. Cannonballs hissed through the rain and emerged from the mist to explode in blinding puffs of orange. Minié balls and shrapnel from shells screeched past the hunched apparition grasping the flagstaff, splashing up mud or thudding into the growing assemblage of gray-clad forms accumulating behind him. There was no opportunity for men to dodge, no sanctuary for shelter. Life and death depended on chance; no one could predict whether a fragment of lead would pass harmlessly by or rip through cartilage and bone. No man, Charles included, expected to reach the angle alive.

wracked by seizures, Charles staggered on, his eyes fixed on high ground at the angle. Behind him came a jumble of men from Mississippi and South Carolina. Some troops clambered over the traverses and leapt from pen to pen, slashing with their bayonets and firing into the Yankees struggling to hold the captured works. Other rebels darted along the cleared stretch of ground immediately below the pens. A few ran along the crest of the main earthworks, braving a steady stream of musketry and artillery fire arcing over the head logs from both sides. Still leading the charge, his flag providing a rallying point, an anchor, an inspiration to the advancing Confederates, was the 1st South Carolina's unlikely flag bearer.

At the head of his motley band of rebels, Charles became the focus of the Union riflemen, who instinctively understood that bringing down the flag bearer would stop the attack. A bullet blazed through Charles's shirt and gouged out a trough of skin along his left shoulder. Ignoring the searing pain, he continued ahead. Nothing mattered to him except reaching his objective. Another bullet broke off the top of the flagstaff, and the banner, its upper end unattached, fluttered precariously from its lower corner.

Charles glanced up at the flag. The cloth was about to tear loose. He could not let the banner fall; the men might think he had been shot, and the charge would falter. Seizing the flag, he ripped it from the staff and wrapped it around his body. On he marched, eyes fixed to the front, a human flagpole in the midst of a leaden storm.

The wave of Confederates surging around Charles hit the defenders of the angle in a frenzy born of desperation. Leaping over the final set of traverses, they jumped into the pens on the high ground. Men from South Carolina and Mississippi fought hand to hand with soldiers from New York, Pennsylvania, and New England. No more was the killing at long range, and no longer were the targets faceless shapes in the mist. Men stared into each other's eyes as they stabbed bayonets into flesh and cracked skulls with gun butts. The accumulated bile and anger from years of war exploded in this narrow stretch of ground where the Mule Shoe made a shallow bend. For many soldiers, the killing at the angle was personal, unlike anything they had experienced in this terrible conflict.

Hacking and shooting into the throng of Yankees packing the angle, McGowan's and Harris's Southerners overran the high ground and a stretch of earthworks several yards to the right. The captured fortifications resembled a charnel house. Mud-caked forms of dead Confederates and dead Yankees sprawled over traverses and floated in trenches. In places, foes still clasped one another in death embraces. "In stooping or squatting to load," a rebel recollected "the mud, blood, and brains mingled, would reach up to my waist, and my head and face were covered or spotted with the horrid paint." Bodies studded the interior of the works like macabre sculptures.

Charles and his fellow Southerners had won the fight to take the Bloody Angle. But an even more grueling task—the battle to hold the high ground—was about to begin.

★ ★ ★

The four rebel brigades now had to hold back Grant's thousands until Lee could construct new fortifications behind them. It was about ten o'clock in the morning, and the frontline troops could only speculate how long they would be called upon to continue their unequal fight. None would have guessed that they faced fifteen more hours of unremitting combat.

Like much of the fighting in the Wilderness, the combat at the Bloody Angle broke down into uncoordinated, vicious squabbles between isolated clusters of men. General Harris, a hundred yards or so to the left of the angle, was unable to influence what happened along much of the line, and Colonel Brown, heading McGowan's Brigade after McGowan's wounding, was off at the far end of the South Carolina troops. Colonel Hunt of the 13th South Carolina ended up at the angle and exercised command there by fiat. Conditions, however, made it largely irrelevant who was in charge. Most of the time, Whilden and his fellow Carolinians were locked in brutal fights for survival in which strategy and tactics played no part.

No sooner had the Confederates captured the angle than the Federals launched a series of counterattacks aimed at recovering that important stretch of ground. "Grant had all the hosts of hell in assault upon us," a Southerner later swore, and so it seemed. Emory Upton, whose charge a few days before had inspired this latest onslaught, marched his troops out of a ravine and onto the tableland next to the angle. Rebels holding the works fired into Upton's men as they emerged into view. "No troops could stand such a fire," a rebel recalled, "and they were driven back in confusion, leaving the ground strewn with their dead and wounded." Another Union brigade attacked next to Upton; some of the soldiers managed to reach the face of the works, but none made it over. A man from Wisconsin recalled that assailants and defenders "shot and stabbed each other until the rebel breastworks were filled with dead in gray, and outside, on the glacis in front, the corpses in blue were piled on each other in heaps."

The Confederates fought grimly on. After each attack, they pitched the dead men out of the trench and loaded all the muskets they could find, propping the weapons against the inside of the works with their muzzles pointing up. When the next charge came, they fired the muskets one after another into the enemy troops trying to scale the works. With each wave, a few enemy soldiers always made it over, and then the fight became even more vicious. "Many times we could not put the guns to our shoulder," a Confederate recalled, "by reason of the closeness of the enemy, so we shot from the hip."

The Yankees also stepped up their artillery barrage, and long-range cannon lobbed hissing bolts of iron at the Bloody Angle, blasting huge gaps in the works and showering the occupants with jagged pieces of metal. Grant also brought out his Coehorn mortars—short, stubby tubes that heaved shells in high, curving arcs behind the Confederate line. Heads, arms, and torsos filled the air after each explosion. The rebels had no protection against the mortars, and the whine of approaching shells was especially demoralizing. Several mortar shells exploded behind the Bloody Angle. One projectile landed between two of Harris's soldiers, blowing a man into fragments and decapitating another. The headless body remained erect while blood spurt from a severed artery. "I sat there watching the fountain of blood spout up on a declining ration like a geyser," a witness remembered.

Determined to break through the rebel defenses, Union gunners rolled a section of artillery onto the shelf of flat land in front of the angle and began firing into the earthworks at point-blank range. The shells punched ragged, smoking holes through the earthen mounds, pulverizing everyone on the far side. A contingent of Pennsylvania soldiers meanwhile pressed close against the face of the works, shooting any Confederates who tried to fire at the men working the artillery. Mississippians vaulted over the barricades only to be blown back by double loads of canister. When too few gunners remained to service the cannon, infantrymen pitched in, blasting solid shot into the earthworks. Mired in mud, the guns finally fell silent. Two more guns and a caisson dashed up, but the horses and men were killed before they could get off a round.

The Confederates had no corner on bravery. As the battle heated, a Union officer noticed that the Federal artillerists were having difficulty hitting the Confederates behind the earthworks and decided to find a way to lower the rebel barrier eighteen inches or so. Someone figured that the task could be accomplished by removing the head logs from the rebel works and gave the assignment to Captain Lewis Wisner, a young engineer from upstate New York. Borrowing axes from a gun crew, Wisner led a handful of men across the fire-swept plain to the face of the rebel fortifications near the angle. He and his companions tried to push a head log off, but the Southerners had wired the heavy piece of wood to the supporting upright members, and the head log would not budge. "I'll do it myself," the exasperated captain screamed. Grasping an axe, he jumped onto the log, swung the axe high, and with two strokes severed each end of the heavy beam. A swift kick sent the log tumbling to the ground on the Union side of the works. Jumping down, Wisner bolted across the open ground and took cover in a hollow. His clothes, a witness noted, were riddled with bullet holes.

Now that the works were lowered, Confederate artillery was able to fire with greater destructiveness into the Union soldiers spread across the plain, and the battery commander who had asked Wisner to lower the works decided that he had made a mistake. Finding Wisner, he directed him to raise the fortifications to their original height by replacing the head log. The captain then darted back across the field, hefted the log, and pitched it back in place. Sprinting back, he again gained the safety of the protective hollow. More bullet holes perforated his clothes, but he was uninjured. After the war, Wisner received the recognition that he deserved and was awarded the Medal of Honor.

The plain in front of the angle rapidly became a field of dead men in blue. Corpses near the angle were pulverized into mush that resembled jelly more than men. One of Upton's officers later counted eleven bullet holes through the sole of a friend's shoe. "There was not four inches of space about his person that had not been struck by bullets," he recounted. New troops marched up to fill the gaps in the line only to discover that dead men were stacked so thickly that they could not move into place. Soldiers broke under the strain and stood erect, firing slowly and deliberately until Confederate balls cut them down.

The scene on the rebel side was equally horrific. "The devil couldn't stand it in there," a Southern officer screamed as he jumped over the works and surrendered. When ammunition ran short, volunteers attempted to run back for more, only to be killed while crossing the cleared ground behind the works. A Mississippian discovered a depression running to the rear that provided tolerable cover, and soon a line of Confederates crawled into the swale and passed ammunition to the front. Volunteers hung cartridge boxes on fence rails and carried them with a man at each end of the load; other men passed cartridges bundled in sacks made from tent cloth. Evacuating wounded soldiers from the front was nearly impossible, and injured troops could only lie in the mud, waiting for darkness to come. For all practical purposes, the rebel soldiers holding on to the recaptured stretch of works, Charles among them, were fastened in place by the pieces of lead howling around them.

As morning became afternoon, Charles and his companions numbed to the ordeal. Men fired blindly into soldiers on the other side of the works, shooting through chinks or reaching over the tops of the ramparts with their rifles. The trenches brimmed with water "as bloody as if it flowed from an abattoir," a survivor recalled. Wounded men drowned in the muck, and bodies lay stacked several men deep in the trenches, some floating in the foul mire. Occasionally a wounded soldier would regain consciousness, crawl from under a corpse, and begin fighting again. Ceaseless musketry scoured the sector, and artillery shells rained in unabated. "The question became, pretty plainly, whether one was willing to meet death, not merely to run the chances of it," a South Carolina man remembered of the dreadful combat.

Soldiers who lived through the experience wrote of it in later years in fragmentary, ghoulish snippets. "Here was nothing of glamour, but unmitigated slaughter, a Golgotha without a vestige of the ordinary pomp and circumstances of glorious war," a participant remembered. Another man remained haunted by scenes of "bloodshed surpassing all former experiences, a desperation in the struggle never before witnessed, of mad rushes, and of as sudden repulses, of guns raised in the air with the butts up and fired over log walls, of our flag in shreds." Indelibly etched in the memory of another warrior was the sight of his rain-soaked companions, "their faces so begrimed with powder as to be almost unrecognizable; some standing ankle deep in red mud, firing, while the edge of the ditch was lined with others sitting and loading as fast as possible and munching hard bread, the crumbs of which were scattered around their smutty mouths and besprinkled their beards." For one Mississippi soldier, the Bloody Angle conjured up the vision of a comrade with a bullet hole in his head, oozing blood and brains. Reaching into his tobacco pouch, the stricken man took out a piece of tobacco and rolled over dead before he could put the chew in his mouth. In later years, veterans festooned battlefields such as Sharpsburg and Gettysburg with monuments and memorials to their valor. Few had any desire to return to Spotsylvania County, much less to the place they called the Bloody Angle.

★ ★ ★

Near two o'clock in the afternoon—although time no longer seemed to matter—Major Nathan Church, commanding a Michigan regiment, managed to work a hundred or so Yankee soldiers tightly against the earthworks near the right end of McGowan's line. Crawling up the muddy face of the fortifications, some of Church's men fired into the rebels defending the angle from so close that their guns and bayonets crossed. Noticing that the return fire from the Confederates was slackening, Church concluded that the defenders had heavy losses and were nearly out of ammunition. His suspicions seemed confirmed when he spotted a white handkerchief tied to a ramrod rising above the barricade.

Deciding that the Carolinians were surrendering, Church ordered his men to stop shooting, but no one could hear him above the din. "In an effort to get the firing to cease," Church later explained, "I took my handkerchief and stepping back a few feet out of the smoke flourished it with one hand, and gesticulating and pointing with the other, tried to signal to our men in the rear and to either side of us that a white flag had been raised." A few other Michiganders pulled out handkerchiefs and waved them to assist Church.

The Carolinians, however, had never intended to surrender, and Colonel Brown, who had moved to the right of the Carolinian's line, was surprised to see the enemy stop firing and start waving white handkerchiefs. Understandably concluding that the Michigan men were surrendering, Brown called on them to lay down their arms and come into the Confederate line. Church stepped forward and announced that it was Brown who should surrender. He had ordered his men to cease firing, he explained, only because the Confederates had raised white flags. "I replied that I commanded here," Brown later related of the incident, "and if any flag was raised it was without authority and unless [Church] came in, firing would be resumed." Church suggested a conference to iron out the misunderstanding and sent a subordinate to parlay with Brown.

While Brown conducted a lively debate with Church's emissary, the rebel Colonel Hunt waged a similar argument a few yards away with another Michigan officer. The men of the 1st South Carolina looked on in awe as the bizarre recess dragged on. "A Babel of tongues succeeded," an officer from the regiment remembered. "Officers ordering the resumption of firing; men calling out to the Federal line, questioning each other, imploring for the fire to be held and the enemy allowed to come in." Everyone recognized the situation was preposterous; both antagonists were fully armed, and neither showed any desire to quit. "So the two sides stood," recollected an onlooker, "bawling, gesticulating, arguing, and what not." A Mississippi man remembered the episode as "the sort of parley in which almost everybody talked, and nobody listened." Concluded he: "Men are not like women, who can talk and listen at the same time."

Hoping to break the impasse, Brown told Church's representative that he would order his men to resume firing unless the Michigan men surrendered. The officer started back and was shot down by a Mississippian who was unaware of the arrangement. "The man was so close that I saw the lint fly from his cap as the ball struck the back of his head and he plunged forward dead," an onlooker recounted. Both sides resumed firing, and the battle roared on as though it had never stopped.

Still Grant pounded. Determined to punch through the meager rebel force holding the head of the Mule Shoe, the Union commander shifted thousands of soldiers from Warren's Corps to join the attack against the angle. Line upon line of Union troops already packed the plain in front of the rebel works and prevented the newcomers from bringing their weight to bear. Lying and kneeling in the mud, they simply added their fire to the unbroken stream of lead engulfing the rebel fortifications. Reinforcements recalled standing in mire halfway to their knees, surrounded by dead bodies, and muskets became so fouled from constant use that some Federal officers formed details to clean the weapons while the rest of the men kept shooting.

Union troops kept coming. A Mississippi man could hear the screams of wounded men over the noise of the fight and used the wails to predict when a charge was under way. The attacking soldiers, he realized, would trample the injured men into the ooze as they advanced, provoking a chorus of piteous howls that served as warnings.

The gray backdrop of rain and gun smoke grew darker as night approached. A soldier noticed bats flying over the angle at dusk, adding a fitting touch to the macabre scene. "We could hear their cries and the swish of their swoops amidst all that racket," he remembered. "It was a different sort of noise from the battle." A mile back, under Lee's supervision, soldiers labored to complete the new Confederate entrenchments. Until they finished, the front line would have to keep fighting. "We were told that if we would hold the place till dark we should be relieved," a South Carolina man recalled. "Dark came, but no relief."

Night also brought no appreciable slackening of fire, and the same four brigades that had recaptured the works that morning still held on. Ammunition was low, and men resorted to firing ramrods, skewering the enemy like insects in a collector's display. "No man thought of eating or even taking a drink of water," a Confederate claimed. "Indeed, no man thought at all," he added. "That function seemed to be suspended." Life resolved into a matter of killing and dying, a slow-motion dance conducted in a ghoulish paste of mud and corpses.

The night was pitch black, and low clouds, their undersides flickering orange from explosions and discharges, hung over the field. "Every flash of the guns lights up the ghastly faces of the dead, with whom the ground is thickly strewn," Charles's friend Armstrong later wrote of the scene. "Some of the dead are leaning against the breastwork," Armstrong noted of his surroundings, "one of whom must have been killed while in the act of firing, his rifle remains in his nerveless grasp."

"Midnight came," penned one of Charles's fellow Carolinians. "Still no relief, no cessation of the firing." Sitting on the edge of a ditch, a Mississippi soldier rested his feet on a corpse floating facedownward that made a little island in the bloody soup. "Near me was a dead Yank, his feet stuck in the mud of the breastwork, and his head in the ditch," the Southerner reminisced. "Lying my head on his leg to keep my face out of the mud, I went to sleep in a moment."

The Bloody Angle absorbed more firepower than any other spot in the American Civil War. An oak tree twenty-two inches in diameter provided the soldiers of the 1st South Carolina with a telling gauge of the intensity of the musketry that the enemy had focused against their few hundred feet of earthworks. All day and into the evening, minié balls had skipped over the top of the fortifications and hit the oak tree, which stood immediately behind their line. The leaves and small branches disappeared first and then the larger limbs went, crashing to the ground. So many balls flattened against the side of the trunk facing the enemy that it seemed encased in lead. Sometime after midnight, the tree toppled over, whittled through by multiple rifle shots as surely as if it had been chopped by a woodsman's axe.[1]

---

[1] A year after the battle, a Union general visited the battlefield and procured the stump from the smokehouse of a local hotel. It presently resides in the Smithsonian Institution's National Museum of American History in Washington.

Near dawn, word arrived from the rear. The new line was finished, and the men passed a whispered command down the trench line. They were to retire slowly and noiselessly from the works, sliding to the left.

Quietly the Confederates crept from the Mule Shoe. Ramseur's soldiers left first, crawling in the mud on their hands and knees. Harris's men passed through the works evacuated by Ramseur. The Mississippi soldier who had fallen asleep propped against corpses woke and took a final look around. Mist still enshrouded the landscape. Injured men cursed, cried for water, begged to have corpses pulled off them, and pled not to be left behind. "I don't expect to go to hell," the Mississippian later wrote, "but if I do, I am sure that Hell can't beat that terrible scene."

Last to leave was Charles and the rest of McGowan's men. "Exhausted, hungry and worn out for want of sleep, we were a sorry looking crowd," a South Carolinian admitted. "Everyone looks as if he had passed through a hard spell of sickness, black and muddy as hogs," one of Ramseur's warriors seconded. All would have agreed with the assessment of one of Harris's dazed troops. "With blackened faces and crisped hand, from lying in the water so long; our clothes stained with red mud and blood, we marched out of this place where more than one-third of our men lay dead to sleep forever."

12

Under a Spreading Oak

As daylight penetrated the mist, Union soldiers on the plain in front of the angle peered warily toward the rebel earthworks. A battery of federal artillery stood less than a hundred yards from the Bloody Angle. The horses, all dead, were still hitched to the caissons, and the gunners, dead as well, slouched against the ammunition boxes. The rebel entrenchments seemed strangely silent as a party of Northerners picked their way through the bodies, mounted the fortifications, and peered over.

The sight appalled even battle-hardened veterans. Corpses filled the trenches, stacked in places four men deep in thick mud that reminded one Union man of hasty pudding. Some bodies were so trodden into the muck as to be barely recognizable as human, and only the occasional twitch of an arm or a leg indicated the presence of a living being. Assistant Secretary of War Charles Dana, who had come from Washington to keep an eye on Grant's progress, was gazing into the rebel trenches when a leg poked up from the fetid brew. The visitors froze in shock while a Union soldier jumped into the pit, tugged on the leg, and extracted a Confederate, badly wounded but still alive.

The butchery of May 12 had taken a horrendous toll on both armies. Nine thousand Union soldiers had been killed, wounded, or captured during the day's battle, and Lee had lost at least eight thousand men, bringing the day's losses to approximately seventeen thousand souls. McGowan's Brigade had been decimated, losing 450 soldiers—the 1st South Carolina accounted for 79 of those casualties—and the service of the wounded general. The 1st South Carolina's command structure was in shambles. Colonel McCreary, Captain Brailsford, and James Armstrong were wounded, and all three Shooter brothers were dead. Another Charleston man, Major Thomas Pinckney Alston, of Company F, became the regiment's new acting commander.

All the killing, however, had bought Grant only a few acres of bloodstained Virginia soil, and Lee now faced him from a line stronger than the one the rebels had occupied when the fighting started.

The Confederates who had been holding the Mule Shoe collapsed in exhaustion behind the new earthworks, about a mile to the rear. The experience had left them numb. Shaking from fatigue and overwhelmed by the realization that they had survived where so many had died, they dipped their hands in pools of rainwater and washed off the accumulated gore. Men cried, unable to contain their emotions, and figures moved about in the hazy light, hunched over as though aged beyond their years, looking for friends and examining one another for wounds.

A Mississippian who had fought at the Bloody Angle attracted special interest. Minié balls had ripped holes in his blanket roll, sliced his trousers in three places, and clipped off both sides of his hat to give it a triangular point in front. One bullet had passed directly through his shirt over his heart, but he had been saved by a deck of cards that he carried in his breast pocket. Word passed around that the bullet had penetrated to the ace of spades, where it had stopped.

Dry beef and hardtack were distributed among the men, who had eaten nothing for a day and a night, but many of them passed up the food to sleep. Bursts of musketry from the front periodically jarred them into consciousness, and wide-eyed, they would grab their muskets and aim into the foggy distance, imagining that they were still in the Bloody Angle. "I don't suppose there is any man that can express the relief we felt in getting out of such a place," a survivor later wrote. "There is not a man in this brigade who will ever forget it."

But there was to be no respite. By noon Union scouts had confirmed that the rebels had abandoned the Mule Shoe and taken up a new position a mile or so back. Ever aggressive, Grant immediately began forming a new plan. Before the Confederates had time to recover, he would withdraw the troops who had been fighting at the Mule Shoe and send them several miles south to hit the exposed lower end of the rebel defensive line below Spotsylvania Court House. That night, thousands of Union soldiers pulled silently back from the Mule Shoe and sloshed along rain-drenched trails on another interminable night march.

Shortly after daylight on the morning of May 14, the head of the column reached a set of fields across from the objective. Soldiers staggered into position, completely worn out from the all-night trek and in no condition to fight. The line of marchers extended miles to the rear. While clusters of demoralized troops straggled up and collapsed in exhaustion, their generals assessed the prospects for success. Six hundred yards away, across a cleared stretch of ground, loomed the familiar form of Confederate earthworks. Holes for sharpshooters pitted the intervening field, and gray-clad figures could be seen milling about on the fortifications, rolling artillery into position. Concluding that he had arrived too late, Grant called off the assault.

Rain pounded down without letup and finished the work of turning the land around Spotsylvania Court House into a vast quagmire. The armies were stuck fast in place, and active hostilities ground to a halt for several days. Charles and the remaining men of McGowan's Brigade spent a miserable time listening to pickets fire at one another and wondering when they would be ordered back into combat. Late on May 14 they marched back through Spotsylvania Court House and set up camp near a small church where Lee had established his headquarters. "We slept in the rain," one of Charles's officers remembered of that night.

Suffering from the shoulder wound that he had received at the Bloody Angle, Charles was admitted to the brigade's field hospital. Armstrong was also there, and Charles was relieved to learn that his friend's injury was not fatal. At five o'clock that evening, Charles penned a letter to his brother William. "We have been in another fight more terrible than the last," he began. "We fought from the 12th at daybreak to yesterday morning daybreak in our entrenchments full of mud and water, and our brigade suffered much. Colonel McCreary of my regiment fell wounded almost in my arms. Lieutenant Colonel Shooter was killed. The top of my flag was shot away and a bullet tore open my clothes and gave a slight wound to my left shoulder, but I am alright. We know very little of how matters are going, as we are moving from point to point all the time, and today is the first rest I have had since I wrote you last."

In a transparent attempt to set his brother at ease about his situation, Charles downplayed the campaign's hardships. "I have from my position as one of the regimental color bearers a very agreeable time in comparison to many of my comrades," he explained, "and am now most of my time messing with Lieutenant Armstrong who has been very kind, as in fact all the officers I know are."

But try as he might, Charles could not hide his true feelings. "And now I want to say that I have never made a will," he went on, "but if it should be the decree of the Almighty that I should lose my life in this war, I wish you to take charge of and destroy such of my papers as you may think proper. I give you my meerschaum pipe, as you are the only smoker beside myself in the family. My watch and chain I wish to be drawn for by your wife, Joseph's wife, Bayfield's wife, Furman and my niece [ ]. I have the pipe and watch now with me. The rest of my property I wish to be equally divided between sisters Charlotte and Ellen Ann—I promised our dear mother that they should never want if I could prevent it."

Realizing that he might never see his family again, he closed with a resounding "Farewell," and signed the letter, "Your affectionate brother, Charles E. Whilden."

★ ★ ★

While Charles recuperated in the field hospital at Spotsylvania Court House, the campaign continued without him. The sky finally cleared on May 17, and the roads firmed. Again the Union commander studied his maps in search of a vulnerable part of Lee's formation, and again he hit upon an ingenious idea. Judging that Lee would least expect an attack across the battleground of May 12, Grant made ready to launch his next round at that very place.

Relying as usual on darkness to conceal his deployments, Grant on the night of May 17 shifted some ten thousand troops back to the Bloody Angle. Soon after daylight the next morning, they started across their former battleground toward Lee's new line, stepping over broken muskets, knapsacks, canteens, and the bloated bodies of men and horses. Suddenly the distant Confederate line came alive with the explosion of artillery, and shells tore into the Union ranks. The charge was a disaster, and few of the attackers got within even musket range of the works. Rarely in the Civil War did artillery alone break a major assault; Grant's attack on May 18 stands as a chief exception.

Persuaded that further forays against the Confederate line were futile, Grant again resorted to maneuver, racing this time with Lee toward the North Anna River, a steep-banked stream twenty-five miles south of Spotsylvania Court House. Directed by Lee to drive the intruders off, Hill sent Wilcox's division into battle at a place called Jericho Mills. Breaking through the Union defenses, the South Carolinians found themselves facing a line of cannon belching double-shotted canister and exploding shells. "I have seen patent mince-meat cutters with knives turning in all directions" a witness later related of the slaughter, "but this double-angled line of fire exceeded them all." McGowan's Brigade lost another 211 soldiers, 43 of them from the 1st South Carolina. Thomas Pinckney Alston, commanding the 1st South Carolina, was mortally wounded, as was the commander of the 12th South Carolina, and Colonel Brown was captured.

During the night, Lee fashioned the Army of Northern Virginia into a wedge, its apex touching the North Anna River's southern bank and each leg extending back from the stream several miles to anchor on a strong natural position. When Grant advanced the next day—here was the cunning part of Lee's ploy—the Confederate wedge split the Union army in half, enabling Lee to shift soldiers from one leg to the other and attack an isolated half of the Federal force. By cleverly exploiting the terrain and Grant's penchant for aggressiveness, Lee had turned a bad situation his way and found a means to use his smaller army to advantage.

Lee, however, fell seriously ill and was confined to his tent, unable to oversee the execution of his plan. And at this juncture, he had no subordinates capable of managing the offensive in his place. Longstreet was gone, Ewell had broken under pressure at the Bloody Angle, and Hill had flubbed an easy assignment at Jericho Mills. Even Jeb Stuart, who had briefly exercised high command after Stonewall Jackson's mortal wounding a year ago at Chancellorsville, was gone, mortally wounded by a Yankee marksman in a cavalry battle near Richmond. Lacking an acceptable substitute, Lee had no choice but to let his opportunity slip away. "We must not let them pass! We must strike them a blow!" aides heard the frustrated commander insist as he lay on his cot, but there was nothing he or anyone else could do.

Resorting again to maneuver, Grant crossed the river system east of Lee. As May turned to June, the two armies sparred and skirmished in a blistering array of battles in the shadow of the Confederate capital. Early on the morning of June 3—a rainy, foggy day reminiscent of May 12 at Spotsylvania Court House—fully half of Grant's army heaved forward in an attempt to break Lee's line at a place called Cold Harbor. Union field commanders, however, had failed to reconnoiter the ground, and none of Grant's subordinates seemed inclined to cooperate with one another. Searing blasts of musketry and cannon fire rippled down from the Confederate fortifications, defeating the uncoordinated attacks piecemeal. Grant's troops well understood the odds against them, and along much of the Union line men simply dropped to the ground and dug. In other places—most notably along Hancock's front—the soldiers charged ahead only to be slaughtered by Confederates firing from behind the protective cover of earthworks.

Grant had lost the Battle of Cold Harbor, just as he had lost the battles in the Wilderness, at Spotsylvania Court House, and on the North Anna River, but still he refused to concede defeat. Once more he turned to maneuver, aiming this time for the town of Petersburg, twenty miles south of Richmond, in hopes of severing Lee's supply lines. But Lee's tattered veterans reached the town before the Federals could overrun its defenses, and Grant's chance for quick success evaporated. The war in Virginia settled into a siege that would last for ten months. Lee had won the battles, but Grant had won the campaign, destroying the Army of Northern Virginia's offensive capacity. Not until April 1865 would Grant bring an end to Lee's army, at a place called Appomattox Court House.

Charles had played a small part in this grand drama, fighting with his regiment for a little more than a week, but his contribution had been remarkable. At the Bloody Angle, the rebel army's salvation had come from McGowan's Brigade, whose indomitable warriors had captured the high ground that held the key to the battle. But McGowan's dramatic rescue had faltered as the brigade's leaders had fallen. Someone had to take charge and restore the momentum. And it had been Charles Whilden who had risen to the occasion, fearlessly leading his comrades to victory with a battle flag wound around his body. Charles never received a medal or official recognition. There can be no question, however, that he was an unsung hero of the Bloody Angle, and that his valor helped deliver the day to the Confederacy.

★ ★ ★

Summer found Charles in the Winder Hospital in Richmond, suffering from epilepsy. Located near the James River, the complex of buildings was one of several hospitals in the city packed with refugees and injured soldiers. Charles had kept with him a few personal possessions, including the battle flag that he had wrapped around himself at Spotsylvania Court House. His blanket had disappeared, and he had petitioned the agent handling matters for South Carolina troops in Virginia for a new one. Much to his surprise, his blanket turned up among the possessions of Thomas Pinckney Alston, who had assumed command of the 1st South Carolina after Wick McCreary's wounding at Spotsylvania Court House and had died in June after his own wounding at Jericho Mills. Accompanying the blanket was a short note from one of Alston's relatives. "I cheerfully and gladly accept it," Charles wrote back, "and although I shall soon be on my way to Charleston on furlough, and I know not whether my peculiar state of health will ever permit me again to return to my regiment, yet believe me that whether for Peace or War, I shall never part with it, but shall cherish it during my life as connected with some of the proudest moments of my entire military career, as well as the most melancholy moment of my Virginian campaign, the death of your relative and my most beloved and distinguished commander, Col. Thomas Pinkney Alston of First South Carolina."

Charles returned to Charleston late in August 1864. His epilepsy kept him unfit for service, and he was carried on the 1st South Carolina's rolls for September and October as "absent, sick in Charleston." On October 25, the authorities issued him a formal Certificate of Disability for Discharge, listing "confirmed epilepsy" as the reason. Charles's days as a soldier were over.

Little had changed in Charleston during Charles's eight months' absence. The Federals had just finished another brutal bombardment of Fort Sumter in which they lobbed some fifteen thousand rounds into the fort over a two-month period, but the garrison had held. Shells also continued to fall with regularity on the impoverished city, and little remained of the neighborhoods within range of the Union guns. The big fear, however, involved General William Sherman. In September, Atlanta fell to the Union armies, and in November, Sherman set off with sixty thousand soldiers on a march toward the coast. His destination was not immediately apparent, but the citizens of Charleston had no doubt that their city was high on his list.

For a time, Charleston's luck held, and by the middle of December, it appeared that Sherman's voracious column was heading for Savannah, a hundred miles down the coast. On December 22, Savannah surrendered and Union troops occupied the city. "I beg to present you as a Christmas gift, the city of Savannah," the general wrote in informing President Lincoln of his conquest.

But Charleston still loomed large in the thinking of the Union brass, and the townspeople would have seen their worst fears confirmed had they been able to read the communications passing between Washington and Sherman. "Should you capture Charleston," Grant's chief of staff wrote the general, "I hope that by some accident the place may be destroyed, and if a little salt should be sown upon its site it may prevent the growth of future crops of nullification and secession." Sherman wrote back the day before Christmas. "I will bear in mind your hint as to Charleston, and don't think salt will be necessary," he advised. "The truth is the whole army is burning with an insatiable desire to wreak vengeance upon South Carolina. I almost tremble at her fate, but feel that she deserves all that seems in store for her."

Throughout the next month, refugees poured from Charleston to Columbia, which many of the city's inhabitants felt was so far out of the way as to be safe. Charles joined the migration, probably taking up residence with William's or Joseph's family.

He could not have made a worse choice. In February 1865, Sherman started north from Savannah, laying waste to a broad swath of

South Carolina. His goal, however, was no longer Charleston; its port was thoroughly blockaded, the city had virtually no military significance, and reaching Charleston required traversing the Low Country's treacherous maze of marshes. Instead, Sherman's army headed for Columbia, intent on bringing the war to the inhabitants of the state's capital.

Chaos reigned as Sherman's hordes approached. Columbia was bursting with refugees from the Low Country who had brought their valuables with them, and they scrambled by the thousands to flee the town. Looting became widespread, and the Confederates set fire to bales of cotton to keep them from falling into enemy hands. On the morning of February 17, Confederate troops evacuated the city, and Sherman's men moved into the town. Alcohol flowed freely, a blustery wind whipped up the flames, new fires were set, and some thirty-six square blocks were reduced to ashes and rubble. Sherman later denied having ordered the torching of Columbia, although he conceded that had he done so, he would have "burnt it with no more feeling than I would a common prairie dog village."

A similar scenario was also playing out in Charleston. During the night of February 17, Confederate troops in the town pulled out, and the next day, Union soldiers moved in. Smoke filled the air from burning cotton, set on fire to keep it from the enemy, and the flames ignited gunpowder in the railroad depot, blowing up more than a hundred people and burning down the neighboring homes. The Confederates had burned the bridge over the Ashley River, and those flames also roared out of control. More explosions shook the city, and many dwellings not already destroyed in the year and a half of bombardment burned to the ground. Weeks of plundering and looting followed, reducing the seat of the rebellion to a wasteland. Passing through Charleston a few months later,

Sherman remarked that "anyone who is not satisfied with war should go and see Charleston, and he will pray louder and deeper than ever that the country may in the long future be spared any more war."

On February 24, 1865, Charles turned himself over to the provost marshal of the Army of Tennessee, comprising part of Sherman's force. He was no longer a combatant, having been discharged from the Confederate army four months earlier, but he was called upon to sign an oath of allegiance, and he did. "I, Charles E. Whilden," he wrote, "do hereby pledge my word of honor not to take up arms against the Government of the United States, or by act or deed to aid the enemy of said Government."

William's Civil War was soon over, too. His outfit, Walter's Light Battery of the Washington Artillery, was among the last Confederate units to surrender, laying down its arms on April 26, 1865. He brought his family back to Charleston, burned his Confederate uniform, and had an earnest talk with Maumer Juno, who was now seventy-five years old. Most former house slaves were leaving their former masters, and he doubtless expected her to do the same. "Well, Maumer, you are free now," William's wife Ellen remembered of the conversation, "and if you want to go and live to yourself with your husband, I will take care of you as long as you live."

"You say that I am free now," she reportedly answered, obviously deciding that staying with the Whildens was in her best interest. She was getting old, she had no children, and while freedom had a compelling attraction, it did not put food on the table. "I never belonged to any of you children," she announced. "No, all of you children belonged to me, and if I was to leave you now, I think I would be disgraced, and if you were to give me up, I think that you would be disgraced. I am going to keep on as I have always lived." And so she stayed with the Whildens, continuing to live with them and serve them in an arrangement that worked for them all.

★ ★ ★

Postwar Charleston was a difficult place to make a living. "A city of ruins, of desolation, of vacant houses, of widowed women, of rotting wharves, of deserted warehouses, of weed-filled gardens, of miles of grass-grown streets, of acres of pitiful and voiceful barrenness," was the pronouncement of a Northern visitor. Slaves liberated from surrounding plantations streamed into town, joyful over their freedom and looking for opportunity. But for white Charleston, the end of the war marked a period of humiliation and hardship. The struggle to prevent the abolition of slavery had ended in failure, and the white population now had to live with the very eventuality that had led it to revolt in the first place.

Charles apparently decided to try his hand once again at lawyering and took up residence at Joseph's house at 81 Spring Street, in the same neighborhood as William. It would be interesting to know whether any of the people he passed on the street each day had any idea of what he had done that rainy May morning in Virginia. The Confederate authorities never gave him recognition for his feat, and nothing appeared in the newspapers about it. One would never have guessed that the graying, bewhiskered gentleman was the unsung flag bearer who had led the charge that saved General Lee's army at Spotsylvania Court House.

Little appears in the written records about Charles until September 25, 1866. It was a rainy day in Charleston—much like that rainy day a little more than two years before, when Charles had carried the flag at the Bloody Angle. Early in the morning,

Charles set off for a walk. And as he stepped down the street, puddles splashing at his feet, he was overcome with an epileptic seizure, fell facedown in a mud puddle, and drowned.

A Dr. Whiting attended to the stricken Charles but could do nothing to revive him. The family arranged for his mortal remains to be buried at Magnolia Cemetery, on the outskirts of his beloved Charleston, and interred him under a spreading oak draped with Spanish moss.

★ ★ ★

After Charles's death, William and his family remained in Charleston. William returned to the retail trade in a few years under the name of William G. Whilden and Company, again selling imported jewelry and silverware. Joseph also prospered, this time in the milling business. Around 1880, William's family moved to Greenville, South Carolina, where William went into business selling insurance. Maumer Juno moved to Greenville with them and died there on October 3, 1883, at the age of ninety-three. "The faithful servant and friend of one family for eighty-three years, this memorial to her worth is erected by the descendants of her first owner," read the inscription placed on her headstone by the family. William lived on, dabbling in history and writing a delightful piece entitled "Reminiscences of Old Charleston" that appeared in the City of Charleston's *Year Book* for 1896. He died that same year and was buried in Greenville. Joseph died in Charleston in 1909, just short of his 89th birthday.

Charles's wartime associates met various fates. James Armstrong survived the war, although just barely. He was wounded a week before Lee's surrender in April 1865, at the battle of Sutherland Station, when a minié ball shattered his right leg. Captured and sent to Washington, he remained in hospitals for some eleven months before the surgeons pronounced him well enough to travel. Returning to Charleston, he received an appointment as harbormaster and served for several years as a member of Governor Wade Hampton's staff. He lived well into the 1920s and spent his later years spinning tales with the aging members of the 1st South Carolina and writing articles about their exploits, including those of his friend Charles.

Wick McCreary was less fortunate. He survived his wound at the Bloody Angle and returned to his regiment. But on the last day of March 1865, he led his command into battle near Petersburg, at a place called Gravelly Run, and there his luck ran out. Retreating after a brutal fight, he was shot through the lungs. His men carried him back on a litter to the rebel earthworks, where he died, and his remains were laid to rest in a family graveyard near Williston, South Carolina.

Sam McGowan returned to command a few months after his wounding at the Bloody Angle and led his dwindling brigade until the Army of Northern Virginia surrendered at Appomattox. Returning to South Carolina, he was elected to Congress, but the body refused to seat him, along with other former Confederates, and he went back home. In 1878, he was nominated to the South Carolina Supreme Court but was not appointed because of opposition by Governor Hampton. Abbeville District sent him back to the state legislature, and the next year he received the Supreme Court appointment over the governor's objection. He served for fourteen years, lost reelection after a quarrel with the then-governor Ben Tillman, and died in Abbeville after a lingering illness in 1897.

Charles's saga did not end with his death. In the years following the war, veterans of the various regiments formed associations where they traded old war stories and supported measures that benefited the aging warriors. The 1st South Carolina had its own vigorous advocate in the person of Edward McCrady of Charleston. An attorney before the war, McCrady had organized a body of volunteers that had formed the core of Company K of the regiment. He had fought from Fort Sumter to the Second Battle of Manassas, where he was severely wounded in the head. Returning to the regiment in time for the Battle of Fredericksburg, he was hit on the head again—this time by a falling tree—was incapacitated from further field service, and finished out the conflict teaching recruits at a camp in Florida.

McCrady was a politician and attorney of note in postwar Charleston. He was also active in veteran affairs, publishing several articles about the 1st South Carolina, and one of his passions was collecting the regiment's memorabilia. He had carried the regiment's state flag—the blue silk banner made by Hayden and Whilden with the state's palmetto tree and half-moon insignia— before he was wounded, and as the elected head of the regiment's postwar organization, he had possession of that flag. His hope was to acquire the battle flag as well.

Learning that William had inherited the battle flag that Charles had carried at Spotsylvania Court House, McCrady asked him for the banner. William, however, was reluctant to part with the heirloom and put McCrady off. On one occasion, McCrady arranged for a photograph of the regiment's surviving veterans and asked to borrow the battle flag for a day, but William did not trust him and refused his request. Still McCrady persisted and finally persuaded William's brother Joseph to agree that he could have the flag. William, however, would not budge.

On the first day of January 1880, McCrady sent companion letters to William's other brothers Bayfield and Furman, forwarding copies to William. "I am the recognized representative of the regiment," he began in his letter to Furman, "and by the wish of survivors, the representative of the regiment, I have the care and custody of the colors of the regiment to which the battle flag in question belongs." He then went, lawyerlike, to make his case for having the flag.

"The battle flag," McCrady argued, "was carried by the regiment in every battle until May 1864 and was borne by many brave men, some of whom fell with it in their hands. I met your brother Mr. Charles E. Whilden in Richmond in January 1864 when he was about to join the army, and by my inducement he entered my regiment which I then commanded. He behaved very gallantly and on one occasion when the color bearer was shot, took up the battle flag and carried it heroically thro the fight. Another battle flag was given to the regiment after the battle of the Wilderness, and this last was carried at Appomattox. It was I believe at the time that this new battle flag was given to the regiment that your brother Charles sent home the one in question.

"Since your brother William G. Whilden has had possession of the flag, I have been pressing him to let me have it to accompany the colors as it used to do. He is very reluctant to give it up, but has consented so far as to say that I may write to your brother Mr. B. W. Whilden and yourself and that if you agree with Mr. Joseph Whilden that it should be given to us he will do so.

"I write therefore to urge you to let us have this battle flag," McCrady said in closing. "For years during the war I lived with this flag in my tent, and slept with it by my side in the bivouac, and fought and literally bled under it. You no doubt value it because of your brother's connection with it. But I think you will recognize mine as the stronger claim. To me personally it has memories and associations it cannot have to you, and as the representative of the regiment I cannot but hope you will agree with your brother Joseph Whilden that it should be given to us to keep with the colors to which it belongs."

William penned a reply five days later. "I have written to my brothers requesting them to withhold their consent in transferring the flag to your custody until they heard from me on what conditions I would consent to the transfer," he informed McCrady. The flag, he explained, had been carried by his dead brother, who had wound the cloth around his waist in battle and had taken it to the hospital with him. "I object to the ground that you take that the battleflag that I have *belongs* to you," he insisted, emphatically rejecting McCrady's claim "as being any stronger than that of any other member of the regiment that 'fought and bled under it.'" William's daughter Ella later recalled that her father "was perfectly willing for the flag to be placed in some collection of Confederate relics, but objected to McCrady having it as his possession."

In 1889, McCrady and other surviving members of the regiment donated the blue state flag to the South Carolina government, requesting that it always be kept at the capitol. William held on to the battle flag, and after his death in 1896, it passed on to Ella. In the spring of 1906, James Armstrong, who had remained a friend of the family, asked her for the flag, and she sent it to him. He wrote back informing her that he had received the flag and that he was attending a reunion where he planned to "communicate with the other officers of the regiment in regard to sending the flag to the State House to be placed alongside of the blue state flag. Until sent there it will be kept in a fire proof vault," he promised, and added in words that would have made Charles blush with pride: "Your gallant uncle Charles was a hero and was as modest as he was manly. I commanded the color company and witnessed his fearlessness and fortitude."

In 1920, Ella wrote Armstrong inquiring about the status of the flag. The now-decrepit warrior was unable to write back because he was undergoing a painful convalescence from the amputation of his leg that had been injured in battle fifty-five years before. His nurse, Rose McKevlin, replied on his behalf. "In regard to the flag given you by your noble natured uncle, his chivalrous comrade of the battle field Charles E. Whilden, he tried to get a meeting of the surviving officers of the regiment to discuss the matter, but failed to do so," she explained. "James Armstrong is now the senior officer," she wrote, "in fact there is but one other, and he is going to send the flag to the Secretary of State to be placed along side of the blue silk flag of the regiment now in the State House. When he regains strength to enable him to write he intends to prepare a notice of your uncle, who was as faithful as he was intrepid."

The current staff of the Confederate Relic Room and Museum in Columbia can find no record of ever having received the 1st South Carolina's battle flag. The regiment's blue silk state flag occupies an honored spot at the museum, but Charles's flag is not there. Perhaps Armstrong died from the effects of his amputation before he had a chance to donate it to the state. Or perhaps it still lies moldering in an attic somewhere in the Palmetto State, as unrecognized and unsung as the man who carried it at the Bloody Angle in Spotsylvania County, Virginia.

EPILOGUE

Whilden is no longer a common name in the Low Country. There is a Whilden Street in Mount Pleasant, and two blocks away, on Bennett Street, the home of Elias Whilden still stands in a pristine state of preservation, home to a local lawyer and his family. The Whilden home on Magazine Street is long gone, but the old jail building still stands. The workhouse is also gone, as are most of the old homes, with the exception of a Charleston single house at 16 Magazine Street, which looks much like the Whilden residence must have looked. A few blocks away, on Bull Street, is Denmark Vesey's home, and a little farther on, at the corner of Wentworth and Rutledge, stands William's house, made much the grander by subsequent owners. The name of Charles E. Whilden, however, appears nowhere, save on a stone in Magnolia Cemetery.

The main monument to Charles is in central Virginia, a few miles below the Rapidan River. The Wilderness is still there, although the saplings are mature trees now, and subdivisions cover the land where soldiers once fought. But if you wander off the roads, the woods grow dark, gullies knife off in all directions, and you will find it easy to imagine what it must have been like when gun smoke drifted through the trees and Grant's and Lee's men went at each other, tooth and claw. Get out at the intersection where Orange Plank Road and the Brock Road crossed, experience the woods, visit Widow Tapp's farm, and then wind south along the Brock Road toward Spotsylvania Court House. The National Park Service has a shelter near Sarah Spindle's farm and maps that will show you the way to where the McCoull family once lived. The house is gone, but the foundation remains, and a trail winds from the house into the woods. Follow that trial downhill to the remains of the McCoull springhouse, cross the little stream, and continue through the forest and up the long, wooded rise. The trail comes out by a parking lot, next to a low mound of dirt that marks all that remains of the Confederate entrenchments forming the Mule Shoe. Turn to your right, and you will see, less than a hundred yards away, high ground where the low mound makes a slight bend to the east. Impressions left by traverses, their wooden supports long rotted away, are still visibly imprinted in the earth. Walk to the high ground, and you will be walking in the footsteps of Charles Whilden. At the crest of the rise, a marker shows the spot where the tree stood that was later sawed in half by bullets, falling into the men of the 1st South Carolina.

Charles's name does not appear on any monuments at the Spotsylvania battlefield, but it does not have to. The place itself is his monument, and standing there, eyes slightly closed—particularly on a rainy spring morning—it is not difficult to imagine what the Bloody Angle was like when he was there, that spring morning so long ago.

SOURCES

1. The Fate of Two Nations

Overshadowed by popular interest in Gettysburg, Grant's and Lee's campaign in Central Virginia in the spring of 1864 has received scant scholarly attention. The first—and still one of the best—history of the military operation, written by Meade's chief-of-staff Andrew A. Humphreys, is *The Virginia Campaign of '64 and '65: The Army of the Potomac and the Army of the James* (New York, 1883). Noah Andre Trudeau's *Bloody Roads South: The Wilderness to Cold Harbor, May–June 1864* (Boston, 1989) and Mark Grimsley's *And Keep Moving On: The Virginia Campaign, May–June 1864* (Lincoln, Neb., 2002) are the best modern accounts. The material in this chapter is drawn from those books and from my own *Battle of the Wilderness: May 5–6 1864* (Baton Rouge, 1994).

Descriptions of conditions in Confederate Virginia are from McHenry Howard, *Recollections of a Maryland Confederate Soldier and Staff Officer Under Johnston, Jackson, and Lee* (Baltimore, 1914); William M. Dame, *From the Rapidan to Richmond and the Spotsylvania Campaign* (Baltimore, 1920); George R. Agassiz, ed., *Meade's Headquarters, 1863–1865: Letters of Colonel Theodore Lyman from the*

Wilderness to Appomattox (Boston, 1922); O. B. Curtis, *History of the Twenty-Fourth Michigan of the Iron Brigade* (Detroit, 1891); and Charles D. Page, *History of the Fourteenth Regiment, Connecticut Volunteer Infantry* (Meriden, Conn., 1906). "The Battlefield of 1864 . . ." is quoted from the Augusta (Ga.) *Constitutionalist,* January 2, 1864.

Grant material comes primarily from the general's *Personal Memoirs of U.S. Grant* (2 vols. New York, 1885); from the comprehensive collection of Grant's writings in John Y. Simon, ed., *The Papers of Ulysses S. Grant* (26 vols. Carbondale, Ill., 1967–2003); from Horace Porter, *Campaigning with Grant* (New York, 1897); and from the best of the modern Grant biographies, Brook D. Simpson's *Ulysses S. Grant: Triumph over Adversity, 1822–1865* (New York, 2000).

For Lee material, I have drawn on Clifford E. Dowdey, ed., *The Wartime Papers of R. E. Lee* (New York, 1961), and from writings by the general's aides, including Charles S. Venable, "The Campaign from the Wilderness to Petersburg," in *Southern Historical Society Papers,* Vol. 14 (49 vols. Richmond, 1876–1944); Walter H. Taylor, *General Lee: His Campaigns in Virginia, 1861–1865, with Personal Reminiscences* (Norfolk, Va., 1906); and R. Lockwood Tower, ed., *Lee's Adjutant: The Wartime Letters of Colonel Walter Herron Taylor, 1862–1865* (Columbia, S.C., 1995). By far the most complete source on Confederate attitudes leading up to the campaign is J. Tracy Power, *Lee's Miserables: Life in the Army of Northern Virginia from the Wilderness to Appomattox* (Chapel Hill, 1998).

General Lee's review of Longstreet's returning troops is based on accounts in Frank M. Mixson, *Reminiscences of a Private* (Columbia, S.C., 1910); D. Augustus Dickert, *History of Kershaw's Brigade* (Newberry, S.C., 1899); and Edward P. Alexander, *Military Memoirs of a Confederate* (New York, 1907).

Charles Whilden's Compiled Service Record in the National Archives and his letters in the Charles E. Whilden Collection in the

South Carolina Historical Society, Charleston, provide Charles's physical description.

2. A City by a Harbor

Details about the Whilden family can be found in the South Carolina Historical Society, in the Whilden family papers at the South Caroliniana Room of the University of South Carolina in Columbia, and in an unpublished monograph by C. Michael Harrington entitled "The Whilden Family in the War Between the States with Genealogical Notes." The sketch of Charles's childhood neighborhood is from William G. Whilden, "Reminiscences of Old Charleston," in *Year Book, City of Charleston, 1896,* and from articles about Magazine Street in the *Charleston News and Courier* of September 6, 1976, April 18, 1977, January 23, 1978, and April 15, 1985, and in the *Charleston Evening Post* of January 30, 1975. Copies of Joseph's *Charleston Gazette* and *Charleston City Gazette* are preserved at the Charleston Library Society. See also William L. King, *The Newspaper Press of Charleston, S.C.* (Charleston, 1872). Reminiscences penned by acquaintances of Maumer Juno are collected in Ellen Ann Whilden's pamphlet, *Life of Maumer Juno, of Charleston* (Atlanta, 1892).

Anyone seeking to understand antebellum Charleston and South Carolina should spend several hours with Walter Edgar's *South Carolina: A History* (Columbia, S.C., 1998), a majestically crafted tome that draws upon centuries of scholarship to reach fresh conclusions. For those wanting to delve into the details of Charleston's past, the place to start is Robert N. Rosen's pithy *A Short History of Charleston* (Columbia, S.C., 1997) and Walter J. Fraser's *Charleston! Charleston! The History of a Southern City* (Columbia, S.C., 1989). It is safe to say that these books, like the city they describe, are never dull.

Denmark Vesey's slave revolt has inspired several recent studies. Those that tell the tale well include David Robertson, *Denmark Vesey* (New York, 1999); Douglas R. Egerton, *He Shall Go Out Free: The Lives of Denmark Vesey* (Madison, 1999); and Edward A. Pearson, ed., *Designs Against Charleston: The Trial Record of the Denmark Vesey Slave Conspiracy of 1822* (Chapel Hill, 1999). The debate over whether the revolt was real or the figment of a few white conspirators' imagination enlivens a marvelous series of essays published in the *William and Mary Quarterly* and republished in pamphlet form under the title *The Making of a Slave Conspiracy* (Williamsburg, Va., 2001). See also Jon Wiener, "Denmark Vesey: A New Verdict," *The Nation* (March 11, 2002).

Definitive sources about the forces that drove South Carolina to secession are Steven A. Channing's *Crisis of Fear: Secession in South Carolina* (New York, 1963) and William W. Freehling, *Prelude to Civil War: The Nullification Controversy in South Carolina, 1816–1836* (New York, 1968). Insight into the secessionists' minds, largely in the words of the secessionists themselves, is provided with unflinching clarity by Charles B. Dew in his *Apostles of Disunion: Southern Secession Commissioners and the Causes of the Civil War* (Charlottesville, 2001).

3. Life Among Scoundrels and Grasshoppers

An unpublished monograph by Manning Alexander Simons titled *Schools in Charleston, South Carolina Before 1860* in the South Carolina Historical Society and more than twenty articles in *The South Carolina Historical Magazine* provide information about Charleston's schools. Source material about Hayden and Whilden includes E. Milby Burton, *Hayden and Gregg: Jewellers of Charleston* (Charleston, 1938), and Charleston *News and Courier,* July 19, 1882. A history of William's house at 73 Rutledge Street appears in Jonathan H. Poston, *The Build-*

ing of Charleston: A Guide to the City's Architecture (Columbia, S.C., 1997).

References to Charles's lawyering appear in John Belton O'Neall, *Biographical Sketches of the Bench and Bar of South Carolina* (Spartanberg, S.C., 1975), Vol. 2. Charles's adventures in Detroit and in the West are all derived from his letters to William, Ellen, and Elias, and from the *Detroit Directory* for 1853 and 1854, copies of which reside in the Burton Historical Collection in Detroit. Some of Charles's letters bearing on his years in Santa Fe were published in John Hammond Moore, ed., "Letters from a Santa Fe Army Clerk, 1855–1856, Charles E. Whilden," in the *New Mexico Historical Review,* Vol. 40 (April 1965).

The train of events leading up to the firing on Fort Sumter is the subject of many books, but none tell it with more verve than Maury Klein in his *Days of Defiance: Sumter, Secession, and the Coming of the Civil War* (New York, 1997). The authoritative narrative of the forces precipitating the American Civil War is James M. McPherson's *Battle Cry of Freedom* (New York, 1988).

4. A Desert Blasted by Fire

For an excellent analysis of Lee's decision to cast his lot with Virginia, see Emory Thomas, *Robert E. Lee: A Biography* (New York, 1995). General Thomas's utterances are quoted in Francis F. McKinney, *Education in Violence: The Life of George H. Thomas and the History of the Army of the Cumberland* (Detroit, 1961).

Charles's mishaps at sea are described in a letter from Elizabeth Hard to the Director of Archives dated October 23, 1869, found in the South Carolina Historical Society. Details of the city that Charles returned to, of the battles around Charleston, and of the Union siege of the city are ably related in E. Milby Burton, *The Siege of Charleston 1861–1865*

(Columbia, S.C., 1970), and Stephen R. Wise, *Gate of Hell: Campaign for Charleston Harbor, 1863* (Columbia, S.C., 1994). The wartime exploits of Elias Whilden's sons are collected in an unpublished manuscript by C. Michael Harrington, "Five Sons for General Lee's Army." Mary S. Whilden's *Recollections of the War 1861–1865* (Columbia, S.C., 1911) describes the Whilden family's exodus from Charleston. For an analysis of why men such as Charles joined the military, see James M. McPherson, *For Cause and Comrades: Why Men Fought in the Civil War* (New York, 1997).

5. General Lee's Shock Troops

Book-length biographies of General Hill abound, but the most recent and definitely the best is James I. Robertson, Jr.'s *General A. P. Hill: The Story of a Confederate Warrior* (New York, 1987). Charles's division commander is the subject of a slim volume by Gerard A. Patterson titled *From Blue to Gray: The Life of Cadmus M. Wilcox* (Mechanicsburg, Pa., 2001). General McGowan and Colonel McCreary have not yet found their biographers, although brief sketches appear in Ezra J. Warner, *Generals in Gray* (Baton Rouge, 1959), and Robert K. Krick, *Lee's Colonels: A Biographical Register of the Field Officers of the Army of Northern Virginia* (Dayton, 1992). I am deeply indebted to William McGowan Matthew and Richard A. McCreary, Jr. for providing details about their ancestors from their personal collections, ranging from McGowan's duel to McCreary's send-off barbeque.

Disappointingly little appears in print about Samuel McGowan's fine brigade. The indispensable source is James F. J. Caldwell, *The History of a Brigade of South Carolinians, First Known as Gregg's, and Subsequently as McGowan's Brigade* (Philadelphia, 1866). Written by a lieutenant in the 1st South Carolina shortly after the war, the work provides an accurate and engaging account of the outfit's battles and its leading personalities. Also authoritative and rich in details about the brigade's jarring battle at the Bloody Angle is Varina D. Brown's *A Colonel at Gettysburg and Spotsylvania* (Columbia, S.C., 1931). Compiled by the widow of Colonel Joseph Newton Brown, the larger part of the book contains speeches and writings by officers and soldiers from McGowan's brigade relating their personal experiences. Information about individual soldiers is from A. S. Salley, Jr., *South Carolina Troops in Confederate Service* (Columbia, S.C., 1913), and from the Compiled Services Records for those troops culled from the National Archives. Details of winter conditions on the Rapidan appear in Patricia J. Hurst, *Soldiers, Stories, Sites, and Fights: Orange County Virginia 1861–1865 and the Aftermath* (Rapidan, Va., 1998).

Flag enthusiasts listed in the acknowledgments helped me ferret out information about the 1st South Carolina's battle flag. For readers interested in Confederate flags and their role in Civil War combat, I strongly recommend Robert F. Bonner, *Colors and Blood: Flag Passions of the Confederate South* (Princeton, 2002); Richard Rollins, *The Damned Red Flags of the Rebellion: The Confederate Battle Flag at Gettysburg* (Redondo Beach, 1997); and Glenn Dedmondt, *The Flags of Civil War South Carolina* (Gretna, La., 2000). The slaughter of the 1st South Carolina's color company is described in Edward McCrady, "Boy Heroes of Cold Harbor," in *Southern Historical Society Papers,* Vol. 25.

6. An Eerie, Inhospitable Region

The first book-length account of Grant and Lee's confrontation in the Wilderness was Morris Schaff's *The Battle of the Wilderness* (Boston, 1910). Written by an officer on General Warren's staff, the author's recollections and sketches of the participants are priceless. A detailed but laborious recounting of the battle is Edward Steere's *The Wilderness Campaign* (Harrisburg, Pa., 1960). My own *Battle of the Wilderness: May*

5–6 1864 is the most recent book-length study. For aficionados of the battle, I recommend Gary W. Gallagher, ed., *The Wilderness Campaign* (Chapel Hill, 1997), which contains an intriguing set of essays, and Stephen Cushman's *Bloody Promenade: Reflections on a Civil War Battle* (Charlottesville, 1999), setting forth insightful observations about the fight through the eyes of a poet and professor of American literature.

For a bibliography of unit histories and personal accounts of the battle, see my *Battle of the Wilderness*. Sources for material quoted in chapters 6–8 can be found there.

7. Like a Saturday Evening Market in Augusta

Details of McGowan's fight in the Wilderness are in Caldwell, *The History of a Brigade of South Carolinians;* William S. Dunlop, *Lee's Sharpshooters: or, the Forefront of Battle: A Story of Southern Valor That Never Has Been Told* (Little Rock, Ark., 1899); and Susan W. Benson, ed., *Berry Benson's Civil War Book: Memoirs of a Confederate Scout and Sharpshooter* (Athens, Ga., 1991). James Armstrong's account of the battle containing references to Charles is from his letter of May 10, 1864, printed in the *Charleston Courier* of May 26, 1864.

8. A Mortifying Disaster

Details of McGowan's retreat through Widow Tapp's farm are drawn from Caldwell, *The History of a Brigade of South Carolinians;* Dunlop, *Lee's Sharpshooters;* and from the H. C. Albright Diary and Samuel Finley Harper letters, both in the North Carolina Department of Archives and History in Raleigh.

An excellent recent analysis of General Lee's encounter with the Texans in Widow Tapp's field is Robert K. Krick, "'Lee to the Rear,' the

Texans Cried," in Gallagher, ed., *The Wilderness Campaign*. One of the best firsthand versions by a Texan who was there is George Skoch and Mark W. Perkins, eds., *Lone Star Confederate: A Gallant and Good Soldier of the Fifth Texas Infantry* (College Station, Tex., 2003). A first-rate analysis of Longstreet's flank attack is Robert E. L. Krick's "Like a Duck on a June Bug," in Gallagher, ed., *The Wilderness Campaign*. The old deacon quote comes from Leigh Robinson, *The South Before and at the Battle of the Wilderness* (Richmond, 1878), and Grant's lecture after Gordon's flank attack and the "Christian men turned to fiends" reference are from Porter's *Campaigning with Grant*.

9. Death Was Always Present

The first book-length treatment of the battles around Spotsylvania Court House was William D. Matter's *If It Takes All Summer: The Battle of Spotsylvania* (Chapel Hill, 1989). Carefully researched, Mr. Matter's work has attained the reputation of a Civil War classic. I also humbly recommend my *Battles for Spotsylvania Court House and the Road to Yellow Tavern: May 7–12, 1864* (Baton Rouge, 1997), which carries the battle up through the Bloody Angle, and my *To the North Anna River: Grant and Lee, May 13–25, 1864* (Baton Rouge, 2000), which completes the fighting along the Spotsylvania lines and follows the maneuvers to the stalemate at the North Anna River. Those curious to learn more about the Spotsylvania operations would do well to consult the essays collected by Professor Gallagher in his *Spotsylvania Campaign* (Chapel Hill, 1998).

For a full listing of books bearing on the Spotsylvania campaign, I refer readers to my *Battles for Spotsylvania Court House and the Road to Yellow Tavern*. Sources for material quoted in chapters 9–11 can be found there.

Several writers have traced the evolution of earthworks during the Wilderness and Spotsylvania campaigns. By far the best modern analysis appears in Brent Nosworthy, *The Bloody Crucible of Courage: Fighting Methods and Combat Experience of the Civil War* (New York, 2003).

Upton's famous charge on May 10 has provoked considerable attention, and both Mr. Matter and myself devote a chapter to it in our respective books on the Spotsylvania campaign. The most recent analysis is Gregory A. Mertz, "Upton's Attack and the Defense of Doles' Salient, Spotsylvania Court House, Va., May 10, 1864," in *Blue and Gray,* Vol. 18 (August 2001).

10. The Mule Shoe

In addition to sources cited previously, Robert K. Krick's "An Insurmountable Barrier Between the Army and Ruin: The Confederate Experience at Spotsylvania's Bloody Angle," in Professor Gallagher's *The Spotsylvania Campaign,* was of help in preparing this and the following chapter. Two marvelous Union accounts are Francis C. Barlow's "Capture of the Salient, May 12, 1864," in *Papers of the Military Historical Society of Massachusetts* (14 vols. Boston, 1881–1918), IV, and John D. Black's "Reminiscences of the Bloody Angle," in *Glimpses of the Nation's Struggle: Papers Read Before the Commandery of the State of Minnesota, Military Order of the Loyal Legion of the United States* (St. Paul, 1898). For gripping Confederate narratives, see the essays entitled "The Bloody Angle," in *Southern Historical Society Papers,* Vol. 21.

11. A Human Flagpole

Details of McGowan's counterattack at the Mule Shoe appear in Caldwell, *The History of a Brigade of South Carolinians,* and in the essays in Brown, *A Colonel at Gettysburg and Spotsylvania.* Incidents of McGowan's charge and of Charles's participation are in James Armstrong, "McGowan's Brigade at Spotsylvania," in *Confederate Veteran*, Vol. 33 (1925); in William Whilden's notations on Edward McCrady's letter, January 1, 1880, in the South Carolina Historical Society; and in Charles's letter home the day after the battle.

Accounts by Mississippians and South Carolinians who fought alongside McGown's men are found in David Holt, *A Mississippi Rebel in the Army of Northern Virginia*, ed. by Thomas D. Cockrell and Michael B. Ballard (Baton Rouge, 1996); Eugene M. Ott, Jr., "The Civil War Diary of James G. Kirkpatrick, Sixteenth Mississippi infantry, C.S.A." (M.A. Thesis, Texas A&M University, 1984); Thomas T. Roche, "The Bloody Angle," *Philadelphia Weekly Times*, September 3, 1881; entries in South Carolina Division, United Daughters of the Confederacy, *Recollections and Reminiscences* (6 vols. Columbia, S.C., 1990–95); and William H. Harris, *Movements of the Confederate Army in Virginia and the Part Taken Therein by the Nineteenth Mississippi Brigade: From the Diary of Gen. Nat H. Harris* (Duncansby, Miss., 1901).

12. Under a Spreading Oak

The final scenes at Spotsylvania Court House and Grant's maneuvers south are covered in my *To the North Anna River* and *Cold Harbor: Grant and Lee, May 26–June 3, 1864* (Baton Rouge, 2002). Charles's letters, his discharge papers, and his parole certificate are in the South Carolina Historical Society. Marion Brunson Lucas provides a thorough narrative of Sherman's occupation of Columbia in *Sherman and the Burning of Columbia* (College Station, Tex., 1976). Events in Columbia from the perspective of a Whilden are in Mary Whilden's *Recollections of the War*, and William's burning of his uniform and the conversation with Maumer Juno came from Ellen Whilden's *Life of Maumer Juno*. Details of Charles's death are provided by Elizabeth Hard's manuscript in the South Carolina Historical Society and by the official death notices for Charleston. Correspondence among William Whilden, Edward McCrady, James Armstrong, and others concerning the 1st South Carolina's battle flag can be found in the Whilden papers in the South Carolina Historical Society. Biographical sketches of McCrady and Armstrong appear in Ellison Capers, *Confederate Military History*, Vol. 6 (Wilmington, N.C., 1989).

ACKNOWLEDGMENTS

C. Michael Harrington occupies the top spot in the list of people who helped make this book possible. A lawyer in Houston, Mr. Harrington has spent years collecting material about the Whilden family and unraveling the clan's complex genealogy. His articles about various Whildens, including Charles, William, and Elias's five sons, appear on the Internet and in various publications. He graciously shared his research with me, helped me find new material, and corrected a draft of my manuscript.

Two descendants of military figures whose lives touched Charles Whilden were especially helpful. William McGowan Matthew, grandson of General Samuel McGowan, has amassed a treasure trove of materials about his illustrious ancestor. During a delightful afternoon at his house in Charleston, he plied me with stacks of letters, newspaper clippings, and other material about the general and sent me away with copies. I also extend thanks to Richard A. McCreary, Jr., of Columbia, who sent me copies of family material about Colonel McCreary.

Several Civil War flag enthusiasts gave unsparingly of their time in my unsuccessful search for the 1st South Carolina's battle flag. I am grateful for the help of Ken Legendre, of Gretna, Louisiana; Gregg Biggs, of Celina, Ohio; and Kerry K. Chartkoff, Director of

Save the Flags, in Lansing, Michigan, all of whom helped me understand the unique role that flags and flag bearers played in Civil War armies. I am especially beholden to John Bigham, Curator of Education at the South Carolina Confederate Relic Room and Museum in Columbia, who helped in my search for Charles's battle flag.

Researchers across the country assisted in ferreting out material. I extend heartfelt thanks to Mary Julia Royall of Mount Pleasant, who introduced my to Charles Whilden; Matthew Reeves, Director of Archeology for the Montpelier Foundation, who located the 1st South Carolina's winter camp along the Rapidan; Bryce R. Suderow, who collected Compiled Service Records for all members of Charles's Company I; Bill Phenix, who researched materials in Detroit; Alfred Young, who shared his impressive tallies of Confederate troop numbers and losses; and the staff of the South Carolina Historical Society in Charleston, the Charleston Library Society, and the South Caroliniana Room at the University of South Carolina, all of whom assisted in my search for material about Charles and his times. I am especially grateful to W. Eric Emerson, Jacqueline McCall, and Carey Lucas Nikonchuk, who greatly eased my research burden. Robert K. Krick, historian extraordinaire of things Confederate, assisted with his encyclopedic knowledge and his near-exhaustive index system. I also extend gratitude to my friends and fellow historians who read the manuscript and helped make it better, including Thomas Alkon, Tom Boggs, Patrick S. Brady, Frank O'Reilly, and Peggy Resnick. Special thanks also to Megan Hustad, who deftly guided my work through the publication maze, from manuscript to finished book.

Without the encouragement of my wife, Catherine, this project would never have left the ground. Thank you, Catherine, for persuading me that I could write this book and for making me do it.

INDEX

ABOUT THE AUTHOR

Gordon C. Rhea is the author of four award-winning books about the Civil War: *The Battle of the Wilderness: May 5–6, 1864; The Battles for Spotsylvania Court House and the Road to Yellow Tavern: May 7–12, 1864; To the North Anna River: Grant and Lee, May 13–25, 1864;* and *Cold Harbor: Grant and Lee, May 26–June 3, 1864.* He lives in St. Croix, U.S. Virgin Islands, and in Mount Pleasant, South Carolina, with his wife and two sons.